THE ULTIMATE ETF GUIDEBOOK

HARRIMAN HOUSE LTD

18 College Street

Petersfield

Hampshire

GU31 4AD

GREAT BRITAIN

Tel: +44 (0)1730 233870

Email: harriman@harriman-house.com

Website: www.harriman-house.com

First published in Great Britain in 2019

Copyright © ETF Stream Ltd 2019

The rights of David Stevenson & David Tuckwell to be identified as the Authors have been asserted in accordance with the Copyright, Design and Patents Act 1988.

Hardback ISBN: 978-0-85719-726-9 eBook ISBN: 978-0-85719-727-6

British Library Cataloguing in Publication Data

A CIP catalogue record for this book can be obtained from the British Library.

CONTENTS

ABOUT THE AUTHORS

DAVID STEVENSON

David Stevenson is a columnist at the *Financial Times* and one of Europe's most influential investment writers. An author of several books, he is a consultant to the ETF industry and a long-time champion of passive investing. A lover of all animals, he is the proud owner of four horses, two dogs and three chickens.

DAVID TUCKWELL

David Tuckwell is the editor of ETF Stream, Europe's foremost ETF trade publication. He has years of experience in the ETF industry, and formerly worked for ETF Securities in London (now WisdomTree Investments). In another life, he was one of Australia's top Tetris players.

FOREWORD

ONE MODERN MALAISE is to complain about too much choice. We, apparently, live in a world of abundance, where investors have a cornucopia of choice. Rather than being a positive, this is increasingly viewed as an ill, resulting in paralysis and indecision.

We think this is rot, tosh and bunkum. Over the last few decades the plight of the ordinary (and not so ordinary for that matter) investor has improved immeasurably – not forgetting the decades long bull markets as a handy bonus.

Back in the bad old days, we were all forced to stick to individual stock picking, almost exclusively focused on domestic stock markets, all implemented at a heinous cost through what now seem like archaic trading mechanisms. In fact, matters were so bad that the only realistic way of checking the state of said portfolio was to either buy a collection of printed papers (called a newspaper) and check the share prices of said portfolio or, god forbid, ring up your stockbroker who'd probably charge you for the privilege of saying 'good morning'.

Good riddance to all that!

And we think it gets better. Not only has technology and product innovation resulted in enormous choice, it has also increased speed, efficiency and liquidity and, crucially, reduced costs. Hallelujah! It has never been a better time to be an investor in global markets.

But that mention of the omnipotent, godly, one also prompts us to introduce a note of caution. Investing is prone, perhaps like politics, to manias and movements motivated by deeply held beliefs. Starting in the middle of the last century, we have witnessed wave upon wave of evangelical investor movements which maintained that only their one way of picking funds/shares would provide above average positive returns. The most powerful evangelical movement – still strong – was the 'Church according to Value Investing', first laid out on tablets of stone by the great Ben Graham. Since then we have seen wave upon wave of investment beliefs ripple through the markets with perhaps the most virulent one being the latest – and the subject of this book.

Exchange Traded funds (otherwise known as ETFs) or more accurately, passively managed funds tracking an index. If you've ever had the good fortune to spend time with investing giants such as the wonderful Jack Bogle, founder of Vanguard, you'll sense an edge of evangelical zeal (and analytical zeal) creep into their enthusiasm for all things passive.

They maintain (largely accurately) that markets are efficient, so don't bother trying to be clever like those value fools. Buy the market, cut costs, keep it simple.

This is an excellent mantra and one which we articulate and discuss in great detail in this book.

BUT, we'd be remiss if we didn't also add a coda, that previously mentioned caution.

Exchange traded funds are, arguably, the single greatest fork of financial disruption to have hit investing in decades.

They have massively increased choice and reduced costs.

They are an essential tool for all investors, and they are a wonderful innovation.

BUT they are simply tools, underpinned by a strong analytical framework. They are, in our view, incredibly useful ways of implementing ideas centred around building a diversified portfolio. They are practical aides to better investing and in the middle of this book we spend page upon page discussing strategies for deploying ETFs within a portfolio.

BUT ETFs are not, in of themselves, the ONLY answer. The authors of this book regularly use ETFs within their own portfolios alongside other fund structures, many of which are actively managed.

There. We've said it.

Active and passive in one portfolio.

Passive funds such as ETFs are just one solution amongst many, although arguably the most important. We strongly believe that ETFs should be used alongside active funds, in varying proportions depending on market conditions, on the availability of products and of course, your own personal preferences.

So, in sum, this book is a practical manual for investors, private and institutional, who want to use ETFs within a diversified portfolio alongside other fund structures.

We discuss what you need to watch out for and what might make sense for your portfolio.

Crucially we'll be updating this book fairly regularly, probably on an annual basis for most years. We'd also maintain that this book should be read alongside our accompanying website www.etfstream.com where you'll find a universe of great content targeted at making us all better investors.

And if you are a professional investor, we also recommend reading our quarterly BeyondBeta publication which focuses on the increasingly important, though controversial area of smart beta, factor investing and ESG.

So, read this book, buy some ETFs alongside other (actively managed) funds, check in at www.etfstream.com and build a diversified, low cost portfolio.

And enjoy!

PREFACE

WHAT THIS BOOK COVERS

This book takes you inside the global ETF industry with a focus on the European and London markets in particular. It walks through how different types of ETFs work, how they are made, how they are traded and how they are managed by issuers. It then addresses some of the key issues concerning the ETF industry today. It ends by taking a look at specific ETFs and how they can be used by investors to build investment portfolios.

WHO THIS BOOK IS FOR

The book is meant for professional and retail investors alike and for anyone and everyone interested in sharpening their knowledge of ETFs. So, this book is not targeted at absolute beginners; it assumes a reader has some grounding in the basics of financial services and has a basic understanding of what an ETF is. It is also, crucially, for any investor who is open to new investment ideas, and especially for investors interested in using ETFs in their portfolios.

HOW THIS BOOK IS STRUCTURED

The first section of this book goes through the nuts and bolts of ETFs. It looks at how indices work, how different ETFs are structured and what the risks are. Section two looks at the debates around passive investing and goes through some of the criticism of ETFs. It then introduces readers to some of the new industry trends – like robo-advice, ESG and smart beta. Section three explores the different asset classes that ETFs offer exposure to and gives a brief overview of the wide universe of indices. Section four puts together several model ETF portfolios and gives investors examples of DIY portfolios made from ETFs.

INTRODUCTION

"The mutual fund industry has been built, in a sense, on witchcraft."
"On balance, the financial system subtracts value from society"
"Don't look for the needle in the haystack. Just buy the haystack!"
"Never underrate the importance of asset allocation."
"Owning the market remains the strategy of choice."
John Bogle

I NVESTING SHOULD BE simple and fun. It should be about long-term wealth creation and sensible financial planning. Necessarily it'll be messy and sometimes a bit fraught, but the result should hopefully be worth all the effort.

Sadly, the opposite is often true.

The fund management industry has quietly led many investors up the path with a promise of outperformance. The traditional model consisted of a well-paid fund manager who would skilfully select a basket of stocks (or bonds) and then charge high fees. But it was worth it, because they hopefully produced more than decent returns.

The overwhelming conclusion of a great many academic and industry reports is that most active fund managers, most of the time, underperform their chosen benchmarks. Yet they continue to charge like the Light Brigade despite underperforming!

Inevitably a new model emerged, first in the US, led by a charismatic evangelist for financial disruption called John (also known as Jack) Bogle. He'd built Vanguard, an asset manager, into a powerhouse through a simple formula: keep it simple and low cost. And as lower costs almost always meant better returns, he focused on a new fund format.

Why just use the index as a benchmark, why not actually copy or track that index and its constituents?

The passive mutual fund was born.

The next step in the story comes a few decades later as a business unit, within what was then Barclays, started to take this idea of tracking the index and turn it into a stock market fund, i.e. a listed entity rather like an investment trust. This exchange-traded fund (ETF) would have a ticker, low fees, and be easy to trade. A business called iShares was born.

Within the space of just a few years this disruption has affected nearly every major developed world market. ETFs are now the fastest-growing segment of the asset management universe. They aren't by any stretch of the imagination, the biggest segment of the funds industry but they are certainly proving immensely popular. And with that enthusiasm has come an inevitable backlash: ETFs will cause the next crash, ETFs will destroy capitalism, or ETFs bake in lower returns. All manner of mud has been slung at ETFs, but they've continued to grow and prosper. Many private investors and their advisers are embracing a new way of investing that is simpler and lower cost.

This book is a celebration of this disruption. It's not meant as a traditional text book telling you, the reader, about every aspect of the construction of ETFs, though we do outline how they work. We also won't be diving into the increasingly arcane academic debates that inform the passive funds and ETF revolution.

This book is about the ETF revolution and how investors can benefit from it, as seen through the vantage of our website ETFStream.com. Over the next few hundred or so pages, we'll examine the key trends and discuss the ideas that have caught our imagination.

Crucially we also want to present the investor with some valuable insight, gleaned from data, about what they might consider investing in. That requires us to outline a long list of potential asset classes that warrant closer investigation. In each case we'll explore the key indices, the things to watch out for and list prominent ETFs (cheapest, biggest, most interesting).

Lastly, this book also takes seriously the idea of building a diversified portfolio of ETFs. We think it should be a simple process, and in the last section of the book we'll outline some novel and sometimes controversial ideas about how to construct a sensibly diversified, low-cost portfolio of ETFs. As we said at the beginning of this introduction, we think investing should be fun and simple to understand.

What this book isn't about should also be obvious.

We're not in the business of offering tips about which ETFs to buy. We simply present a range of obvious choices, which you, the reader, the investor, can go away and investigate.

We're also not in the business of painfully taking apart the existing model of active fund management. If you're looking for a polemic against the traditional fund management industry, look elsewhere. This is a practical book about new ideas. We also happen to believe that successful active fund managers still have a very valuable role to play. The sensible and engaged investor probably mixes and matches ETFs and actively managed funds in one portfolio. By way of background, that's certainly what the authors do in their own portfolios – combine ETFs and listed investment trusts.

But whatever investors decide to do, if ETFs are a consideration this book is here to help.

Section 1

FUNDAMENTALS

A BRIEF OVERVIEW OF ETFS

THE FOLLOWING IS not meant to be an introductory guide to ETFs for beginners. If you are looking for that, there are plenty of adequate books and online guides. Rather, we highlight here some specific issues of ETFs that we think are worthy of note.

Our journey starts with the core building block of ETFs: the index, which is tracked by the fund or product. Without an index, you can't have an index tracking fund (of which ETFs are just one version). Active managers make reference to indices – as benchmarks – but are in effect free to invest in whatever they choose as long as it's allowed in their prospectus. ETFs and other index tracking funds must, by their very definition, invest in the constituents of an index. But indices, as we're about to discover, are far from being simple creations. Or perhaps more accurately they once were simple, and easy to understand, but over time they've become much more complex, forcing investors to understand exactly what's inside the 'box'!

UNDERSTANDING INDICES

The first ever index was invented by a journalist called Charles Dow back in 1896. His core insight was to build an index that would track and measure human progress, which he believed was best achieved by tracking the share prices of the major companies in the US, building the industrial world in the 19th century – miners, railways and factory owners. Mr Dow's method of calculating the index was simple. He added together all the share prices and divided them by the number of companies in the index (chosen by him – 12). It gave him a reading of 40 for the index, which he adopted as the starting point for this index. The first stock market index was thus born, but over the following 120 years we've seen an explosion of indices – there are now literally tens of thousands of different stock market indices in existence plus many tracking other financial markets such as bonds and commodities.

But despite this profusion of indices most investors still focus on the well-known benchmark indices such as the Dow Jones or their equivalents in the UK, run by FTSE Russell. The oldest continuous index in the UK is actually something called the FT 30, also known as the Financial Times Index or the FT Ordinary Index (FTOI). This index was established in 1935 and nowadays is largely obsolete – it's been replaced by a bigger and more widely used index called the FTSE 100. The FT 30 is similar to the Dow in that it tracks the share price of companies in the industrial and commercial sectors. Financial sector companies and government stocks are excluded. But four of the companies in this index are included in a much more familiar name, the FTSE 100 – those four businesses are GKN or Guest Keen & Nettlefolds, Tate & Lyle, Imperial Tobacco and Rolls-Royce.

The FTSE 100 Index is itself a major component of a wider index series called The FTSE All-Share Index, which was launched in 1962, and today covers 621 constituents with a combined value of over £2 trillion – approximately 99% of the UK's market capitalisation, according to the FTSE Russell Group. The All-Share is a market capitalisation-weighted index representing the performance of all eligible companies listed on the London Stock Exchange's main market.

The FTSE All-Share index was enhanced with the addition of FTSE 100 in 1984 and FTSE 250 in October 1992. The Dow and the FTSE series are just a few examples of the leading share indices for different countries – there's also the S&P 500 in the US, the CAC 40 in France, the German DAX and the Japanese Nikkei 225, to give a few examples.

Relatively few will know that there are major differences in the index compilation technique used to calculate these benchmarks. The S&P 500, the FTSE 100, CAC 40 and DAX are based on something called capitalisation-weighting, while the Dow Jones Industrial Average and the Nikkei 225 indices use a system called price-weighting. Capitalisation-weighting means that each constituent company's importance in the index is determined by the market size of the company. The larger the company (calculated as the number of shares in issue multiplied by the share price), the larger the index weighting it gets. The Dow and the Nikkei, by contrast, are price-weighted – so that the index allocates greater importance to companies whose share prices are higher in absolute terms, regardless of the actual economic importance of the companies concerned. A company with a share price of £10 automatically gets ten times the weight of a company with a £1 share price.

And there are many more index compilation techniques than just these two. Indices tracked by ETFs often weight their components equally, by weight of dividends or compiled according to some quantitative model. See our later section on smart beta strategies for a more detailed discussion of these alternatively-weighted indices. Recently there has been a vigorous debate between the proponents of different types of indices, with some claiming that certain index construction techniques are better than others when used as the basis for an investment portfolio. A key argument in this debate has been the one between the supporters and the opponents of capitalisation-weighting – we'll encounter this debate later when we look at trends in the smart beta space.

Market capitalisation allocates each company a share in the index in accordance with its market footprint – its share price times the number of shares issued, aggregated to all the market capitalisations for firms in the index. Because of this, critics say that company and sector weightings can be thrown out of line with economic reality by the impact of the market bubbles and busts. This becomes easier to understand if one looks at some examples from history. When Japanese stocks hit their peak in 1989/90, Japan represented over 40% of the MSCI World Index, and anyone buying an index fund based on that benchmark at that time would have had to devote nearly half their portfolio to Japanese shares at the time of the country's peak valuation. More recently, the internet bubble of 1999/2000 and the financial sector overvaluation in 2007 would have caused investors to allocate a large part of their assets to those sectors, if investing according to a capitalisation-weighted index, such as the S&P 500.

This criticism is rejected by many indexing specialists, who maintain that markets are broadly efficient, and they are merely replicating what the market buys, also called the market portfolio when using capitalisation-weighting. Nonetheless, much research effort has recently gone into different methods of index construction – as we'll discover in the section on smart beta. Nevertheless, it's also worth considering the reality that many of these newer indices do not necessarily result in higher turnover when tracking portfolios are set up. While market capitalisation-weighted index portfolios need to adjust their weightings only when constituent companies fall out of the relevant size bracket, to be replaced by others, the model-driven portfolios rebalance their portfolios more frequently, incurring greater costs. This can have more or less of an effect on the tracker funds and their end-investors, depending on the secondary market trading liquidity for shares in the market being tracked. ETFs tracking non-traditional indices typically also come at a significant premium in fees to the established index ETFs, something investors also need to take into consideration.

Investors might also want to factor in two additional considerations relating to the index used by an ETF. The first is whether your index is actually capturing the sensitivities and processes that you want to track. Take the FTSE 100 which is hugely popular with investors – this index has become a default choice for investors in UK stocks. Yet in practice the FTSE 100 Index is a thoroughly international index where the constituents of the index just happen to list their shares on the London market. In fact, many investors would argue that the FTSE 250 Index is a better gauge for the performance of the UK as opposed to the global economy.

The second issue is the actual structure of the index itself, especially in the commodity space. Many indices in this specialist and very alternative space simply use rolling one-month futures contracts as a measure for the trajectory of futures prices. This may be simple to understand but not necessarily optimal, as these futures-based structures encounter the force of contango and the cost of rolling futures contracts forward.

One last question about indices – should you invest in an index which tracks the total return (where the dividends paid out are rolled up into the total return) or one that pays out the income? In simple terms, a total return index rolls up the dividend income into a total index value (usually net of any withholding tax) whereas a distributing fund pays that income out as a regular payment. Many income investors will, of course, prefer that convenient, regular payment but historical evidence suggests that reinvesting the dividend (via a total return index) makes most sense over the long term – with distribution payments, too many investors forget to reinvest the proceeds and thus lose out on any subsequent capital gain. The bottom line? Dividend or income reinvestment at low cost nearly always makes most sense unless you require a regular income stream.

WHY ETFS DO NOT HAVE DISCOUNTS

Exchange-traded funds are listed stock market funds with a ticker and a bid/offer price. There are other listed funds on the stock market, especially in the UK, called *investment trusts*. These are also called *closed-end funds* i.e. they issue a fixed number of shares and may even have a limited life. But investment trusts, though popular with private investors, have one drawback – many can trade at a discount to the aggregate value of all their assets. Discounts of 10% or more are common. In effect if you bought a share at £1 and it now trades at 90p but its assets total the equivalent of 100p per share, you have seen 10% of your investment vanish. Some investors love these discounts because they offer trading opportunities as the discount fluctuates, but they can be a real challenge.

ETFs avoid this problem almost always with some clever financial engineering. Remember that a tracker fund invests in the underlying securities of a well-known index – or at least that's the case most of the time with physical replication. This allows ETFs to operate a system that removes the possibility of a discount (or a premium) by using what are called *authorised participants (AP)*.

Let's say we are tracking the FTSE 100 Index. If a discount opens up in an ETF, an authorised participant can simultaneously buy the ETF and sell the exact same bunch of shares (FTSE 100 constituents), in the same proportion as in the index. The authorised participant can then exchange the ETF for the basket of stocks which make up the ETF by presenting the ETF to the ETF issuer. If the discount was say 10%, the AP might buy the ETF for £0.9m and sell the underlying stocks for £1.0m and this would make a profit of £0.1m. But in practice, because of this creation and redemption process, the discount is nearly always arbitraged away (by those APs). Thus, discounts are never a major problem for what are open-ended, listed funds such as ETFs.

FX RATES REALLY DO MATTER

A great many underlying indices are denominated in US dollars. There's no inherent problem with this if you also happen to be a dollar-based investor, but for British investors who use sterling funds there's an obvious risk: you are always also exposed to the currency of the index that you are tracking. Why? Because the assets that the index is tracking are in that currency. For example, if a UK investor buys an S&P 500 tracker, and the US dollar falls 10% against the pound, then the UK investor will lose out as assets in US dollars are now worth 10% less! Some investors choose to control this risk using hedging, which can be useful over some periods of time, but which comes with an obvious cost.

Other investors choose to simply buy hedged ETFs – which are ETFs that build in a currency hedging and spare investors the work (we discuss these more later in the book).

FUND STRUCTURE – PHYSICAL TRACKING FUNDS

The most common form of index tracking (which could involve tracking a major index such as the FTSE 100) is through a fund. Funds are closely regulated by fairly stringent UCITS regulations and must have – among other key characteristics – some form of diversification built within the holdings as well as fairly strict fiduciary and custodian requirements. The UCITS stamp has gained broad acceptance as an assurance that basic regulatory standards are met, to the extent that many investors outside Europe have become familiar with it.

The simplest choice is between an exchange-traded fund (an ETF) or a more traditional unit trust accessed via an IFA-orientated platform. In practice many unit trusts access the same holdings as an ETF, so the main difference between these two structures is whether the fund is stock market listed or not in the case of the index mutual or unit trust fund!

Most of the earliest index trackers originally devised in the US used what was called physical tracking; this tracking methodology is still dominant stateside and many large European providers (including iShares and Vanguard) also make use of physical replication. These funds use 'physical' or 'in specie' replication to track indices. Under this methodology, the ETF's manager will purchase all the stocks, or a representative or optimised sample of the stocks in the index and hold them. This was the original ETF structure and this type of fund represents the majority of ETFs run by Europe's largest manager, iShares, as well as many of its main competitors.

To understand how this works, imagine you wanted to track the FTSE 100 Index. A physically replicating ETF would look at the contents of the FTSE 100 Index and then systematically buy every stock in that index. But how does the fund choose how to weight its key holdings within the fund?

The answer comes from the index's market capitalisation-weighting. If for instance, the entire FTSE 100 was worth (in aggregate) £1 trillion, and HSBC (one of the largest companies in the index) was capitalised at £50 billion, its weighting within the index would be 5% (£50bn/£1000bn = 5%).

Unsurprisingly a FTSE 100 tracker would aim to have 5% of the fund's total value in HSBC shares. Crucially it would actually buy those shares in the open market and then hold them in a segregated, secure account on behalf of the investors.

On paper this sounds easy, but in practice the value of the FTSE 100 and the companies within the index are constantly changing – how does the manager of this physically replicating fund pull off this constant daily tracking? The answer is that it is mostly done automatically. How? Well, if the price of HSBC declines by 10% in value on one day, then it would decline equally both in the index and in the FTSE 100 ETF, as the weighting of HSBC shares in the ETF simply mirrors the index. This means that, day to day, the fund manager does not have to do too much to monitor the valuations of individual companies. Where the work comes in for the fund manager is when the companies within the FTSE 100 change. These changes called 'rebalancing' happen every quarter for the FTSE indices and require fund managers to sell whatever companies are dumped from the index and buy whichever new ones are added. (ETFs, while passive, are still professionally-managed funds with trading desks and capital markets teams.)

Nonetheless, the mechanics of how this fund works are a little more complicated than this simple explanation, and involves professional investors called authorised participants who constantly look to arbitrage away any differences between the fund price and the value of its holdings. But, in simple terms, you are buying into a fund that actually copies the index by buying the stocks (or bonds for that matter) within your chosen index.

Physical tracking or replication works very well if one is tracking a very broad, very liquid, well-known index such as the FTSE 100. This index contains well-known names trading in the world markets, where there are literally tens of thousands of professional institutions operating on a real-time basis.

But some indices aren't quite as liquid, or efficient. These indices might track for instance Indian equities or track a very specialised part of the US mainstream equity space such as small cap US stocks that pay a high yield. Within these specialised indices there may be all manner of complications including a relatively small number of underlying stocks – or the index might contain stocks that might be more illiquid, with wider bid-offer spreads. In some cases, there may not even be a liquid market at all and the fund manager cannot easily buy the underlying stocks.

For whatever reason, physically tracking a specialist index might be more complicated than tracking the FTSE 100. This needn't prevent a fund provider from setting up an index tracking fund – they could use a technique called *optimisation* for instance – but their management costs might be a little higher.

Also, we might begin to see something called *tracking error* emerge.

TRACKING ERROR

Tracking error is where the performance of an index and the performance of a fund tracking that index diverge. For example, if the FTSE 100 provides a performance of 6% in a year, but an ETF tracking it only delivers a 5.5% return, the difference is called tracking error.

Tracking error represents a cost (in some rare cases tracking error can be positive). Hence institutional investors always ask about tracking error before committing to buy an ETF. While tracking errors are usually small, in some cases they can be substantial and shoot over 1% a year. While a 1% tracking error may sound unproblematic, if it persists over several years, the effect it can have on compounding can be substantial. This means tracking error is of particular importance for long-term buy and hold investors.

There are many reasons why tracking error might emerge. The main ones are:

• Management fees

• Cash drag

• Transaction costs

• Replication methods (i.e. optimised sampling)

Management fees effect all ETFs. ETFs cost money to run. These running costs – including the fees charged by the ETF provider – are recovered from the fund, usually its distributions. This causes a difference in performance between the fund and the index it tracks, as indexes assume no fees or running costs.

Cash drag, like fees, effects all ETFs. When ETFs invest in the securities underlying an index, there is always some uninvested cash left over (even if only a tiny amount). This leftover cash creates a 'drag' on performance, causing some drift between the index and the fund, as indices assume that all cash is invested. Cash drag can cause more tracking error during dividend payments as the fund will contain more cash.

Transaction costs are incurred when a fund buys and sells securities. In ETFs, this typically occurs when an index rebalances and the fund needs to sell the securities that are removed from an index and buy the new ones that are added. Transaction costs create tracking error because indices are calculated in a 'frictionless' market without transaction costs. Funds that hold illiquid securities – like emerging market debts denominated in local currencies or micro-cap stocks – will incur higher transaction costs.

Different replication methods produce different tracking errors. Synthetic ETFs, which we discuss in the next section, have the least tracking error. Optimised and sampling replication – where the fund managers pick and choose between securities in an index, and never invest in them all – have the most. Tracking error plagues optimised sampling because it is impossible for ETF managers to pick securities so perfectly that their cherry-picked selection matches the performance of an index.

Tracking error effects all ETFs, to various degrees. For this reason, astute investors keep an eye on it.

FUND STRUCTURE – SYNTHETIC ETFS

The other major type of ETF is synthetic. In most respects as far as an investor is concerned, synthetic ETFs are similar to physical ETFs: they're funds that track an index and trade intraday on an exchange. But with one crucial difference: they use swaps.

Swaps are a type of derivative. A swap, when it comes to ETFs, is just an IOU from an investment bank (often the parent bank of the ETF issuer) that can be used to provide the performance of an index. A synthetic ETF following the FTSE 100 will give the performance of the index, much like a physical ETF. But rather than holding all one hundred FTSE stocks, it will just use a swap.

How swaps get used in ETFs is complicated. In brief, UCITS rules prohibit funds from having derivatives exposure to a single institution exceeding 10% of the fund's value. This means that cash that comes into a synthetic ETF is used to buy a *collateral basket*, which is then held by the fund as collateral for a swap. So, a synthetic ETF will own a collateral basket and a swap, which are used together to give the performance of an index.

Why were synthetics developed in the first place?

There were four main reasons why synthetic ETFs were introduced.

1. ACCESS

The main driver behind synthetic ETFs is that they allow ETF providers to give exposure to markets that are hard to access or hold. Examples of this include equities in emerging markets or, as with bond markets, it may be judicious to use synthetic structures when there might be a proliferation of illiquid securities.

2. TAX LAW

Synthetic ETFs were first introduced in Europe in 2001 and their success in part is driven by regulatory and taxation factors. Notably, in the US swap-based ETFs come under a less favourable tax treatment than traditional ETFs, helping to explain why synthetics only account for less than 3% of net ETF assets in the US.

3. COSTS

The TER of synthetics tend to be lower than with physical ETFs. Portfolio rebalancing due to changes in a benchmark index will involve trading costs that erode an ETF's returns, albeit it helps a fund do a better job of matching an index's return. The need to rebalance is eliminated in synthetic ETFs, since they do not physically track the index, in the sense that they do not trade the actual securities underlying an index.

4. TRACKING ERROR

There can be a significant difference in tracking errors between physical and synthetic ETFs, according to Morningstar. As a general rule, synthetic ETFs have less tracking error. This is because the performance of a synthetic ETF is guaranteed by contract.

Physical ETFs, however, have to buy and hold the underlying assets. While for big famous indices like the FTSE 100 or S&P 500 this is usually easy, for other indices like emerging market debt or super-large indices with thousands of constituents, it can be very tough indeed. And obviously the harder it is for physical ETFs to get a hold of the assets within an index, the harder it is for the physical ETF to track that index...

What about counterparty risk?

A vital element of synthetic and physical ETFs alike is counterparty risk. Investors in physical ETFs may think they avoid counterparty risk because their ETF holds all the shares that make up an index. But both physical and synthetic ETF investors are exposed to counterparty risk. Synthetic ETFs take a gamble on the creditworthiness of the investment bank that provides the swap. If the investment bank goes bust, the swap it's providing goes bust with it. But physical ETF investors are also taking on counterparty risk because the shares in their ETFs are usually lent out to short sellers, who might not bring them back. Issuers and investors are generally not prepared to take credit risk, or they use certain techniques, and it is to these – collateral and stocklending – which we now turn.

COLLATERAL

In the beginning, there was no collateral in ETFs. Investors had faith in things like swaps, stock lending and investment banks. ETFs never used collateral, and no one ever asked for it. Then the 2008 financial crisis occurred and suddenly investors sought more security. Now collateral is everywhere. Despite its ubiquity, collateral remains one of the opaquer wings of the business. Investors rarely know how it works, what collateral their ETF holds, or what claim they have to it in the event of a default. But how does collateralisation work? What gets used as collateral? And what are the costs?

Swaps are used in synthetic ETFs, which we touched on above. In the past, the majority of European ETFs used swaps to track their indices. This number peaked at 60% almost ten years ago, but is now down to around 22%, according to Morningstar data (see following chart).

Europe ETP AUM by replication method

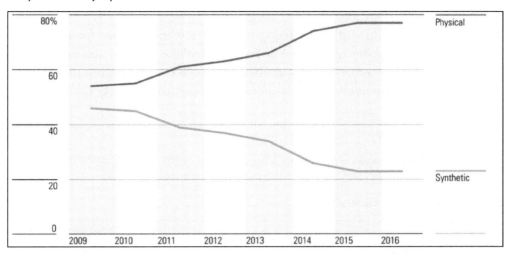

Source: Morningstar, A Guided Tour of the European ETF Marketplace

Swaps have benefits and drawbacks, which we detailed above. Just to refresh, the benefits are:

- access

- tax efficiency

- low cost

- low tracking error

But they also have an important drawback: counterparty risk from the swap provider. This is where collateral comes in.

ETFs use two different kinds of swaps when tracking an index: funded and unfunded. Unfunded are more common, and typically occur when the swap-providing investment bank and ETF issuer are owned by the same parent company.

Unfunded swaps

In an unfunded swap, ETF issuers enter into a swap agreement with an investment bank. As part of the agreement, the ETF issuer uses the cash they received from investors to buy a collateral basket – a mix of assets that are liquid and safe. In practice, a collateral basket is usually full of government bonds and sometimes blue-chip shares.

The assets in this collateral basket, which are often sourced from the parent company's balance sheet, are then put in a custody account. After paying a swap fee to the swap provider, the ETF issuer then swaps the desired exposure – be it emerging market construction companies, junk bonds or whatever else – against the return of the collateral, usually benchmarked against LIBOR. (Note: swap fees are paid every year and form part of the running cost of a synthetic ETF.)

The value of the collateral is marked-to-market every trading day. Under UCITS rules, the collateral basket must equal at least 90% of the value of the fund. But in practice, most ETF providers post more than 90% collateral; some even maintain full or over-collateralised positions. This collateral helps offset counterparty risk that comes from the swap.

Unfunded swap model

The unfunded swap model is the most commonly used synthetic-replication method.

Simplified unfunded swap ETF structure

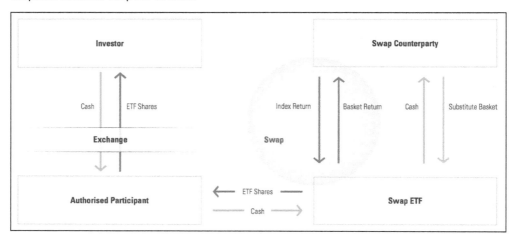

Source: Morningstar Research

Funded swaps

Funded swaps are different, and in many ways function more like an exchange traded note. Funded swaps receive the performance of an index from an investment bank, as with unfunded swaps. But instead of giving the investment bank a collateral basket, they give them cash. The investment bank then goes and turns this cash into a collateral basket themselves.

Funded Swap Model

Under the funded – also known as fully funded – swap model, the portfolio manager transfers investors' cash to a swap counterparty in exchange for the index performance (adjusted for a swap spread) plus the principal at the future date. The counterparty posts collateral assets in a segregated account with a third-party custodian.

Simplified funded swap ETF structure

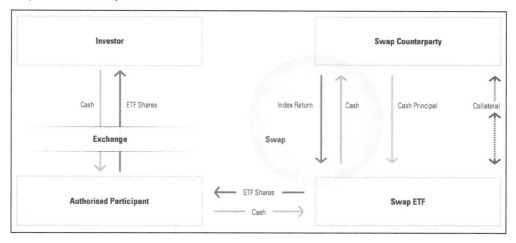

Source: Morningstar Research

What happens next, however, is crucial and something any investor considering a funded-swap-backed-ETF should know. In some cases, the investment bank will give the collateral to a segregated account with a transfer of title in place. But other times they will put it in a pledge account. This difference is important because it can determine what rights investors have to collateral. When a default occurs in ETFs using a segregated account, the transfer of title means that the collateral is transferred from the segregated account to the fund's account and the ETF issuer has direct access to the collateral. The pledge account can be more complicated. When defaults arise, a pledge must be enforced. In this scenario, it is possible that bankruptcy administrators – whoever they may be – freeze the assets in the pledge account.

STOCK LENDING

ETFs are getting cheaper. At the time of writing, the annual fee for some plain vanilla ETFs is close to zero. If pricing trends continue, in a few years' time some ETFs may cost absolutely nothing.

But ETF issuers have to make money somehow. And it's stock lending that allows ETF issuers to charge close to nothing for these new ETFs.

ETFs, like every fund, hold stocks, which the fund's managers can lend out. ETFs are very attractive for stock lenders because they have large holdings and little trading activity – meaning there are many idle stocks which can easily be lent out. (This is different, say, from some mutual funds where there is heavy churn and fewer stocks.)

Stock lending is common and widespread – and not just in physical ETFs. In 2016, for example, the global value of stocks on loan at one point in time exceeded $2 trillion. It is also very important because it provides an additional source of revenue – around three basis points per ETF, according to Vanguard – in a time of declining fee revenue.

In a typical lending scenario, the potential borrower of a stock – usually a large financial institution with a view to short selling – goes hunting for a potential lender. The potential borrower rarely goes looking for a lender directly. Rather, they go through agents, such as broker-dealers, who can connect them to a lender. The agent will then take a share of the rental fee, usually 30%.

When a borrower has found a lender, the lender requires the borrower to post collateral before they agree to lend them the stock, this way the lender has security if the borrower defaults. The lender will also spell out the terms of the loan. This includes the loan's duration, how much rent the borrower must pay, and an agreement to pass any dividends or coupons a stock pays on to the fund. Unwinding the loan is the reverse process. The stock borrowed is returned to the fund from which it was borrowed. Collateral is then released via the agent who arranged the loan. All fees are then settled.

How much of an ETF's holdings are lent out depends, in the first instance, on the issuer. Some issuers have policies in place limiting the amount that can be lent out – with typical limits varying from 30 to 50%. Others – but very few – have policies prohibiting securities lending altogether. Such limits are subject to change and purely voluntary. As a rule of thumb, it's safest for investors to assume that their ETF issuer will engage in stock lending and that it can lend at least 50% of its holdings out.

Another important consideration for investors is what lending model their ETF issuer is using (if it is possible for them to find out). Here, Vanguard divides stock lending into two kinds models: value and volume. Value involves lending out stocks that few other issuers are lending out. This means they attract a scarcity premium and higher rental fees can be charged. Volume lending, by contrast, is picking stocks that are most likely to get lent out, meaning an issuer can maximise the number of loan transactions made.

Here, it can be worth noting that academics have found that issuers tend to hold stocks that are most likely to get lent out (whether for value or for volume reasons). That is, ETF issuers skew their funds' holdings towards what short sellers want to borrow.

As well as between issuers, lending also varies between ETFs. ETFs with different holdings engage in different degrees of securities lending. As another rule of thumb, ETFs that hold government bonds are extremely likely to engage in securities lending. Government bonds are the most borrowed stocks around the world – by far. According to a recent study around 40% of all stock lending is in government bonds.

Should investors be worried about stock lending?

There are two kinds of risks involved in stock lending: borrower default risk and collateral reinvestment risk. Borrower default risk is when the borrower cannot return the stock they've borrowed. Most often, this is because a short-seller's (and borrowers are usually short sellers) gambit has backfired and the stock they borrowed, rather than dropping, rallies strongly, forcing them to default. How often does this happen? Very rarely. According to BlackRock, since the company's founding in 1981 there have only been three cases of borrowers defaulting. And in every case, BlackRock says, they were able to repurchase the stocks borrowed with collateral posted.

There are also safeguards. Stock exchanges and industry practice almost always require that short sellers post collateral exceeding the value of anything they've borrowed. In the United States, industry practice dictates that collateral exceeds 102% of the value of the stock borrowed. Rules are similar in other countries.

Collateral reinvestment risk occurs because ETF issuers tend to lend out the collateral they receive, as well as the stock. This is usually into low-risk money market funds. Here the danger is that a financial crisis – or some other event – can wipe out the value of the collateral. This happened during the 2008 financial crisis, for instance. Such situations are rare but do happen.

The major criticism of stock lending is about who gets the spoils. Some say that the gains (the rental fees charged to borrowers) should go to investors – not the issuers. After all, it's the investors' assets being lent out and investors who ultimately bear the risk. Here it can be worth noting that some issuers do in fact offer investors the spoils of stock lending.

But this coin has two sides. Stock lending is what enables big issuers to offer ETFs at such low costs. They are, after all, commercial beasts and they have to make money somehow. If they don't do that through management fees, it has to come from stock lending, they say. It is stock lending that makes free ETFs free.

Another major criticism is that stock lending blurs the distinction between physical and synthetic ETFs. Synthetic ETFs expose investors to counterparty risk because they're based on swaps. Thus, if the swap provider defaults, then the synthetic ETF goes bust with it. But stock lending complicates this. Because physical ETFs lend out their stocks and the collateral backing it up, investors are exposed to the same sort of counterparty risks you'd find in a synthetic ETF. That is, they can lose their stock and collateral in the type of event, like a financial crisis, that would threaten the solvency of a giant investment bank that provides the swaps.

ETNS

Investors tracking more adventurous indices may encounter what are called *exchange traded notes* or *certificates* and are generally issued by banks to their sophisticated investors. These are yet another variation on the theme of synthetic replication. In essence these notes and certificates are almost exactly the same as their synthetic ETF cousins with four key differences:

1. They are **not funds** and thus can track relatively undiversified indices such as commodities or futures. This allows for greater flexibility in construction.

2. There is **no collateral**, just a simple swap-based structure that operates like an IOU against the issuer. In effect they are a kind of debt-based security.

3. The **downside risk in the structure is greater** because of that lack of collateral, i.e. if the issuer goes bust, you could be faced with a capital loss as you will be a creditor like any other bondholder in the bank or issuer.

4. They often include **options** embedded within the pay-off, such as giving downside protection in return for reduced income or upside.

Investors will find many ETN and ETC structures within the alternative asset space where the construction of a traditional diversified fund is almost impossible. That means that these products are probably best left to adventurous investors who are capable of understanding the dynamics of a particular alternative asset class, options pricing and the risks (and potential rewards) of the counterparty risk.

ETCS

Investors interested in exposure to commodities can gain access through the exchange-traded vehicles built specifically for commodities exposure: exchange-traded commodities. ETCs can track any and every type of commodity: from agricultural goods like wheat and cocoa, to industrial metals like zinc, to livestock like lean hogs. Because they are not funds as such, they are therefore not bound by any diversification rules. This means that ETCs can provide exposure to a single asset class like gold.

In terms of structure, ETCs fall into two main categories: physically-backed and synthetic. Physically backed are by far the most popular type of ETC, making up more than 90% of assets. They are most commonly used for precious metals, like gold, silver and platinum. A physical ETC is a brilliantly simple financial instrument and is, in effect, nothing more than an IOU note for a physical bullion sitting in a bank's vault. Legally speaking, they're usually structured as "zero coupon bonds", where the debt owed is precious metal bullion. When APs want to create physical ETCs, they deliver bullion to the ETC issuer (in a manner similar to creating physical ETFs, discussed above). Physical ETCs are a very safe structure and have no credit risk. For this reason, they are popular even in countries where ETF markets are quite small, such as in sub-Saharan Africa and India.

Synthetic ETCs work in a manner much like synthetic ETFs discussed above. They typically involve picking a commodity index, like the Bloomberg Commodity Index, and then finding a swap counterparty to deliver the performance. As with other synthetic ETFs, they are also collateralised.

Summary of the types of ETF

Structure	Risks	Upsides
Physically replicating ETF or fund	Stock lending Tracking error Can be more expensive in terms of management fees	Simplicity of construction Very low counterparty risk (though there may be some with stock lending)
Synthetically replicating ETF	More complicated structure Counterparty risk if swap becomes worthless	Low tracking error (fund expenses will still produce a small tracking error) Can be less expensive in terms of management fees
ETN or ETC	Counterparty risk based on issuer Likely to be more complicated underlying index Some ETNs might not be hugely liquid for day-to-day trading with possibility of higher bid offer spreads	Low tracking error Access to more adventurous asset classes Can be structured to increase leverage or gearing

WHY COSTS MATTER

When looking at a potential ETF investment many investors will start by looking up the fund's total expense ratio (TER); understandably so, since one of the key attractions of ETFs is their low cost, especially when compared with actively-managed mutual funds, with their 1.5–2% annual management fees, and initial charges of up to 6% of the invested amount.

Of course, since ETFs are traded like shares, an investor will need to pay a stockbroker's commission on any purchase or sale. Fortunately, since the arrival of internet-based discount brokers, such costs are pretty modest. It's worth ensuring that the broker you use operates a segregated custodial account for client securities, since this will ring-fence your assets in the case of the failure of the institution concerned.

In addition to the TER, the investor should consider the likely bid-offer spread that the ETF commands in the secondary market. The spread – the difference between the buying and the selling price – can be minimal in the most liquid ETFs – usually around a few basis points (hundredths of a percentage). But in the less liquid ETFs it can jump to 1% or more.

Bid-offer spreads generally represent the real trading costs of the securities underlying the ETF, so if you're investing in an emerging market small cap fund or a corporate bond ETF, expect to pay more in percentage terms as spread than in a large benchmark ETF, such as one of the EURO STOXX 50 Eurozone equity funds, or in one of the money market ETFs that have become very popular in Europe as an alternative to bank deposits.

However, there may be structural problems underlying high bid-offer spreads. The larger the number of market makers trading in a particular ETF, the greater the chance that the arbitrage mechanism which underlies the ETF's creation and redemption process (where market makers, acting as authorised participants, exchange ETF units for the underlying securities, discussed above) will work efficiently. If there's only one market maker, perhaps part of the bank that owns the company promoting the ETF, the arbitrage mechanism may not work so well. This information should be available on the issuer's website. If it isn't, ask.

But at the end of the day, ETFs are very liquid instruments and were created with low trading costs in mind. Unlike investment trusts (close-ended mutual funds), ETFs are open-ended, meaning they can be created and redeemed without limit, helping to ensure liquidity. And unlike unit trusts (open-ended mutual funds), ETFs can be short sold and traded throughout the day – again helping to improve liquidity and lower trading costs. At the time of writing, State Street's SPY, the first ETF ever listed, is the most liquid equity security in the world and currently has a spread of 0.00% – the only equity security in the world that, essentially, trades freely. And if investors are of the buy-and-hold variety, a spread of 1% for an ETF that is held for 10 years may not be too high a price to pay. For those interested in frequently trading ETFs, however, spreads have to be watched.

TAX REPORTING

For a UK investor, there are a few important tax rules to be aware of. Tax, as always, can be a complicated subject, and investors should check with their own advisers to be absolutely sure of their tax position. Since most ETFs sold in the UK are domiciled in established overseas fund jurisdictions such as Dublin or Luxembourg, where the funds pay little or no tax, distributions to UK residents will be considered to be foreign dividends and subject to dividend tax rates, which are currently 32.5% for higher-rate taxpayers, and 10% for basic rate taxpayers.

When listed for trading in the UK, most of these foreign-domiciled ETFs have 'distributor' status, meaning that gains made on ETFs for taxable investors are subject to capital gains tax (CGT), rather than income tax. Since the CGT rate is currently 18%, and income is taxed at rates up to 40%, ETFs with distributor status are clearly preferable for a tax-paying UK investor.

European-domiciled ETFs are generally eligible for inclusion within tax-protected savings accounts such as ISAs, PEPs and SIPPs. ETF issuers' websites should confirm if a particular fund has distributor status, and whether a fund is ISA-, PEP- and SIPP-eligible.

A big obstacle to the popularity of ETFs in the UK was removed in 2007, when stamp duty on secondary market trading was removed. This has led to a big increase in the number of ETFs listed for trading on the London Stock Exchange, giving UK-based investors greater variety.

If you're UK-based and investing in a taxable account, the decision on whether to invest in bond ETFs or direct bond holdings is a tricky one. While capital gains on direct bond holdings are not taxable, gains on bond funds such as ETFs are liable to CGT. On the other hand, investing in bonds via an ETF gives you immediate diversification and may be the only practicable route for an investor with a few thousand pounds to devote to the sector.

WHY LIQUIDITY, AVAILABILITY ON PLATFORM AND SIZE MATTER

If you look up the actual trading volumes for European ETFs on the issuers' or exchanges' websites, you'll find that while some funds are very actively traded, there's a long tail of funds in which activity is very subdued. ETF issuers often point out that reported trading statistics (*on-exchange volumes*) are not entirely representative of the real liquidity of their funds, since in Europe a lot of institutional trading in ETFs takes place over the counter, that is, away from the official exchanges. Therefore, the true liquidity is probably greater than the reported figures suggest and, as issuers like to say, an ETF is as liquid as its underlying components.

Nevertheless, the reported trading volumes and bid-offer spreads are likely to give you a good feel for the trading liquidity of a particular fund. Spread information can be found on the websites of the German XETRA exchange, the Borsa Italiana in Milan and the NYSE Euronext exchange in Paris. They all publish monthly or quarterly reviews of ETF secondary market liquidity and it is certainly a good idea to look up the trading costs for any fund you're considering buying. As European ETFs tend to be cross-listed in different countries, such data should be broadly applicable across the region for particular funds, in case your local exchange doesn't publish the data.

This data on trading should also give you a clue about another key issue – whether a fund is big enough to survive. Or in simple terms, whether your ETF is economic. As a rough and ready rule, funds with a total market capitalisation – or assets under management, another parallel term – of under £100m are unlikely to be economic or profitable. As the average total expense ratio of a fund can vary between 20 basis points (0.2%) and 1% per annum, the fees will probably only amount to between £200,000 and £1 million for our £100m fund. Out of that there are many fees to pay including the trading fees, the trustees and custodians, and of course the fund managers' own internal costs. Many issuers may be happy to run a fund with less than £100m because they think it'll grow over time, but they might also be tempted to close it if profits slump in the future. Once AUM gets below, say, £50m, and especially £20m, these issues become more acute.

One last factor to watch out for is the platform you trade your ETF on. Many investors might find themselves attracted to more adventurous structures such as ETNs only to discover that their fund/dealing platform doesn't offer access to products aimed at sophisticated investors. This sophistication test isn't quite as daunting as it first seems largely because most stock-broker platforms will simply require the investor to sign a suitable risk declaration form. But investors who work through a financial adviser need to be aware that many IFAs use platforms that offer no access to any listed products whatsoever, be they ETFs, ETNs or even investment trusts.

THE BOTTOM LINE: DIFFERENT STRUCTURES FOR DIFFERENT INVESTORS

Which fund and product structures make sense for the average investor and their adviser?

The answer is that it greatly depends. The table below sums up the key differences between the most popular structures.

Clearly the appropriateness of a fund largely depends on your attitude towards risk and return and the frequency of your trading. As you can see there are a great many different variations but as a general rule the simplest distinction should be between a *strategic* investor (boasting low trading volumes within their portfolio and a long-term focus) and a more *tactically* inclined investor who wants to change their asset allocations on a very regular basis.

By and large, options-based structures and leveraged trackers are most appropriate for the tactical investor who wants to increase their potential for geared, short-term returns. By contrast most strategic investors should probably avoid all geared, leveraged structures and focus instead on ETFs (and ETNs for the more sophisticated investor) as well actively managed funds such as investment trusts where appropriate.

And what of the distinction between physically and synthetically tracking an index – how important is that debate around structure?

For many cautious investors, synthetic replication in funds might worry them, especially if they focused on counterparty risk. Yet these investors also need to realise that many illiquid equity markets (for instance some emerging markets) and most alternative assets can only be accessed via some kind of derivative.

We find the debate between physical and synthetic a slight side show – other issues such as cost, bid-offer spreads and the quality of collateral matter more than the generic structure of a fund. Yet there is also no getting around the fact that you need to understand not only the product structure itself but also the cost of that structure (and that means looking at the bid-offer spreads and, tracking error, which crucially includes fees), the index that it is tracking and whether that index is appropriate for your diversified portfolio.

ETF checklist

Here's a summary of useful checks to perform when selecting a particular ETF or other tracker product:

1. Is it UCITS-compliant?

2. What is the ETF structure and replication method, and do I understand what counterparty risks the product carries?

3. How is the index constructed, and could there be any drawbacks in the construction method (excessive concentrations, index turnover, roll costs, tracking error over time)?

4. What's the secondary market liquidity like? How large are bid-offer spreads for the ETF I'm considering buying?

5. Is the fund company or fund likely to close, and if so what costs might arise?

6. Is the ETF's tax status suitable for me?

Summary of ETF structure characteristics

Likely Tracking Error for an ETF	Product
Lower or zero tracking error	Synthetic ETF especially in less liquid underlying market
Higher tracking error	Physical replicating ETF
Likely Counterparty Risk Level	Product
Lower risk	Physical ETFs
Higher risk	Synthetic ETFs
Duration of Investment Term	Product
Days and weeks	Leveraged trackers, turbos
Months (up to 12 months)	Covered Warrants, ETNs and ETFs
Years	ETFs and structured investments including listed structured products
Use of Leverage	Product
Low or no leverage	ETFs and ETNs
Medium leverage	Covered Warrants
High leverage	Turbos and Leveraged Trackers
Risk Inherent in Structure	Product
Lower risk	ETFs and some structured investments such as structured deposits
Higher risk	ETNs and other options-based structures including covered warrants
Ease of Availability on IFA and Dealing Platforms	Product
Widely available	Unit trusts, and some ETFs
Available largely on stock broker platforms, and require investor to have signed risk notice	ETNs and most options-based structures
Cost in Terms of TER	Product
Under 0.50% TER pa	Many ETFs, physical and synthetic
0.50% to 1% TER pa	Many ETNs and other options-based structures, some investment trusts
1% or more TER	Most unit trusts (except index tracking)

Section 2

ETFS NOW

PASSIVE INVESTING IS NOT TAKING OVER

THE HEADLINES IN the financial pages often make it seem that passive is taking over the world, but the data makes it clear that this is far from the case. Recent analysis from BlackRock shows that the relative scale of index investing is still small – at around 20% of all global equities. In fund terms, index and ETFs represent around 12% of the US equity universe and 7% of the global equity universe.

But even this simple breakdown might be misleading. Data regarding asset management is sometimes hard to obtain and verify, but the BlackRock team make the point that active mutual funds are also a relatively small percentage of the market with the largest percentage of the market consisting of assets not owned by any manager. As can be seen from the BlackRock chart (below), ETFs are a very small slice of the overall market at 4%, or $2.7tn of the investable equity universe.

	$ trillions of market cap owned	Percentage of total market cap owned
Index	11.9	17.5%
Mutual funds	2.3	3.4%
ETFs	2.7	4.0%
Institutional indexing	5.4	7.9%
Internal indexing	1.4	2.1%
Active	17.4	25.6%
Mutual funds	8.0	11.8%
Institutional	7.5	11.0%
Hedge funds	1.9	2.8%
Assets not managed by an external manager (excl. Internal index investing)	38.7	57.0%
Corporate (financial and non-financial)	25.2	37.0%
Insurance and pensions (defined benefit and defined contribution)	8.5	12.5%
Official institutions	5.0	7.4%
Total	67.9	100%

Source: BlackRock

But is it growing?

Yes, but there might be a natural self-regulating balance that will apply as and when passives become an even larger part of the market. It is the relative underperformance of active mutual funds which has contributed to the appeal of index strategies; should index funds grow large enough to affect price discovery in parts of the market, then active managers would be able to exploit the mispricing and hence encourage flows back into active strategies. "Improved active performance would attract flows back into active strategies. Intuitively, the market will continuously adjust to an equilibrium," says the BlackRock analysts.

Still, active funds assets must have been going backwards?

Not necessarily. It is a more nuanced picture, suggest the BlackRock team, with index strategies often being used as low-cost building blocks in actively managed portfolio asset allocation strategies. "Moreover, active funds that have exhibited strong performance net of fees have still been able to generate significant inflows, indicating that this shift is about performance and fees rather than the style itself," they write. The team suggest that investment flows into index strategies are primarily from active funds that are themselves benchmarked to a passive index. In effect, it is perfectly possible for that flow to take place in a way that makes zero net change in the demand for given stocks.

So why all the current chatter about passives?

Partly, it might be argued the newsflow at present is reflecting a movement in investment fashion. BlackRock points out that 40 years ago, balanced funds containing both stocks and bonds were popular, run in the US by bank trust departments and in Europe by pension funds, banks and insurers. A number of investment professionals then left to create their own firms, mostly to focus on equity funds. Broad equity portfolios were then segmented further, such as by company size, industry, or region. "Over the past few decades, individual investors have moved from owning individual stocks to investing in the equity market via mutual funds," they write. "Most recently, there has been a shift from traditional active strategies towards index."

So, it's a fashion thing?

No, this is a question of performance. According to the BlackRock team:

> Index strategies are often used as low-cost building blocks in actively-managed portfolio asset allocation strategies – which again suggests that active or index are not clear distinctions. Moreover, active funds that have exhibited strong performance net of fees have still been able to generate significant inflows.

What about the impact of pricing pressure on fees?

What is interesting are the drivers behind the price pressure. While investor enthusiasm for cheaper index products is partly down to underperformance by more expensive mutual fund options, the push and pull on prices is also down to a greater regulatory focus on fees.

In the US it has been the Labor Department's mandated transparency on fees on 401k plans, in the UK it was RDR and now across Europe it is MiFID II which are encouraging a greater degree of insight for consumers on what they pay for their investment plans. As BlackRock suggest, many intermediaries involved in offering products to individual investors have interpreted these regulatory actions to mean that low-cost products are a safe harbour. "By choosing low-fee products, they are in essence fulfilling their responsibility towards their clients," they suggest.

PASSIVE FUNDS WON'T DESTROY EFFICIENT MARKETS

INIGO FRASER-JENKINS, AN analyst at Bernstein, made a splash recently when he argued that "passive investing is worse than Marxism". His argument was that a largely passive stock market will no longer be able to allocate resources sensibly, so we'd be better off with a communist central planner making those decisions.

It's an interesting argument, but we think it's wrong. Even though money will continue to shift into passive investments for some time to come, we doubt that markets will be significantly less efficient than they are now.

What are efficient markets anyway?

Before we go any further, let's quickly clarify what efficient markets are. The efficient market hypothesis (EMH) says that a company's share price should represent all the information and analysis that is available for that stock at any one time. If new information comes to light, then the share price should change.

The rise of the EMH is one factor behind the huge growth in passive investing. If markets are 100% efficient, it should be impossible to beat the market, and if it's impossible to beat the market, you might as well invest in plain vanilla passive funds that allocate money on the basis of company market caps.

But if the whole market is held by passive investors, how can new information be incorporated into share prices?

For the market mechanism to work, you need investors who respond to new information and who are also analysing a company in depth and looking for new information and insights.

This would be a valid concern if there was any likelihood of the whole market, or nearly the whole market, becoming passive. But we don't think that's ever going to happen. For starters, the market is more active than you might think. Index funds, including passive ETFs, still represent less than 20% of global equities, according to BlackRock. What's more, we shouldn't forget that a large proportion of equities aren't held by fund managers whether active or passive. Stocks are also held by pension funds, insurance companies, direct retail investors, and other companies with stakes in a business.

We also shouldn't forget the dividing line between passive and active is a bit blurry. Passive isn't just about investing in a fund tracking the FTSE 100 or S&P anymore. Strictly speaking, smart beta funds are passive not active because the stocks are still selected according to a rules-based process, but they feel more active than a Footsie tracker. And even if your portfolio wholly comprises passive ETFs, your overall asset allocation decisions – which markets to invest in – are still active.

Perhaps more importantly, if we do ever get to a stage where 70% of the market is passive, that should offer exciting opportunities for active investors. If 70% of money is just following existing market caps, it'll be easy to spot companies that are clearly under-valued – paying high yields or trading on low price/earnings ratios even though profits are growing fast.

Because of that, we're fairly convinced that a self-correcting mechanism will kick in if passive investing truly starts to dominate the market. That self-correcting process might take a while and you might argue that such a market – where it takes a while for share prices to react to circumstances – wouldn't be truly efficient. And that's fair comment. But we'd argue that even the S&P 500 isn't 100% efficient now, and anyway, the self-correcting mechanism we've described should at least mean that the market will allocate resources more effectively than Marxist central planners.

Shorting

There's also an aspect of passive investing which helps to make the market more efficient, not less. That's the process of stock lending which is an essential part of the shorting process. When an investor wants to short a stock, he normally borrows that stock and sells it immediately. He hopes that the share price of that stock will then fall, so he can buy the stock back more cheaply when he has to return it to the stock lender.

Currently around 65% of loanable assets are provided by passive investors, and as Peter Sleep, Senior Investment Manager at Seven Investment Management says: "By contributing their assets to the stock lending market, passive investors are helping prevent individual securities from getting over-valued. This allows short sellers to borrow from a plentiful inventory of shortable assets."

The investors who short stocks aren't traditional passive investors driven by market cap, but they don't just include active hedge fund managers. Sleep says that some smart beta passive investors are also shorting stocks.

So, in summary, we don't think markets are 100% efficient now, we don't think the rise of passive investing is making them a lot more inefficient, and we don't think passive is worse than Marxism.

PASSIVE AND ACTIVE
IS NOT A BINARY CHOICE

THE WAY INVESTORS like decisions to be framed as either/or questions is natural given what is often at stake. At a basic level, investing itself is a decision to either invest or to not invest and even market sophisticates are drawn to the simple analogy of markets being either risk on or risk off.

No prizes then for guessing that the debate regarding active and passive management is often cast as a binary choice. A simple question of yes or no. Yet like many other apparently simple decisions, this over-simplifies a more complex picture.

"Differentiating between active and index strategies is often a useful shorthand," say the capital markets team at BlackRock. "However, whereas much of the current dialogue pitches active and index investment strategies against each other as opposites, the investment landscape is in practice more nuanced."

The BlackRock team make the point that the investment landscape is better understood as a continuum of investment styles where absolute definitions are increasingly blurred. Specifically, the chosen investment style will be delivered via a set of products which will be driven to a greater or lesser degree by either active or index management and with a proportionately greater or lesser relationship to the index.

BlackRock go on to define the four common investment styles; active-absolute return, active-relative return, active and index factor strategies and finally purely index strategies. As BlackRock point out, the first of these categories is effectively dominated by hedge funds which employ investment techniques that generally are not available in traditional asset management products, such as short selling, use of borrowed funds, more sophisticated financial contracts or physical positions in commodities. They also, not coincidentally, charge the highest fees.

Welcome to ETF-land

In the last three investment styles we see ETFs in one form or another enter the equation. Fully active ETFs clearly fall into the active-relative return category. But this is also the area where, according to active management's critics, we would find the index-hugging funds, charging an active premium for an effectively passive return.

Then we get the factor strategies and the world of smart beta. The latter might be a new term, but as BlackRock point out, investing in size and style factors has a long history going all the way back to the 1930s and Benjamin Graham. Smart beta formalises many of these factors into some key strategies such as value, volatility, momentum, dividend yield and/or size.

"In this way, smart beta incorporates elements of both active and index: the benchmark is the result of an active process and the resulting portfolio replicates or tracks the benchmark," say the BlackRock team. "Factor strategies have generated increased interest as investors try to implement investment exposures that target risk and return profiles that differ from traditional market capitalisation indices."

Then we finally get to 'pure' passive index funds. Yet, as BlackRock point out, using the term index strategies "may give the false impression of a fully automated approach to investment management".

"These strategies do seek to track the composition and performance of an index closely, but require specialist portfolio management expertise to do so," they say. There are three characteristics that index providers and index funds will generally look to in order to construct and track benchmarks.

1. **Transparent** – meaning that the rules of the index, its risk-return profile and the constituents are disclosed.

2. **Investable** – meaning that a material amount of capital can be invested in the index constituents and the index's published return can be tracked.

3. **Strictly rules-based** – meaning that no portfolio manager intervenes in determining the investment universe and holdings of the fund (away from managing the minimisation of tracking error, transaction costs or other restrictions). The portfolio management process for index investments does not rely on fundamental analysis of individual stocks and maintains economies of scale that tend to facilitate lower expense ratios.

The development of indices

A vital ingredient in all this are the indices themselves. As BlackRock say, they have become indispensable parts of the capital markets and investment process and are used for myriad purposes: tracking the performance of markets or sectors; measuring portfolio manager skill versus a benchmark; as building blocks for portfolios; and as key inputs to stock price discovery in global markets.

The growth of index investing has, then, 'catalysed' new questions about index investing and the ownership of company stock, and renewed those questions posed in the early years of index markets regarding the impact of index investing on efficient price formation for stocks.

But it also makes plain that the issue of active versus passive is now, more than ever, not an either/or issue. To coin a phrase, it's more complicated than that.

NOT ALL ETFS TRACK EQUITY

ETFs ARE OFTEN taken to be mostly, or even exclusively, about equities. When investors look to invest in ETFs, they almost always are looking for equity products or index trackers: what's called plain vanilla.

The same is true of investment pundits and the press. In commentary discussing whether ETFs are in a bubble, to take a popular recent example, the ETFs being referred to are almost always equity trackers.

The view that ETFs are mostly – or even exclusively – equity funds has some historical justification. ETFs, after all, began as index funds.

When Jack Bogle listed the world's first index tracking fund in 1976, it was all about equity, and 'Bogle's folly' was targeted at active equity management. When State Street listed the world's first ETF in 1993, it was likewise an equity tracker. Other kinds of ETFs and ETPs came later.

To date, of the $4.5tn locked in ETFs globally, $3.6tn of it is in equity funds — that's 80%, according to BlackRock data. But this also means that 20% – and a growing percentage at that – is in different kinds of ETFs.

Not all ETFs are equity trackers

The types of assets ETFs track is widening every day. Twenty years ago, there were only equity ETFs that tracked a narrow range of famous indices. Now, there are ETFs for whisky, marijuana and fallen angel bonds. At the time of writing, ETF issuers and exchanges are working to put blockchain and cryptocurrency ETFs into play – showing just how far things have come.

Fixed income ETFs growing rapidly

Not only are more and more non-equity ETFs emerging, but on the current trend the share of ETFs taken by non-equity funds is expanding – particularly in fixed income. As KPMG explained in a recent report, entitled "Index Investing":

> Investors are increasingly looking beyond equities and are using index products to gain exposure to other asset classes. A majority of investors use index products for some fixed income exposure.

Global ETP assets

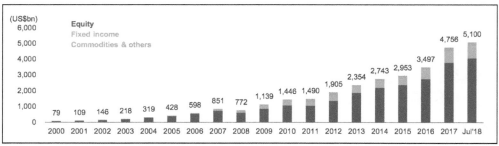

Source: BlackRock Global ETP Landscape, Nov 2017

One reason for the growing popularity of fixed-income ETFs is that they offer retail investors exposure to bonds that were, before ETFs, available only to institutional investors. Crucially, this includes investment grade bonds from blue-chip companies, whose debts were only sold to other institutions.

Other reasons include the growth of actively managed ETFs, which allow investment professionals to sit and watch over the performance of the underlying bonds. This benefit is acutely felt for high yield bonds, which can be riskier and benefit from oversight from experienced professionals watching the market. But it is also because fixed-income investors, as with equity, like the transparency and low-cost structure of ETFs.

The growth of fixed-income ETFs has been particularly pronounced in the US, where the biggest five fixed-income ETFs all have more than $20bn assets under management. They are also highly liquid, with spreads lower than 0.01%.

Commodities ETFs

Another major area for ETFs outside equities is commodity products – particularly gold. Gold ETFs are some of the oldest and began with Gold Bullion Securities in Australia in 2003. They're also some of the largest: GLD by State Street in the US has more than $34bn. They are also, interestingly, some of the first to be listed in new countries. In many sub-Saharan African countries, for example, where the ETF markets are very small, gold ETFs are all they have listed.

This makes sense. Gold is familiar to investors and its investment benefits do not need explaining. But it's also a good bet because most gold ETFs are backed by physical bullion. This means that investors can cash in their ETFs and ask for bars of gold in some instances. For example, Gold Bullion Securities (LSE: GBS) allows investors to trade their ETFs in for bars of gold, providing they have an LBMA account and own enough of the ETF that it adds up to a whole bar's worth. This kind of physical backing is only available with precious metals ETFs.

VIX ETFs

The other major kind of ETFs for investors to get their heads around are ETFs that track VIX futures. This is one of the more obscure corners of the passive investing universe. VIX is known as the fear gauge and is meant to measure how much fear is in the market. ETFs that track the VIX "are some of the most complex ETPs trading," explains David Nadig, the CEO of ETF.com. They can also be quite risky (as was seen in early 2018) and more expensive than more conventional funds.

Nevertheless, they've developed a large enough following among sophisticated investors, particularly hedge funds, to merit special mention as a third major class of product.

INVESTING IN BONDS USING ETFS

IN THE LAST three to four years, the ETF revolution has finally swept through the fixed income space, with hundreds of new bond-focused index tracking funds opening up for business in the last year or so. This sudden popularity of bond ETFs is in part a consequence of the decade-long bull market for fixed income investors, with many supposedly boring, lower risk bonds actually turning in far superior (positive) returns when compared to equities. But bond ETFs have also become much more popular simply because there's a huge amount of choice around. Put simply, virtually any form of mainstream fixed income security can now be tracked by an ETF.

That huge variety is a simple reflection of an economic fact that fixed income markets are hugely important for global investors. There are hundreds of governments, thousands of quasi-governmental organisations (including municipalities in the US) and tens of thousands of corporations around the world that issue bonds of one form or another. Getting a handle on just how huge this potential market is isn't actually that easy – for example hundreds of different towns and municipalities in the US issue their own debts and some of them are rarely if ever traded on any public exchange, while the European Investment Bank may have several hundred bond issues trading at any one time. Given this immense size, it's little surprise that back in the world of ETFs you'll find a huge choice, with three main categories of funds:

- **Mainstream government securities**, called gilts in the UK. These come in varying shapes and sizes, with conventional issues the mainstay, all with varying durations. There's also a growing index-linked gilts space plus of course a huge international choice of different governmental issuers.

- **Mainstream corporate bonds**, mostly issued by the bigger, more reputable companies with lower risk ratings and excellent reputations. In this hugely popular – and higher yielding – space the key differentiators are based around underlying currency (sterling, dollar or euro), riskiness of issuer (expressed in the credit rating) and a focus on including or excluding certain sectors (notably financial services and especially bank bonds).

- **Newer bond market indices** tend to focus on innovative ideas such as risk weighted indices or newer issuers from the emerging markets.

BOND ETFS: THE BASICS

A bond ETF is simply a collection of bonds that are grouped together so that instead of buying an individual bond issued by say the UK government security, or a big European corporation, you can gain exposure to a whole selection of bonds in one simple trade. You can't buy a bond index directly, but you can get exposure to one by purchasing an ETF.

For investors in bonds there's essentially two big initial choices, based around who issues the bond. **Governments** are by far the most prolific issuers of bonds, with lots of different time lengths and structures. The big issuers include the US and UK governments– their governments borrow a very substantial amount of money every single week! These governments are regarded as very reliable and thus the yield or income they pay out is relatively low. But yields can vary substantially from government to government. Some government bonds, such as those from emerging markets, have very high yields because they are judged to be riskier.

Corporate issuers are typically bigger companies that want to raise some money for a specific business reason, maybe to fund an acquisition or build a new factory. The sheer variety of corporate bond issuers is huge ranging from massive, very reliable big corporations such as McDonald's or Royal Dutch Shell through to much smaller, riskier businesses. As these businesses by and large are riskier than say the US or UK government – they could conceivably go bust – the regular income paid out, the yield, is usually a bit higher than for government securities.

Whatever issuer of bonds you favour, bond markets provide huge choice and deep liquidity – this means there's lots of buyers and sellers. These markets are also conveniently tracked by a variety of indices.

The world of govies or government bonds

Generally, government securities such as UK gilts are perceived as very low risk, which means the income yield is also low. But these assets are very attractive if equity markets look volatile and dangerous. And even within this broad spectrum of government bonds you have a choice over the length of time you loan your money out – short duration bonds with a time span of just a few years are less risky than long duration securities where you are lending for ten or even fifty years!

Gilts are issued by HM Treasury and are rated as AAA in risk terms (more on these ratings below) by all the major credit ratings agencies and can be viewed as effectively risk-free from the point of view of default – neither the UK nor US government has ever defaulted or missed a payment on their bonds.

Crucially the notes or bonds issued by the government to fund its public services will fluctuate from day to day in the market, depending on the outlook for interest rates. And it's not just the UK government that issues bonds – nearly every major government in the developed world currently runs a deficit and needs to borrow via bonds on the global markets although it's worth noting that the US, Japan and Europe (primarily the UK, Germany, France, Italy and Spain) dominate the government bond market, accounting for more than 84% of all government bonds outstanding! Within this broad category of government bonds you may also encounter two different types of bond.

The most popular bonds consist of **conventional gilts** – these represent the largest part of the gilt portfolio and are in effect a guarantee by the government to pay the holder a fixed cash interest payment (half of the coupon) every six months until the bond matures. On maturity the holder receives the final coupon payment and the nominal capital amount invested. The prices of conventional gilts are quoted in terms of £100 nominal or par. A conventional gilt is denoted by its annual coupon rate and maturity – with that duration varying between a few months and as much as 50 years. The range of maturities is usually broken down into three main groups:

- *shorts*: 1–7 years

- *mediums*: 7–15 years

- *longs*: over 15 years

The most popular gilts for private investors are maturities between two and ten years although in recent years the government has concentrated its issuance programme around the 5-, 10-, 30-, 40- and 50-year maturity areas. Investors in gilts may also run into a variety of names including Treasury Stock, Exchequer Stock, Conversion Stock, War Loan and Consolidated Stock.

You may also encounter another form of government bond namely **index-linked gilts**. In the UK, these bonds were first issued back in 1981 and these *linkers* as they're popularly called now account for just under 25% of the government's gilt portfolio. Index-linked gilts are still bonds issued by the government to pay for spending but their structure of payouts is very different from that of conventional gilts – with linkers the semi-annual coupon payments and the principal (the final payout) are adjusted in line with a measure of inflation called *General Index of Retail Prices* (also known as the RPI).

Corporate bonds

British-based investors looking for a superior yield should look at the range of corporate bond indices and most probably the sterling variant. Be aware though that corporate bonds can move in sympathy with equities and if corporate defaults gather pace these funds could be in for a hard time as capital values fall – it's not a great hiding place in a recession, unlike most traditional gilts.

Virtually every major listed company issues some form of fixed income debt – the most popular form is something called a *corporate bond*. Like government bonds or gilts this promises to pay the holder a fixed income coupon regularly until the bond is redeemed.

Investors have flooded into funds comprising corporate bonds for a wide range of reasons including:

- They're another form of bond with different risk characteristics compared to gilts, thus allowing the investor to build a **diversified portfolio** of bonds from different issuers.

- Most corporate bonds provide an **income** that is both steady and greater than that provided by government bonds.

- Corporate bonds are also increasingly **easy to trade** in and out of. In fact, corporate bonds are often more liquid than other securities and stocks. Astonishingly the highest quality segment of the corporate market (investment grade – for a description of this market see below) now exceeds the gilt market in size.

- **Risk can be easily measured** using the credit scoring system used by the likes of S&P to assess the risk of investing in a particular bond. These measures are now widely used and understood, and investors can sensibly assess the basic risk of a corporate bond within just a few seconds. Other factors being equal, the better a bond's credit quality, the lower the credit spread. Broadly speaking, lower rated BBB rated corporate bonds do, on average, trade on lower prices and higher yields compared to highly rated, low-risk bonds with a rating of AAA.

Within this vast global universe of corporate bonds, you'll encounter two basic distinctions – between *investment-grade* and *speculative-grade* (also known as high-yield or junk) bonds. The first category of bonds (investment grade bonds) itself encompasses a vast range of 'risk levels' – see our discussion of credit ratings later in the chapter – while speculative bonds or junk bonds are clearly regarded as riskier and must pay a higher interest rate to compensate the investor for the possibility of future default.

In practice though the very term junk is itself misleading, implying that the issuers are close to rubbish and thus are likely to go bust. In fact, the majority of these bonds will never default, and all interest coupons end up paid – investors might even make some money by buying them cheaply second hand on the market and then waiting around (collecting those regular coupons or interest rate payments) until they redeem at par, paying back the entire principal.

What are the risks with corporate bonds?

No major OECD country has ever defaulted on its debt but plenty of corporations have! That risk is quantifiable and is expressed in the yield – the riskier the company, the higher the yield. Crucially it's important to understand that not every high yielding, high risk bond issuing company goes bust – the vast majority carry on paying their interest coupons. But it's also true that the highest quality, most blue-chip companies – especially those given the term *investment grade*, for the very lowest potential risk – are the least likely to go bankrupt and stop paying their debts.

In recent years that investment grade status has been taken to bizarre lengths – in recent years for instance corporations like McDonald's had possessed better rated debt than some Western countries. Italy may be forced out of the Euro but global hamburger specialists will probably continue paying their interest coupons.

Sadly though there's a big problem facing most ordinary private investors – big corporations issue their bonds in big bundles requiring an initial outlay of £50,000 or more. Direct ownership of corporate bonds by private investors is unsurprisingly very low as a consequence.

Step forward corporate bond funds and indices. These aggregate the most liquid, most popular bond issues into one structure – usually compiled by an index company such as Markit (through its iBoxx index structure) or MTS. Only the most liquid bonds get into this fund – although it's important to say that not all the bonds in the fund are of the highest risk grade. Investors use ratings firms to assess the potential risk of default and the safest companies tend to get the coveted AAA rating with the lowest rating (outside junk bonds) getting BBB ratings.

GOING GLOBAL AND BUILDING RISK INTO BOND INDICES

Over the last few years a growing number of fixed income investors have begun to express some concern that these traditional bond indices tend to weight their holdings towards those bond issuers who have the biggest debt – not the safest credit rating! The concern here is that in effect an investor is buying a bond ETF which has the highest exposure to the most indebted company or government. Surely the smarter alternative is to weight an index towards those with either the lowest debt levels or more generally the better perceived risk? An alternative version of the same idea is to weight a bond index towards the economic footprint of a company or country, using key fundamental measures such as value, yield, and indebtedness.

Scratch away at these criticisms and a constant worry emerges – in traditional actively managed funds, there was always a manager who was alert to the specific risks of investing in certain types of country or company, and thus avoided them or at very least weighted them at a very low level. With many bond ETFs, investors are blindly putting their money into the most indebted issuers, not necessarily the safest issuers.

A new generation of risk weighted bond indices has thus emerged that address this specific issue – they are constructed using measures that look to weight those issuers with the least risk either at the balance sheet level or at the security volatility level.

This cautious approach to screening out the most risk bond issuers contrasts with a move to include riskier countries and companies from around the world. Traditional government and corporate bond indices have always given the investor a chance to buy US government securities for instance – usually through a global bond index. In practice most UK-based investors have tended to stick with their UK government issuers, largely to avoid any FX or taxation issues.

But a growing number of investors are eager to look at riskier countries, especially emerging market sovereign issuers. With these countries the attraction is that you are in effect buying into countries that are growing fast but yield more in terms of income – they are the growth stocks of the bond world, riskier but potentially more appealing. An even more recent version of this global yield scramble is to invest in emerging markets corporate bonds, where the income yield is even higher, although risk levels are also much greater.

WHAT FACTORS SHOULD YOU WATCH OUT FOR IN BOND ETFS?

What you really care about is being repaid at the end of the loan period – just being paid interest and not receiving any capital back at the end is a very unappealing combination. That forces investors to think about the quality of the issuer and their 'credit risk'. Generally speaking the US and the UK governments are viewed as very low risk whereas sovereign emerging market issuers – local governments – are viewed as much higher risk.

Investors also care deeply about the length of the loan – the duration of the loan. The shorter the period the less risky but equally the lower the income. Longer durations are riskier – who knows what might happen over the next ten years – thus tend to pay a higher income yield.

And if interest rates do start rising you might need to find some buyers for your bonds as conventional bonds tend to fall in value as interest rates start rising. Put simply higher interest rates imply that cash rates are suddenly much more attractive, which prompts investor to sell their low yielding bonds, pushing down prices. So, this means that bonds tend to underperform if economies are booming and central banks are increasing interest rates. Also, most bonds underperform if inflation rates are rising – a process that usually results in higher interest rates!

Last but by no means least bonds are impacted by FX rates – if you own a fund that tracks US bonds for instance, you'll need to keep a close eye on how US and UK FX rates move about. Corporate issuers are usually riskier, which means they pay a higher income yield but there is a greater chance of not getting back all your capital – many businesses can and do default on their debts. As an economy recovers from a recession for instance corporate bonds can outperform strongly as investors stop worrying about businesses going bust and chase that yield. This yield chasing behaviour can drive up the prices of corporate bonds, which means existing bond owners can reap capital growth as well as yield.

ACTIVE ETFS

THE VAST MAJORITY of ETFs are passive. They follow a particular stock market index or a particular commodity such as platinum. If an index, including dividends, rises 8% over a year, then a passive ETF tracking that index should rise by 8% minus the tracking error. There's no fund manager picking stocks here.

When ETFs were first launched, all ETFs were passive, but more recently we've seen the arrival of active ETFs where a fund manager makes the final investment decisions. Just like any investment fund, these active ETFs still have benchmark indices. So, if a fund's benchmark is the FTSE 100, that should be your first point of comparison when you evaluate that fund's performance. But crucially a manager of an active ETF can deviate from that benchmark if he wishes. He can avoid a stock or sector just like an active manager of a traditional fund.

Same as smart beta?

Active ETFs aren't the same as smart beta ETFs. That's because all smart beta ETFs track an index. Granted, not a well-known index such as the S&P 500, but an index nonetheless. Often a new index is specially created for a new smart beta ETF and once that's done, the new ETF does nothing more than track the index. The ETF is following a clear set of rules that were set at inception – there's no opportunity for a human to back his/her judgement and tilt the composition of the ETF. An active ETF can still stay pretty close to a smart beta index or it can strike out more on its own.

What's the point?

You might think that active ETFs are pretty pointless. If you want to invest in a fund run by an active fund manager, there are countless unit trusts and OEICs out there. And if you want to invest as cheaply and simply as possible, then a passive ETF fits the bill.

But of course, cost and simplicity aren't the only attractions of ETFs. The other big plus point is that ETFs are traded just like shares on a stock exchange. The share price of an ETF changes all the time and you can trade in and out of an ETF several times a day if you wish to do so. With a unit trust or OEIC, you can't do that. The price of the units is set once a day.

That said, in the UK there is another kind of investment fund that is also traded on the stock market like a stock – the investment trust. The first investment trusts were launched in the nineteenth century and they are hugely more popular than active ETFs.

Premiums and discounts

A crucial feature of investment trusts is that they often trade at a premium or discount to the net asset value. The net asset value is the value of the underlying assets that an investment trust owns. The share price is set by supply and demand for the investment trust on the stock market. If the share price is higher than the net asset value, the trust is trading at a premium. If the share price is lower than the net asset value, the trust is trading at a discount.

Conventional unit trusts and OEICs don't trade at discounts or premiums. If someone wants to invest in a particular unit trust, the trust simply creates new units in the trust for the investor. And if someone wants to sell, the units are cancelled. And as we said earlier, the price is set once a day – that price reflects the value of the assets held by the trust. There is no discount or premium.

The crucial point about active ETFs is that they're traded on the stock market, but they don't normally have significant premiums or discounts. That's down to the unique structure of ETFs.

Each ETF has several authorised participants (APs) which are usually investment banks. They can force the ETF provider to create new shares or redeem them. If a large investor wants a substantial number of shares in an ETF, the investor – perhaps a pension fund – can approach an AP with cash or securities to pay for an ETF purchase. The AP can then hand over some securities to the ETF provider in return for fresh shares in the ETF. The ETF provider is obliged to create new shares if the AP wants them.

Similarly, an AP can hand some ETF shares back to the ETF provider and receive a basket of securities – normally shares held by the ETF – in return.

If a premium or discount appears for the ETF, the AP has an opportunity to make money. If there's a premium, the AP can short sell shares in the ETF and then, having bought the underlying securities on-market at a cheaper price, hand them over to the ETF provider in exchange for more ETFs. These shares are more valuable than the securities and so the AP is able to make money. As a result of this arbitrage process, the gap between the share price and the NAV quickly narrows.

If the ETF is trading a discount, the AP can buy shares in the ETF on-market and then sell the underlying securities at a higher price, bagging the difference as profit. This arbitrage channel should quickly narrow a discount.

Transparency

If you're wondering why there aren't more active ETFs out there, one big issue is transparency. To work best, ETFs really need to disclose their portfolio daily and many active managers don't like to do this. They're more used to quarterly disclosure which they prefer as it makes it harder for other investors to copy their strategies.

Bonds and equities

Active ETFs are more common in the US than Europe and it's worth noting active bond ETFs have attracted more cash than equity ETFs. That's probably because when it comes to bonds, the case for passive investing isn't as strong as with equities. A passive bond fund will end up buying the most bonds from the most indebted companies or countries, which creates opportunities for active bond managers.

Featured ETF

Vanguard Global Value Factor UCITS ETF (LSE: VVAL)

Vanguard offers four active ETFs in Europe and the Global Value Factor Fund is the biggest of the four with $71 million under management. It's heavily weighted to the US (57% of the fund) and financial services (37% of the fund). The fund mainly invests in stocks in the FTSE Developed All Cap Index. The ongoing charge is 0.22% a year. The same charge applies for Vanguard's other three active ETFs in Europe: Vanguard Global Momentum Factor (LSE: VDMO), Vanguard Global Liquidity (LSE:VDLQ) Vanguard Global Minimum Volatility (LSE:VMVL).

NOVELTY ETFS

NOVELTY FUNDS ARE the truffles of the ETF world. They're exotic, hard to find and add flavour to ETF portfolios. And the past two years they've been in season, with new funds popping up like mushrooms. But what are they? Here are some examples:

- ProSports Sponsors ETF (FANZ:US), which tracks companies that sponsor major American sports teams like baseball, gridiron, ice hockey and basketball.

- Quincy Jones ETF (QJ:US), named after Michael Jackson's producer, which tracks online entertainment companies such as those that stream music.

- American Energy Independence ETF (USAI:US), which tracks energy companies across North America thought to help boost the US independence.

- AdvisorShares VICE ETF (ACT:US), which invests in companies that make most of their money in 'vice' industries like tobacco, alcohol and marijuana.

- Point Bridge GOP Stock Tracker ETF (MAGA:US), which tracks companies with ties to Republican politicians that win elections.

- Medical Marijuana Life Sciences ETF (HMMJ:CN), which tracks companies in medical marijuana.

Sign of the times

If sport, celebrities and marijuana do not catch investors' eyes then not much will. And if these ETFs seem very eye catching, well, that's because they're designed to be. But as well as highly marketable, these ETFs are in their own way a sign of the times. Like funky designs on T-shirts and edgy labels on wine bottles, there seems a sense in which these products are targeted at the young. In recent years, ETF issuers have picked up the scent of young investors, who are coming to inherit family fortunes but have different tastes to their parents. (Discussed further in the chapter on ESG investing.)

They also illustrate just how widespread the *ETF-isation* of asset allocation has really become. The investment strategies that novel ETFs use are not so different from what active managers often try. Picking stocks in nascent industries, as with the newly legalised marijuana, is a strategy that active fund managers have used for years. So, has picking companies based on political changes, as in the GOP Stock Tracker ETF.

The trend to ETF-isation is visible elsewhere too. 2017 saw the launch of event-driven and market-neutral ETFs, both of which transplant hedge fund strategies in ETF wrappers. Like novelty ETFs, they do their part in pulling the rug out from under active management.

These funds also come at a time when investment conditions globally are unusually benign. With central banks pouring liquidity into capital markets and governments cutting corporate taxes returns are higher and volatility is lower than ever before. This has created the hunt for yield that has left investors open to quirkier opportunities, like bitcoin and other cryptocurrencies.

Who's impressed?

The success of novelty ETFs has varied greatly from product to product. HMMJ has had the best of both worlds, collecting C$429m in assets while delivering returns over 60% this year. (Not bad for a fund that was only listed May 2017.) Another novelty ETF listed in 2016, the ETFMG Video Game Tech ETF (GAMR) has returned 60% the past 12 months while gathering US$62m in assets. But other novelty funds, while often performing admirably, have often struggled to bring in bigger numbers.

But it is still early days yet and in asset management, collecting the first $100m in assets is always the hardest. And if novelty ETFs do not collect assets then they aren't alone.

Why are they popping up?

Most of the drive behind novelty ETFs comes from smaller issuers. While some are supported by Exchange Traded Concepts, an Oklahoma-based firm that provides white labelling services to small advisers, none are listed by a big issuer with tens of billions under management. This is no accident.

The ETF universe is crowded and almost every few months a new US issuer comes along. The crowded marketplace means that small new issuers have to do more to stand out.

But the need to stand out often sits alongside modest marketing budgets, meaning smaller issuers need ways of standing out that do not cost millions of dollars in marketing. This is where novelty ETFs can come in. Interesting and unusual ideas are free (at least to come up with) and have a tendency to market themselves. People talk about them, the media reports on them and investors' ears get pricked.

Scroll through a Google News feed and you can see just how much coverage the Quincy Jones ETF received. Sure, some was negative: "Quincy Jones ETF is a joke, but it's no laughing matter", wrote the *Seattle Times*. "You could invest in the new Quincy Jones ETF, but Quincy doesn't recommend it," wrote the popular blog the Heisenberg Report. But if you're a small issuer, it can make sense to risk the bad press and enjoy the cheap marketing ride.

Another reason that small issuers tend to be the ones listing novelty ETFs is the fee war. When ETFs got going in the 1990s, most charged more than 40 basis points. Today, however, big money managers have driven fees down to only a handful of basis points for ETFs that track famous indices like the S&P 500. Their fees are so low that these issuers need $10 billion-plus in AUM in order to be cash flow positive.

This scale-before-profits approach acts as a barrier to entry for small issuers, and often means they have to look to collect assets in alternative spaces, where the fee war has yet to crowd them out. And can mean that – in ETFs as in other corners of the economy – smaller new firms can be the first to bring new ideas to market.

SMART BETA PERSPECTIVES

IN THIS CHAPTER we'll explore the fast-evolving world of smart beta – and how investors can navigate their way around the confusing terminology. But before we dive into the deep end of quantitative finance, we first need to provide the wider context to the smart beta revolution. In essence, smart beta builds on the insights provided by active fund managers over the last 50 years – but codified into a set of rules-based criteria that can be turned into an index. Once in an index, an issuer can build an ETF which tracks this sub set of stocks or bonds.

But how can we define a small group of stocks or bonds that can be turned into a smart beta index? Welcome to the world of the stock screeners and quantitative finance experts.

Over the last few decades there have been numerous longitudinal studies which involve a deep dive into financial market returns. These historical analyses involve mining huge amounts of data on returns from shares (equities), bonds, commodities and cash. By and large these academic studies have all revealed one essential truth – that if the past is any guide, investing in equities has been a rewarding if volatile pursuit. Bonds can be relied to churn out anything between 0 and 5% per annum over the long term (by which we mean decades) whereas equities have produced something between 5 and 10% per annum. The increased return from equities (which includes both changes in the price and accumulated dividends paid out) is what's called the equity risk premium i.e. the extra return from investing in equities over say cash or bonds.

But virtually every one of these deep-dive historical studies has also revealed another important truth – not all risky equities are equal. By and large these longitudinal studies have revealed that some kinds of stocks produce better returns than others. That general return of 5 to 10% per annum hides huge variations between countries (pity the poor investor in pre-Communist Russia) and between different types of stocks. For instance, smaller companies (by market capitalisation) have returned, on average, more than larger companies over most extended periods of time. Academic economists have also revealed that if you screen through a wide universe of stocks in say the S&P 500 or the FTSE 100 you can quickly find some other measures or signals which help identify stocks with greater likely returns than the average – they might be stocks with strong relative momentum behind them for instance or stocks with high dividend payouts.

These two simple truths – that equities have outperformed but some different types of equities have outperformed their peers – represent the founding myths of a brand of investing called quantitative finance. This rarefied world of pointy-head maths types involves crunching huge databases of stock returns to find measures that outperform. But quantitative finance doesn't need to be the exclusive preserve of well-paid quants. Ordinary investors can use cheap or free online tools to screen through stock markets in search of the 'right kinds' of stocks. Stock screening, as it's called, has been around for decades and can produce fabulous returns, well above the average. The first and perhaps most important piece of evidence for the efficacy of stock screening is from a truly fabulous organisation called the AAII or American Association of Individual Investors, based in Chicago with a website at www.aaii.org.

Any thoughtful UK investor would be strongly recommended to buy an annual subscription if only because of the AAII's thorough and comprehensive analysis of more than 60 individual stock screens. Their evidence is that pretty much the majority of these individual stock screens based on key filters or measures works i.e. it produces superior returns to simply investing in a broad basket of stocks in the S&P 500 Index. In fact, a cursory check at their home page for stock screens reveals that of the 43 main strategies defined just three have underperformed the market since 1998.

Suitably cynical types might already be starting to ask questions – what about longer time frames and do these summarised results really tell you the whole story? Luckily the AAII's research has been tested by two academics. In a paper for the *Financial Services Review* Frederick P. Schadler and Brett D. Cotton dig deep into the data and test out the AAII's ambitious claim that 91% of its screens beat the market – a claim which they suggest has some "support" based on their finding that:

> Of the 54 screens with full data 50 earned higher gross returns than the S&P 500 index. These results translate to a 92.6% out-performance rate versus the S&P 500.

They then rigorously tested those 54 different screens used by the AAII, over eight years and found that if you ignore transaction costs "75.9% of the AAII portfolios significantly beat the S&P 500". Their overall conclusion:

> We agree with AAII that many of their screens may be a good starting point in the portfolio selection process.

And Schadler and Cotton aren't the only academics to have looked carefully at attempts to use strategies and screens to better the returns from investing. In a study published in 2000, James Choi, a professor of finance at Yale, looked at Value Line, one of New York's most prestigious research firms, which uses screens and comprehensive analysis of company data to focus investors on to a smaller number of stocks. Choi's study concluded: "I find that Value Line continues to outperform relative to current models of expected return… with mean abnormal portfolio returns reaching magnitudes of up to 45 basis points a month even after controlling for size, book-to-market, momentum, and earnings surprise effects. This in itself is a remarkable result, for it suggests that a system that requires no human input other than the entry of publicly available numerical data can perform as well as high priced Wall Street professionals." (Prof Choi qualifies this, however, noting that Value Line's outperformance is heavily watered down after transaction costs are built in.)

One of Wall Street's most brilliant commentators and fund managers has also looked in detail at how you can attempt to beat the market average by using strategies and screens in an intelligent and relatively easy way – and then subjected it to rigorous academic analysis. Back in the 1990s James O'Shaughnessy produced his results in the hugely successful book *What Works on Wall Street*. In the book he applied a number of straightforward screens to a massive database of US shares (called Compustat) from 1954 to 1994. A screen that hunted down stocks where the share price was very low compared to the 'book value' (a measure of the assets in a company) demonstrated annual compound returns of 14.4% compared to just 7.5% for firms where the share price was many times the book value. It also showed that a screen based around another popular measure – the share price relative to the sales generated by the firm – produced annual compound returns of 15.6%.

THE RISE OF FACTOR-BASED INVESTING

Many experts in stock screening – using measures to identify a subset of more successful stocks – are employed by active fund management groups. The key insight here is to use the various measures to build a shortlist of stock picks that can then be traded by the active fund manager.

But the same insight – that certain types of stocks outperform – can also be used by professionals working in passive or index tracking fund managers. If say stocks with a high dividend yield can be seen to outperform, then why not test the measure to see if its good at selecting the right stocks, then build an index and finally construct an ETF which follows the rules of the index?

The key is to find these measures or *factors* as they're called and then isolate them and build indices around them. Many mainstream investment economists who've spent decades staring at historical returns from investing in stocks maintain that these factors are just a way of taking *extra risk*, for extra reward.

One of the easiest to understand factors has been called the *size risk* by economists – this simply suggests that smaller companies grow faster than bigger companies and thus produce greater returns. Thus any strategy that focuses on small caps or even tiny micro-caps (sub £10 million in market cap) will produce exceptional returns over certain periods of time. Eugene Fama, a Nobel laureate at Chicago University, and his colleague Kenneth French examined this concept of a size factor. They examined data from 1963 to 1990 and divided all shares into deciles according to their size as measured by total capitalisation. The results, according to the two professors, showed a clear tendency for the deciles made up of portfolios of smaller stocks to generate higher average monthly returns than deciles made up of larger stocks.

Another extra form of risk is sometimes called *distress risk*, although it's also known as the *value premium*. This is the risk of owning companies that the market perceives as being in some form of financial trouble. While none of us would choose to invest in a single company in potential big trouble – that distress could be defined as a poor balance sheet or falling earnings or even loss – indices of 'value' stocks have historically offered very high returns precisely because most investors follow the crowd and target what are called growth companies i.e. companies growing fast, that sport expensive share prices relative to their profits. From this simple observation – noted time and time again by analysts for over 50 years – has emerged a whole new world of value-orientated factor investing. This school of investing even has its own moniker – the fundamentalists – and a belief system that suggests that the key measures of value (using key balance sheet and profit measures) are crucial to explaining why some shares do better than others.

The hard work digging into the numbers that 'prove' the value premium comes from Fama and French again. In a separate study published in 1998, the two professors looked at the international evidence on how value stocks performed compared to growth stocks. They found that "value stocks have higher returns than growth stocks in markets around the world. For the period 1975 through 1995, the difference between the average returns on global portfolios of high and low book-to-market stocks is 7.68 percent per year, and value stocks outperform growth stocks in twelve of thirteen major markets."

French and Fama's body of work the past three decades suggests that if investors take on extra risk and invest in both the size and value premiums, they can earn an additional 4–7% more per year.

Historical simulation results ($)

Time Span	Index	Annual Compound Return	Annual Standard Deviation
1964 – 2000	Fama/French US Large Value Index	14.28%	17.83%
	S&P 500 Index	11.90%	15.92%
	Fama/French US Large Growth Index	11.49%	18.65%
1964 – 2000	Fama/French US Small Value Index	15.66%	25.89%
	CRSP 6 – 10 Index	13.35%	25.52%
	Fama/French US Small Growth Index	10.15%	30.40%
1975 – 2000	Fama/French International Value Index	18.26%	20.61%
	International Small Company Index	18.07%	27.44%
	MSCI EAFE Index	13.69%	20.58%

Source: Fama/French

Another variant on this idea of the value premium is to look at what some called *cheapo stocks* – or bombed-out shares to you and me – shares that have crashed in price. A strong school of contrarian thinking suggests that buying these unpopular stocks can produce huge long-term outperformance for those willing to be patient, mainly because markets over-react in their punishment of certain shares and eventually the market is forced to admit the error of its ways by marking up prices. DeBondt and Thaler (1995)[1], for example, argue that investors are subject to waves of optimism and pessimism which cause prices to crash below their fundamental value (the value of assets for instance) – give the market a few years and these prices revert to mean and reward the brave contrarian. Looking at very long-term horizons they found that "stocks which have underperformed the most over a three- to five-year period average the highest market-adjusted returns over the subsequent period, and vice versa".

Dividend payouts also feature prominently among factor enthusiasts. Academic economists such as Jeremy Siegel at Wharton Business School argue that buying high yielding stocks cheaply makes analytical sense – we'll explore this dividend or equity income argument shortly in more detail. But dividend savvy investors also need to be cautious. In his famous book *A Random Walk Down Wall Street*, Burton Malkiel, a professor at Princeton, found that:

> Investors who simply purchase a portfolio of individual stocks with the highest dividend yields in the market will not earn a particularly high rate of return.

Simply buying the highest yielders doesn't always produce abnormal returns.

Which brings us to the question of practicalities – all these quantitative ways of dividing up the universe of stocks sounds great in theory, but how does it work in practice? If we do spot a factor and then build an index around it – with defined rules – how do we make sure the fund actually delivers on the promise?

Welcome to the smart beta revolution. In the world of ETFs, we'd suggest that four groups of factors absolutely stand out. These are:

1. Buy good quality businesses where profits have been growing steadily and balance sheets are strong.

2. Buy good value businesses where the share price doesn't truly represent the underlying value of the business, especially when focused on the dividend payout.

3. Buy a proper mix of small and large cap stocks because small caps have a tendency to outperform their bigger brethren over the longer term.

---

1   Financial Decision-Making in Markets and Firms: A Behavioral Perspective. In *Handbooks in Operations Research and Management Science: Finance*. Edited by R.A. Jarrow, V. Maksimovic, and W.T. Ziemba. Elsevier: 385–410.

4. Buy stocks of businesses where the share price has been increasing in value more than the benchmark i.e. some stocks exhibit greater positive momentum.

There are some other factors wandering around in the copious academic literature on this subject. (In fact, academics claim to have discovered hundreds of factors.) But you get the gist: certain styles of stocks (determined by the factor) outperform.

As index tracking funds have become mainstream, passive fund managers have become expert at building alternative, new indices which capture every kind of factor imaginable! A far-sighted investment manager called Robert Jones at Goldman Sachs is credited as being the first to ponder these issues back in 1990 – and then turn them into what was the first smart beta fund. He designed and ran a fund based around earnings, but the fund was closed down after it failed to beat the inhouse enhanced index fund. Since then the main proponents have been Rob Arnott of Research Affiliates, and Jeremy Siegel of WisdomTree, a US-based issuer.

SMART BETA IS BOOMING

The hard numbers suggest that all kinds of investors are buying into smart beta. According to London-based research firm ETFGI, assets invested in smart beta equity ETFs/ETPs listed globally reached a "new record of US$647 billion as of mid-2018."

Other notable statistics relating to smart beta include a report which suggested that smart beta ETFs have a greater than 80% satisfaction rate with investors. Another recent report concluded that in the US 67% of ETF investors are using ETFs to gain exposure to smart beta strategies, compared to 49% in 2014.

Cynics will argue that smart beta is successful because it's been marketed aggressively, to both institutions and private investors. But talk to smart beta users and you'll discover that they use these structures largely because they work.

To understand this crucial point, consider the work done by analysts and researchers at big Swiss private bank Lombard Odier – they've been using ETFs for many years but recently they've embraced the idea of using these factors to help build their ETF portfolios. Carolina Minio Paluello of Lombard Odier Investment Managers reckons that:

> Factor-based investing may introduce some timing risk, but over the long term, evidence shows that factor based outperformed significantly and that this out-performance should persist in the future.

So, for a long-term minded investor with a 20-year time horizon, using factor-based investing will add value.

In practical terms one could for instance buy US stocks through something like an S&P 500 tracker or alternatively you could buy only those US stocks that are either best value, showing the strongest momentum or have the best quality business. Simply by excluding the trash stocks that are too volatile, loss making and profoundly unloved, can deliver you an extra 0.50 to 2% per annum in returns over the long term.

What is Beta?

If you're wondering what Beta is, it's a measure of the volatility of a security or portfolio when compared to the market as a whole. A beta of 1 indicates that a security's price moves in line with the market. A beta of less than 1 means that the security should be less volatile than the market whereas a score of more than 1 indicates that volatility should be higher than the market.

It's also important to understand that smart beta indices have gone through numerous iterations in recent years. The very first wave of smart beta indices focused on a small number of simple 'risk factors' or risk premiums i.e. fundamental indices that used value-based ideas centred on the balance sheet or dividend payouts as a key measure.

Optimised strategies such as low or minimum variance represented the next generation of indices but even these relatively innovative products are now being overtaken by multi-factor models – where momentum and say low-volatility measures are used to construct an index.

At the core of this revolution though is the acknowledgement that not all shares are created equally – thus our initial discussion about stock screens. Different shares are impacted by different factors, nearly all based around some measure of risk.

At ETF Stream we've tried to get to grips with the dizzying variety of different smart beta strategies available. The final result of our head scratching is in the table below – our classification of the weird and wonderful worlds of smart and thematic beta. The latter term – thematic beta – is another iteration of the stock screening idea, focusing on selecting stocks based on a key theme or idea such as robotics or businesses that sell to China.

We've identified eight sub categories of smart and thematic beta, all used by ETF issuers. The two biggest belong in the first two boxes. Fundamental factors include many of the ideas identified by the stock screening experts mentioned earlier. Here we see a real focus on what are fundamental measures of a stock's attractiveness, with dividend yield or the value of the biggest focus. But this fundamental category also includes factors and measures which identify fast-growing stocks, measured by say advancing earnings growth.

Another huge sub category of smart beta centres on variance and risk. In this category we find a focus on screens and measures which identify stocks that don't move up or down as much on a daily basis (low variance or volatility). The key insight here is that boring stocks, with low variability or volatility, can end up producing better long-term returns.

Our next sub category of smart beta measures centres on the size effect, a factor we've already encountered. In simple terms, smaller businesses in terms of market capitalisation can be riskier but over time they tend to outperform their larger peers (discussed above). This could mean focusing solely on small cap companies or it could mean building an index where all the stocks included are 'equally weighted' – which has the immediate effect of boosting the weighting of small cap stocks.

Indices built around environmental, social and governance-based measures (ESG) are hugely popular at the moment – and the subject of the next chapter – and represent a real focus for many index developers. ESG indices based around religious and moral ideas have been around for most of the last decade – Islamic indices were the first to appear – but in recent years we've seen an explosion of new ideas, many of them based around global warming and sustainable business practices. The only slight challenge for this large universe of indices is that most ESG indices tend to underperform the broader indices.

A small number of index developers and smart beta experts have latched on to the idea of popular shares and taken it to the extreme – they've used technical and momentum based measures to select a shortlist of shares. The most popular variant of this is to focus on stocks with strong momentum behind them as measured by the relative strength measure versus the broader market.

In simple terms, for much of the time during a stock market boom, simply selecting only those stocks with positive price momentum (defined as superior relative strength versus the market over 20 and 200 days) will produce superior returns. Unfortunately, this strategy of chasing momentum also has a nasty tendency of 'blowing up' and making huge losses when a bull market turns sour.

Multi-factor strategies do what they say on the tin – they select a bunch of different factors including say fundamental and momentum-based measures and then combine them in one index. In practice this tends to take different forms. One is a small selection of factors which concentrate on a smaller number of stocks (or bonds), in order to produce extra returns. A second variant looks to build multi-factor indices with the broadest possible diversification, thus producing a better risk-adjusted return. We explore this world of multi-factors in more detail shortly.

Our last two boxes or sub categories represent the cutting edge of index construction. *Thematic Beta* is popular with index developers and involves what is essentially supersectors i.e. groups of stocks in a bunch of sectors which all respond to a big structural driver. This 'driver' could be growth in China or an aging population. *Alternative* beta strategies represent a collage of strategies designed to focus on more alternative assets such as commodity futures or FX (foreign exchange). In this box we've also included more bond (and FX) focused strategies looking at exposure to changing interest rates.

The many varieties of Smart and Thematic Beta

VARIANCE AND RISK Target volatility – low volatility, minimum volatility Risk weighting – risk weighted, equal risk, risk parity Defensive style premium – low beta Stability – dynamic and defensive (vol, leverage, ROC, multiple factor)	**FUNDAMENTAL** Value Yield – dividend weighted, quality dividend growth, select dividend, progressive aristocrats, high dividend yield, equity income Composite value – CAPE, value enhanced, RAFI Buyback Quality Growth
SIZE Equal weight Small cap	**ESG** Broad ESG Moral and political – Islamic, Christian, Evangelical, Political Green – low carbon, green bond, exclusive indices (fossil fuels and coal) Impact
SENTIMENT AND MOMENTUM Momentum Big data Earnings surprise	**MULTI-FACTOR** A – Diversified B – Concentrated, alpha seeking Number of factors Two factor – value beta Three factor – MSCI Factor Mix, FTSE Qual/Vol/Yield Four factor (and Four Plus) – Comprehensive Factor indices Scientific Beta – EDHEC incorporating diversification and multi factor
THEMATIC BETA – ECONOMIC EXPOSURE Geographical exposure – China Consumers Thematic sector exposure – Robo and Cyber and Demographic Exposure	**ALTERNATIVE** Commodity futures – long dated, enhanced commodity futures, daily roll Currency basket (FX) Foreign currency carry Interest rate exposure

MULTI-FACTOR INDICES EXPLAINED

When multi-factor indices were first launched back in 2010, the implication from much that was said at the time by providers was that it marked another staging post in the evolution of smart beta. In short, if smart beta is passive investing that has an undergraduate degree, then multi-factor is well on its way to gaining a doctorate.

Multi-factor indices have grown out of long-established single-factor products that seek to assess stocks according to certain criteria or factors which, have been proven to offer returns that can beat the market.

The most well-established and recognised factors are as follows. We discussed some of them above:

- **Value** – stocks with high versus low book-to-market value

- **Momentum** – stocks with high versus low returns over the past 12 months, but omitting the most recent month

- **Quality** – stocks that are characterised by low debt, stable earnings growth and other financial quality metrics

- **Low size** – stocks with low versus high market cap

- **Low volatility** – stocks based on the estimate of their volatility and correlations with other stocks

- **Yield** – stocks that appear undervalued and have demonstrated stable and increasing dividends

When it comes to the multi-factor indices, depending on the index provider, the multi-version will encompass all or some of these factors in combination in order to provide diversification and an adjusted weighting to suit the investment needs and objectives of investors.

All of the major index providers have opted to construct multi-factor indices including MSCI, EDHEC-Risk, FTSE Russell, Solactive and S&P, though there are key differences in how these are constructed. These differences bear some examination along with some of the issues that affect single-factor indices which multi-factor attempt to address.

Bottom up versus top down

An important issue with single-factor index returns is that this type of exposure is highly variable. Each individual factor will offer different return patterns depending on which underlying trend it seeks to exploit. In particular, single factors can suffer extended periods of underperformance as they are driven by very different market factors which can pay off at different times in the economic cycle. S&P has provided research with regard to the S&P 500 Low Volatility Index which shows that though the index outperformed the benchmark over the 20 years between 1995 and 2015, it also underperformed the benchmark for protracted periods within that timeframe.

The research points out that in the 69-month period between December 1995 and August 2001, the index suffered long cyclical downturns. The cumulative return peaked in September 2002, but it took another 72 months to reach the same height in August 2008.

It goes on to add that similar extended periods of over- and underperformance can be seen in other single-factor indices. Such is the variability that it has engendered much academic debate regarding factor timing and factor rotation. Yet another approach, though, has been to construct fixed combinations of factors that can address the problem of cyclicality but in a lower cost way. Hence, we get to the concept of multi-factor indices. Another index provider, FTSE Russell, provides an examination of three routes it identifies as approaches that can be taken towards constructing a multi-factor index.

Composite index

This is the simplest multi-factor index. At its most basic it takes the weighted average of just two single-factors indices – FTSE Russell suggests as an example a 50/50 split between value and quality. The advantage of this approach is its top-down simplicity. In principle, this is no different from replicating single-factor indices in their chosen weights but by having both factors together the index provider maintains the fixed weights, thus relieving the customer of having to adjust index-replicating products.

Composite factor

The next step in the evolving landscape of multi-factor indices has been to combine a weighted average of the individual factors in a bottom-up approach. This takes better advantage of the interaction between factors and offers potential trading economies: if a stock is eliminated from inclusion in one factor but added to another, then no trade needs to take place to maintain index replication.

Tilt-tilt

This is the most recent evolution in multi-factor indices and the most sophisticated. The approach sees the provider construct the index according to a tilt towards one factor or another rather than looking to average out. This is also known as a multiplicative approach or sequential tilting.

Behind such simple definitions lies a whole mathematical library of equations and calculations which underpin both the single-factor indices and the multi-factor versions that seek to address issues around weightings and exposures.

There are also basic disagreements between the various providers over which is the best and most consistent approach, but the basic tenet of all multi-factor indices holds true for all. Namely, any multi-factor approach – however it is reached – will provide diversification of the specific risks and lead investors away from concentrated benchmarks that are exposed to often undesired and unrewarded risks. It is also true that within funds notionally covering the same factors, the differing approaches to index composition can lead to differing sector exposures.

Multi-factor performance: evidence is weaker than on single factor

While multi-factor indices sound like an obvious and obviously good idea (why not roll all these factors into one great index and get a one-stop-shop?) evidence suggests they don't work as well as single-factor indices.

Index provider MSCI – which takes four of the factors to go towards its Diversified Multi-Factor Indices dropping low volatility and yield – said its multi-factor world index substantially outperformed its famous World Index over the 16-year simulation period before launch in 2015. However, as critics would point out, this outperformance was both a simulation and retroactive – meaning it only existed on paper and MSCI's index managers could pick which stocks went into the index already knowing how they performed.

Before investors commit to multi-factor indices, they may want to see more evidence that it can work. The EDHEC-Risk Institute conducted a survey of 211 fund managers in 2016. The survey found that fund managers wanted to know there was good empirical evidence backing up the idea that factor investing can work.

THE FUTURE – YET MORE FACTORS

Regardless of whether they work, multi-factor indices remain popular. According to FTSE Russell's 2017 smart beta survey, multi-factor combinations have become the most popular type of smart beta index among index providers. This suggests that if the coming years are anything like the last, more multi-factor ETFs will likely emerge. The EDHEC-Risk Institute's survey found something similar, with one-third of respondents saying they wanted more multi-factor ETFs developed in the coming years.

A small detour: the importance of dividends and equity income

We think that one smart beta strategy stands head and shoulders above its peers – value and dividend-based investing. We do think it is worth repeating some key observations on why the humble, boring, regular dividend cheque makes a huge difference to long-term returns.

The following table comes from French bank BNP Paribas and looks at US and European dividend growth over the very long term.

US and UK long-term nominal and real dividend growth

Average	Dividend Growth %	Real Dividend Growth %	Inflation Rate %	Earnings Growth %	Payout Ratio %	Dividend Yield %	10-Year Bond Yield %
US : 1871 – 2008	3.5	1.4	2.1	2.7	63	4.5	4.7
UK : 1970 – 2008	8.4	1.9	6.5	9.7	56	4.4	8.9

Using long-term data from the US stock market, it suggests that US equities have not only risen consistently faster than inflation but have increased by a fairly steady 1.4% per annum in compound annual terms – an extra 1.4% every year, compounded makes a huge difference to returns data as we shall discover.

Dividend income as a % of monthly total return of the S&P 500

Decade	Dividend Income as a % of Monthly Total Return of the S&P 500
1940s	53%
1950s	28%
1960s	39%
1970s	50%
1980s	26%
1990s	14%
1926 to 2004	34%

Source: Standard and Poor's

Turning to the academic research it's clear that the long-term case for dividends and their importance to private investors rests on all these factors – the dividend payout itself, the rating attached to a high yielder and the stable growth in the dividend payout over time. But it's the reinvestment of dividends that really makes the huge difference over time. The hard spade work on this analysis comes from the London Business School Professors Elroy Dimson, Paul Marsh and Mike Staunton – featured regularly in their Credit Suisse Global Investment Returns Yearbooks. Like many analysts they break the long-term returns from equities down into four components:

1. The actual **yield** itself (usually compared to the risk-free rate of return from holding cash or index linked gilts).

2. The **growth rate of real dividends** (increased dividends above the inflation rate).

3. The way that the **market rewards a company because of its dividend** i.e. the rating it will give the shares via a measure like the price to dividend ratio and last but no means least.

4. The **reinvestment of the dividend** using schemes like the dividend reinvestment investment plans or DRIPs.

According to Dimson et al: "the dividend yield has been the dominant factor historically" and "the longer the investment horizon, the more important is dividend income". Dimson's point is that the long-term real dividend growth rate is only 1% per annum and this low growth can't make that big a difference while the rerating of stocks based on its multiple to dividends is also very variable over time and also doesn't appear to make that much difference. As the authors note "dividends and probably earnings have barely outpaced inflation".

But the actual payout is dwarfed by the importance of reinvesting those dividend cheques. Looking at the 109 years since 1900, Dimson et al. suggest that the average real capital gain in just stocks plus the dividend payout is about 1.7% per annum (an initial $1000 would have grown six-fold), but over the same period dividends reinvested would have produced a total return of 6% per annum (or a total gain of 582 times the original $1000 i.e. $582,000). Dividend reinvestment really matters, and luckily most big progressive dividend payers have their own easy-to-use dividend reinvestment plans.

CASE STUDY: EM DIVIDENDS

One of the most interesting developments within global investing over the last few decades has been the inexorable rise of emerging markets (EM). This growth-orientated asset class has come from virtually nowhere in the 1980s to become a major focus for many investors.

But this relentless increase in prominence has masked another fascinating trend which is that more and more emerging market businesses are actually becoming relatively mature. That has meant that many businesses within emerging markets are happy to pay out a dividend to their shareholders. This has profound implications – academic studies have told us that over the very long term, equity investors have received the highest returns from a value strategy, which in practice means focusing on cheaper stocks that have a higher propensity to pay dividends.

Emerging markets by contrast have been typified as 'growth stocks' i.e. shares in businesses where markets perceive that profit growth will be strong, resulting in strong positive momentum in the shares. Growth-based strategies can and do outperform value strategies in some years, especially bullish ones, but over the long-term investors inevitably end up over-paying for the promise of growth tomorrow! This simplistic way of looking at investing styles would have traditionally suggested that patient, long term capital investors should steer clear of emerging markets.

But if the percentage of dividend paying businesses is rising, maybe we need to think again?

According to a 2015 report by Aye Soe, Senior Director, Global Research and Design at S&P Dow Jones Indices, over the past 16 years the percentage of companies paying dividends has increased at a faster rate in emerging markets than in developed markets. S&P reckons that the percentage of dividend-paying companies in developed markets varies between 60% and 70% yet for emerging markets, the percentage of companies paying dividends has steadily increased from 60% in 1998 to 70%–80% in 2014, surpassing the levels observed in developed markets. According to Soe from S&P, the Czech Republic, Poland and South Africa have made the biggest impact in terms of dividend growth. The aggregate annual dividend payout ratio has been climbing steadily in emerging markets although the S&P analysts also point out that "the dividend payout ratio, which indicates the percentage of earnings that is being returned to shareholders, has been declining in developed markets".

Percentage of dividend-paying companies in developed and emerging markets

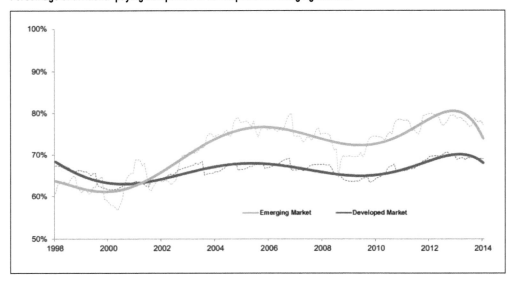

Source: S&P Dow Jones Indices LLC. Data from 1998 to 2014. Charts and graphs are provided for illustrative purposes.

Crucially investors who'd put money to work in emerging markets stocks would have discovered that dividend payers in EMs have outperformed non-payers, with much lower volatility.

The S&P research argues that "studies have shown that dividend payers have historically outperformed non-dividend payers". However, much of the available dividend research focuses on the US and other developed markets. A study published by Morgan Stanley Research showed that there is a strong relationship between dividend yield and total return in developed and emerging markets, with this link being the strongest in emerging markets. "Our analysis of emerging markets shows that, on average and similar to developed markets, dividend payers earn higher risk-adjusted returns than non-payers."

Cumulative performance of emerging markets dividend payers versus non-payers

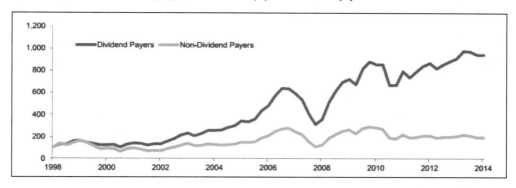

Source: S&P Dow Jones Indices LLC. Data from Dec. 31, 1998, to Dec. 31, 2014. Past performance is no guarantee of future results. Charts and graphs are provided for illustrative purposes.

One last crucial observation – many emerging market dividend ETFs have significantly underperformed their actively managed peers in recent years. This weakness can almost always be accounted for by investing in the wrong kinds of businesses, in the wrong countries! Successful active managers within the emerging markets space have usually made a conscious decision to avoid countries where the corporate governance culture is poor and returns not very visible – ETFs with their focus on quantitative measures built into an index have by contrast found themselves over-invested in some of the wrong nations.

Our bottom line? Investors within the broad emerging markets space need to increasingly focus on dividend yield as a key indicator for picking the right national ETFs. Look at the businesses and sectors the local market features prominently, understand the yield, and see how it has been growing over time. In particular seek out those countries where corporate governance is strong, respect for dividends/external investors widely publicised and the dividend payout robust and increasing over time.

PRACTICAL CONSIDERATIONS – HOW TO USE SMART BETA

To many cynics smart beta smells mightily of what's called data mining. Grab a huge series of data points, mine it intensively for 'trends' or 'factors', and then build complex methodologies that can be turned into indices – which can then be commercialised and turned into fee charging ETFs.

The only slight fly in the ointment with many data mining projects is that as soon as someone turns it into an actual practical 'strategy' – to make money – it collapses. Many factors look interesting but once tested via funds, the strategy proves ineffective. This doesn't surprise critics of smart beta like Vanguard's founder Jack Bogle. He thinks most smart beta strategies are a waste of time – data mining designed to charge investors extra money. His view is that most markets such as those stocks tracked in the S&P 500, are fairly efficient and thus won't give you an extra reward for choosing a factor. In his – and many others' view – factor mining is actually all about taking on more risk. Better, Bogle thinks, just to buy the main market via say a cheap S&P 500 tracker and sit tight over the long term.

Many institutional investors aren't quite as cynical as Bogle, with many big investors especially in pension fund land embracing quantitative investing. Two recent surveys on smart beta by the French business school EDHEC – sponsored by Société Generale – throw valuable light on the use of smart beta products. Crucially they offer all investors (institutional and otherwise) valuable lessons about what to watch out for when using smart beta funds. What's clear is that whatever the variety of smart beta, a growing number of institutional investors are using these 'intelligent' products – the EDHEC research showed that 25% of the managers surveyed already use products tracking smart beta indices, while another 40% are considering investing in them in the near future.

But what's also clear from the EDHEC survey is that among active users of smart beta products, most are still sticking with first and generation products – with low-volatility and fundamentally weighted indices by far the most popular as seen in the chart below.

For each of the strategies, this exhibit indicates the percentage of respondants that already invest in it, together with the percentage of respondants that are likely to increase their investment in the future. It also shows the percentage of respondents that do not invest in the strategy at the present time, but are considering a possible investment in the future.

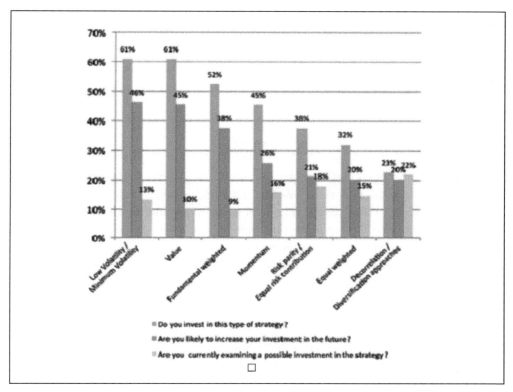

Source: EDHEC

Yet, as we dig deeper into the EDHEC research some very valuable learning points start to emerge.

The first is that smart beta products are overwhelmingly used for risk mitigation, within the equities space and on a long-only basis. The EDHEC analysts reveal that:

Among long-only strategies, Low Volatility, Equal-Weighted and Value Strategies have the highest....Decorrelation/diversification strategies have the lowest familiarity, among long-only strategies, even lower than some long/short strategies.

The relatively low usage of momentum-based trackers is hugely important – these surveys suggests that investors are looking to manage their downside risk by investing in low vol stocks or shares. Investors are *not* using these products to gear up positive returns or make money by going short. One last observation – as the next box below indicates – most of those surveyed in the reports think that value-based indices will continue to provide the best returns moving forward.

Rewarded factors. Which equity risk factors do you think will be rewarded positively over the next ten years, after accounting for transaction costs and other implementation hurdles? The level of confidence was rated from 0 (no confidence) to 5 (high confidence).

Value	3.28
Small-Cap	2.93
Low Volatility	2.68
Liquidity	2.65
Momentum	2.55

Source: EDHEC

WATCH OUT FOR SMART BETA OVER-TRADING

The smart beta revolution may be picking up speed but as we've just seen it also presents many challenges for the uniformed investor. The devil is very much in the detail. How does the index work? What are the rules behind the index and how are different stages of the investment cycle likely to impact different factors? More to the point, is the factor just a statistical artefact or a robust, permanent phenomena i.e. has the index developer simply used data mining to find a trend that has now vanished or is the factor actually robust over many decades?

The good news is that plenty of highly trained stock market analysts have been turning their attention to this smart beta revolution. Their results bear some scrutiny – not least because they raise some important challenges.

One challenge in particular keeps re-appearing in reference to smart beta – over-trading.

Smart beta might involve identifying a smaller subset of stocks (or bonds) which could reduce risk but it also involves lots and lots of trading. Or at least that's the conclusion of another research paper produced by French bank SocGen, this time by a research team headed by Andrew Lapthorne working alongside index specialist John Carson.

In a report entitled "Global Style Counselling", the SG researchers challenge the conventional idea that passive indices are…well…passive i.e. they don't trade very much. If as is increasingly obvious these indices are actually fairly active, then surely smart beta indices will be even more active? This might in turn open up investors in these tracking funds to extra trading costs and the risks of front running by experienced institutional investors.

Let's start with that point about mainstream passive indices being more active than we first thought. The report's analysts observe that the:

> MSCI World, an index of around 1,600 stocks, saw over 4,000 weighting changes last year. Yes, you did read that correctly, 4,000 weighting changes! Little wonder the Index Watch team is busy. Of course, many of the changes are so minor that they require little if anything in the way of trading, but the Index Watch database records around 1,100 weighting changes in 2014 that they do consider to be significant. Once added up, all these changes can amount to significant two-way turnover.

The table below shows the turnover of a wider series of mainstream benchmark indices.

%	2010	2011	2012	2013	2014
MSCI World	9.21	7.86	9.32	8.44	10.01
FTSE World	11.91	9.39	6.65	14.61	11.08
MSCI North America	9.92	8.94	11.33	9.75	11.94
FTSE North America	14.56	9.80	7.68	13.11	11.65
MSCI Europe	7.29	6.80	7.01	7.72	9.00
FTSE Europe	8.52	10.95	6.91	16.31	13.22
MSCI Pacific	11.56	7.37	6.06	5.87	5.51
FTSE Asia Pacific	12.50	8.91	5.82	17.43	8.81
MSCI Emerging World	19.1	15.1	12.5	12.8	13.7
FTSE Emerging World	21.0	15.2	13.9	25.6	15.4

Source: SG Cross Asset Research/Equity Quant

All of these transactions might well have an impact on trading costs – and thus returns. The SG report notes that:

> Since 2003, the performance spread between MSCI World index review additions and deletions has averaged around 10% from the period 20 days prior to the announcement date to 20 days post the announcement date. And even as recently as two years ago, these returns were much higher. So for the passive fund rebalancing on the effective date, new entrants will cost more and the deletes will be sold at a discount to where they stood. Sadly, for the passive fund, that does not seek to mitigate these rebalancing issues, the "delete" losses occur in the index, while the "add" gains happen outside the index.

The study argues that investors can already witness the impact of this trading in real-world markets. Observing that when WisdomTree announced the latest adds/deletes to its increasingly popular currency-hedged European index, there were notable share price movements in those companies affected. "Yet the ETF tracking this index is just $20bn in size."

The next three tables contain the incendiary results of the detailed SG analysis: that turnover is massively increased in smart beta funds, with trading costs also rising substantially, producing an inevitable hit on total returns. In each table authors compare a traditional market cap based index (MCAP weight) with four factor versions and an equal weight index over the period 1995 through to 2015.

Total turnover (%, 1995–2015)

	MCAP Weight	Equal Weight	Fundamental Weight	Momentum	Quality	Value	Profitability
Total turnover	14.0	62.0	58.4	379.2	212.6	224.8	138.2
Index changes	6.1	15.9	6.0	353.8	187.9	192.2	101.3
Reweightings	7.9	46.0	52.5	25.4	24.7	32.6	36.9

Source: SG Cross Asset Research/Equity Quant, MSCI, Factset

Trading costs (based on US$1bn trade, 1995–2015)

	MCAP Weight	Equal Weight	Fundamental Weight	Momentum	Quality	Value	Profitability
Theoretical performance (%)	7.0	8.4	6.6	10.1	10.9	12.8	10.4
Trading impact (basis points)	0.2	8.9	1.2	127.3	65.9	88.2	34.9
Trans. costs (basis points)	0.7	3.1	2.9	19.0	10.6	11.2	6.9
Total cost (basis points)	0.9	12.0	4.1	146.2	76.5	99.4	41.8
Net performance (%)	7.0	8.3	6.6	8.7	10.2	11.9	10.0

Source: SG Cross Asset Research/Equity Quant, MSCI, Factset

Net performance after transaction and impact costs

	US$0m	US$100m	US$500m	US$1bn	US$2bn	US$3bn	US$4bn	US$5bn	US$6bn	US$7bn
Value	12.8	12.6	12.3	11.9	11.0	10.1	9.2	8.3	7.4	6.6
Market Cap Index	7.0	7.0	7.0	7.0	7.0	7.0	7.0	7.0	7.0	7.0

Source: SG Cross Asset Research/Equity Quant, MSCI, Factset

BUILDING A SMART BETA CHECKLIST

We think the key insight from these studies is that the construction of the indices and their investability is massively important. Although some of these clever, intelligent indices might produce outperformance in the long run – and in some cases dampen down volatility – it's not a risk-free trade. Transactions increase substantially, as do costs and investors might find returns lagging over long periods of time.

So, as investors you need to be on your guard, and understand the very real risks. The analysts from SocGen conclude their exhaustive analysis with some sage advice for investors contemplating using smart beta funds:

- Be careful when using an index as the basis for your smart beta exposure. Use the concepts, factors and constructs, yes, but deploy them in a bespoke way.

- Rebalancing on one day along with everyone else, especially when the market knows what you need to trade, is madness. Trade away from the crowd and over multiple days if possible.

- Multi-factor approaches at the stock rather than index level work best. The opportunity to net off trades, minimise volumes and market impact should reap benefits in the long term.

Transatlantic fund management group Invesco PowerShares has also recently issued a gaggle of academic research papers by Cass Business School at the City University London, with one in particular of direct relevance – it's called Smart beta: Monitoring Challenges[2].

The authors are Prof. Andrew Clare, Prof. Stephen Thomas and Dr. Nick Motson and they argue that "investors will need to be certain that the 'production' of the index is of a very high standard and that all the rules are laid out clearly in the published description of the index". The main international association of securities commissions, IOSCO, has in fact suggested that investors should focus on issues such as how the index is governed, benchmark quality, detail of methodology and accountability. "Before investing in a smart beta fund investors might wish to check that the index provider is committed to the high index production standards laid out in the IOSCO paper", suggest the academics. More importantly looking at the ETF, investors need to satisfy themselves then that the manager has the operational skills and capabilities to replicate the smart beta strategy in an efficient manner.

Not to be outdone, US analysts at research firm Morningstar have also been tracking the rise of these smart beta funds and they've developed their own checklist of factors to watch out for. Some of the language may be a bit challenging for the ordinary investor, nevertheless it is worth a read[3]. Here's Morningstar's own checklist for using smart beta products – they suggest looking for some of the following:

- What does this fund do?

  - Find out which index it tracks and read the methodology document.

- Does this fund attempt to leverage a well-known factor?

---

2   http://www.invescopowershares.co.uk/PowerShares/pdfs/Part-4-Monitoring-challenges-Cass-Business-School-Invesco-PowerShares.pdf

3   http://images.mscomm.morningstar.com/Web/MorningstarInc/%7b9bb270bb-cb36-43eb-bcd1-14e1078f611b%7d_Morningstar_Manager_Research_-_A_Global_Guide_to_Strategic_Beta_Exchange-Traded_Products.pdf

- What does the fund own?

  - Sector tilts

  - Style box characteristics

  - Quality and profitability

  - Portfolio concentration

- Are there other funds that offer similar exposure?

  - How does the fund's expense ratio and portfolio compare?

- Has the fund performed as expected? Look at peer group relative performance.

- What are the risks?

The ETF Stream smart beta checklist

These varied studies into smart beta and its efficacy allow us to compile what we think is an essential checklist for smart beta investors – what we call a due diligence list of potential smart beta snags:

- Find out more about the index and how it has performed in various markets in the past. Crucially investors need live and after-cost daily performance numbers for any smart beta index. If the index provider does not give this information, avoid it!

- Also consider using this performance data to look at how much the index changes in composition terms every month or quarter, i.e. examine how the index turns over on a regular basis.

- Ask whether there is any independent research available on the ideas behind the smart beta index i.e. white papers and research notes.

- How much extra in terms of fees – in basis points – are you paying for the index construction? A range of between say a few basis points and 0.20% seems reasonable but anything much above 0.40% needs some explaining.

- Understand the index rules and explore any white papers that give a deeper, research-based understanding.

- Look at the investment debate and see whether particular styles of investing – value or growth for instance – are becoming more popular. Not every investment style (expressed in a smart beta index) works all the time. Quite the contrary in fact – some investment styles such as value investing can underperform for many years.

- See how concentrated the index is in individual stocks. One index might contain only 50 stocks, another 500. One is not better than the other but you do need to understand how your index is built and how concentrated the holdings are.

- Be aware of how much turnover there is in the index and what the likely impact of trading costs will be on performance.

- Is the smart beta index a genuinely independent, third party creation? On a related theme see if there's any independent academic evidence – or research cited – that backs up the central insight of the index.

- Closely examine any white papers or background guides which explain the thinking behind the smart beta strategy and which explore past performance.

- Be cautious about smart beta back tests. In our experience any data of this kind has limited value unless the back test goes back over many decades.

- Transparency matters. More than a few smart beta indices are built on black box approaches where the key investment metrics are not revealed.

- Monitor your smart beta picks carefully. The Cass academics note previous Invesco PowerShares research among professional investors which suggests that 38% of respondents said that they were reviewing their clients' smart beta investments on a monthly basis; 45% on a quarterly basis; 13% every six months.

Which smart beta factors to use in a portfolio?

Some of the factors discussed in this chapter are amazingly resilient over the long term. Our own hunch is to just 'tilt' (another jargon term) towards a small number of key factors if you are in the game of investing for the next 20 years. For those of you who are adventurous consider a tilt towards smaller caps, while defensive types might go for dividends and arguably quality stocks. More tactically inclined investors might by contrast go for momentum i.e. you might go bullish on fast growing equity prices when markets are bullish overall and then sell them when markets turn bearish.

FURTHER READING ON SMART BETA

To date academics have identified more than 300 factors although based on the current status of academic research, there is a consensus on just four consistent factors: volatility, value, momentum and size. But are factor ETFs the same as smart beta ETFs? For most, factor investing is a broader category which subsumes smart beta but is much more comprehensive. Other unresolved background disputes include:

- Is the benchmark for these funds equal weighted or market cap-weighted indices?

- Is the value added in smart beta ETFs from the factors like value, which can be arbitraged away over time, or is it in their rebalancing?

- Is there such a thing as alpha?

- Is there an observation effect, where people see a smart beta ETF work well so they flood into it, killing its success through overvaluing it?

Arguably the most cited research article on smart beta comes from academic economist Burton Malkiel – the analysis is called "Is Smart Beta Really Smart?" and is published in *The Journal of Portfolio Management* 40.5 (2014).

Malkiel's core observations? That smart beta portfolios do not consistently outperform and when they do produce appealing results, they flunk the risk test. Malkiel observes that:

> Smart beta portfolios have been the object of considerable marketing hype. They are more a testament to smart marketing rather than smart investing....All smart beta strategies represent active management rather than indexing.

Malkiel suggests when smart beta outperforms it's because it takes on more risk i.e. there's a huge amount of evidence of reversion to the mean. Thus, smart beta funds don't produce alpha – in effect it's an academic bubble. Malkiel argues that the:

> Actual records of smart beta portfolios run with real money do not in general replicate the results suggested by academic studies. For example, an examination of mutual funds' returns of funds with value and growth mandates starting in the mid-1930s shows that both types of funds had similar 70-year average annual returns.

Another crucial – and critical – paper comes from Ben Johnson, Hortense Bioy, and Dimitar Boyadzhiev – the paper is called "Assessing The True Cost of Strategic Beta ETFs", and is in *The Journal of Index Investing* Summer 2016, Vol. 7.

This analysis suggests that smart beta ETFs are more expensive. Three reasons are suggested: higher replication and indexing costs, more thought goes into smart ETFs which thus incurs higher staff costs, and last but by no means least, issuers are looking for profitable territory given fee cuts in plain vanilla ETFs. The 'impending' good news? Fees are declining.

Johnson, Bioy and Boyadzhiev's key message is that issuers don't appear to be willing to lower their fees on smart beta ETFs. This contrasts with plain vanilla ETFs where there has been an intense fee war. In essence, the suggestion is that investors care less about fees of smart beta ETFs than on plain vanilla ones – the authors wonder whether in practice investors benchmark smart beta ETF fees relative to active management fees:

> The average total expense ratio (TER) of strategic-beta ETFs using the S&P 500 as a parent index is three times higher than that of ordinary S&P 500 ETFs.

Smart beta also comes under some attack in a paper called "How Smart Are Smart Beta Exchange-Traded Funds? Analysis of Relative Performance and Factor Exposure" by Denys Glushkov published in the *Journal of Investment Consulting*, Vol. 17, no. 1, 50-74, 2016.

The author finds:

> No conclusive evidence to support the hypothesis that smart beta ETFs outperform their benchmarks on a risk-adjusted basis.

The author also rejects the claim of smart beta advocates that rebalancing boosts smart beta ETFs, finding no evidence. Crucially this paper reminds investors that smart beta also has unintended factor tilts, as well as intended ones. These unintended ones might offset the intended factor tilts!

A more positive account of smart beta comes in a paper called "The asset manager's dilemma: How smart beta is disrupting the investment management industry", by Ronald N. Kahn , and Michael Lemmon in *Financial Analysts Journal* 72.1 (2016). This paper argues that smart beta is a disruptive innovation, using Clayton Christensen's definition of the term. The authors (two BlackRock staff) argue that smart beta, in effect, roots out active managers charging alpha-level fees while delivering only beta exposure. It also argues that active managers will survive, but only those who provide pure alpha. Kahn and Lemmon suggest:

> Many traditional active managers deliver a significant fraction of their active returns via static exposures to smart beta factors while charging active fees. Active management will evolve into two separate product types: smart beta products with lower fees and pure alpha products with higher fees.

Another positive take on smart beta comes from Jie Cao, Jason C. Hsu, Zhanbing Xiao, and Xintong Zhan in a report entitled "How Do Smart Beta ETFs Affect the Asset Management Industry?" This paper argues that smart beta ETFs make investors more critical of mutual funds and active managers. The authors report that:

> (Smart Beta) ETFs changes investors' way of evaluating mutual fund performance. With intensified competition from Smart Beta ETFs, mutual fund managers now must provide an outperformance after adjusting for the influence of easily replicable risk factors.

The authors also argue that:

> The trading of smart beta ETFs has led to a structural change in the mutual fund industry by altering the way investors assess active mutual fund managers' skills. Investors no longer reward managers for being exposed to common risk factors when ETFs, which could replicate the return to such risk factors, are actively traded.

But even Cau et al concede that:

> Smart beta portfolios have been the object of considerable marketing hype. They are more a testament to smart marketing rather than smart investing.

One last notable paper comes from Rob Arnott, Mark Clements and Vitali Kalesnik, available on the ETF.com website. In a note entitled "Why Factor Tilts Are Not Smart 'Smart Beta'", the Research Affiliates analysts argue that factor-loading portfolios and smart beta strategies (i.e. smart beta ETFs) are very different. The authors observe that:

> Factor-replicated portfolios are poor substitutes for their smart beta counterparts: performance is poor, turnover is high, and capacity is terrible. Why? The simple answer is that construction details matter in achieving both lower trading costs and higher performance.

ESG INVESTING

O NE OF THE defining themes for ETFs during the past few years has unquestionably been the growth of environmental and social governance (ESG) products. There is now more than US$22.9tn of assets being professionally managed under responsible investment strategies (not just ETFs) according to the Global Sustainable Investment Alliance. Yet defining the movement – what is ESG? – is notoriously slippery. As the *Financial Times* observes:

> The ESG phenomenon has blossomed in spite of an absence of detailed, globally-agreed definitions on what constitutes ESG standards. Indeed, the trend feels more like a freewheeling movement with index providers, investment managers, pension fund executives and others making discretionary decisions.

Attempts to define ESG with any precision are more or less absent in studies and commentary on the asset class. Most commentators and investors are happy to settle with what Supreme Court Justice Potter Stewart said of porn: "I know it when I see it." And most investors are happy to leave ESG as a generic term for non-financial performance indicators that evaluate corporate behaviour. And most are unbothered if exact definitions vary from person to person.

With this in mind, ESG ETFs have been many and varied recently. It's to this we now turn.

HISTORY

By general consensus, ESG investing began in the late-1970s with the South African divestment movement. Like many of the late twentieth century's innovations – blue jeans, the internet, political correctness – ESG investing began on university campuses. Students were unimpressed with South Africa's apartheid regime and thus pressured university fund managers to divest from businesses profiting from South African apartheid.

The pressure worked, at least in twisting the arms of universities' endowment managers. By the mid-1980s many universities had divested their South African holdings. Following the success of the South African boycott, activists put other targets in their crosshairs. Thus Exxon, after the Valdez oil spill in 1989, was subject to activists crying out for divestment much as South Africa had been in the decades before.

Today much is different, and much is the same. The spiritual centre of the ESG movement is still university campuses. Students and faculty continue in pushing universities to divest, or more precisely to invest in a manner that aligns with the views of activists. The logic is also still the same: activists see investment as a paintbrush for politics. But much is also different.

For one the strongest arm of the ESG movement today is environmental (discussed more below). But more significantly, ESG is being driven as much by conservatives, institutions and rich family offices as it is by campus activists.

ETFS AND ESG

While 'campus snowflakes' get much of the attention when it comes to ESG, investors should know that the biggest driver behind ESG are generational divisions within rich families. As baby boomers retire in increasing numbers, they are passing control over tens of trillions of dollars in assets to a younger new millennial generation who want social governance screens on their investments. As Accenture, the consultancy, explains in its report entitled, "The Greater Transfer of Wealth: Capitalising on the Intergenerational Shift in Wealth":

> [The] wealth transfer is… estimated at over $30 trillion in financial and nonfinancial assets in North America…[which] makes this massive transfer of wealth between generations a defining issue for the wealth management industry… what makes this transfer strategically difficult to manage is that firms cannot rely solely on their advisors to manage this… many current advisors are nearing retirement and might be less motivated to build foundational relationships with their clients' children. Capturing the heirs and earning their long-term loyalty – even though many of these prospective clients are not yet in what are seen as desirable client segments – is going to be crucial for firms as they navigate this transfer. Firms can gain this loyalty by understanding and acting upon the heirs' needs and expectations, including creating client experiences in both advisor-led and direct channels that can profitably meet those needs and expectations today.

This wealth transfer matters because it means those building financial products, like ETFs, will have to take on board the world views of millennials in the not-too-distant future. And while millennials may be of little interest to money managers for now, once they inherit their parents' fortunes they certainly will be. And this is the central fact: ESG has gained ground with ETF issuers in recent years because we are crossing a threshold in intergenerational wealth transfer.

There is no ambiguity about the fact that ESG-investing is millennial-driven. Studies are more or less unanimous in finding that millennials have greater faith and interest in ESG investing than previous generations, including the boomers who drove through the South African boycott. A particularly striking study came in 2015 from Bank of America's private wealth division, which deals with rich families and their children. It found that 85% of millennials believe ESG matters to investment decisions, compared with only 49% of boomers.

Investment managers are being urged by their advisers to respond. In a recent report, Scorpio Partnership, a family wealth management research firm, found that wealth managers "urgently" need to cater themselves to the changing cultural beliefs and preferences of high net worth families. The report said:

> As it relates to millennials, updates that favor connectivity, transparency, and social responsibility provide wealth managers with an opportunity to win loyal customers.

REASONS FOR ESG: INSTITUTIONS

Besides millennials inheriting, the other important driver on ESG is institutional – again, breaking with the campus activist image. The industry is mostly behind ESG and is happy to drive the change. This shows up in a number of elements. One is the way advisers are going. Greenwich Associates, the finance research firm known for its ETF advocacy, found that 80% of advisers believe that ESG investing will only grow in the coming years.

It also shows up in SEC filings. By all accounts, investors are increasingly asking companies to disclose what actions they are taking to improve their sustainability. Thus, in more than 80% of SEC entries, companies made some kind of disclosure on environmental impact.

In ETFs specifically, ESG is showing up most obviously in indexing. Index providers are of particular interest and significance. This is partly because they act as gatekeepers, deciding which companies qualify as ESG and thus which receive investment from ETFs. But also importantly because index providers can act as weather vanes: they only roll out indices if they believe that investors will be interested in them. Thus indices can symbolise broader market trends.

When it comes to new indices, the trend to ESG indexing is nothing short of stunning. In MSCI's index universe alone, there are currently more than 720 indices that can be characterised as ESG[4]. A remarkable growth considering there were virtually none at the turn of the millennium.

The final type of institutional driver is that big institutions are directly asking asset managers to create ESG products. As far as ETFs go this is quite rare. But one example has been State Street's award-winning gender diversity ETF (SHE) which was seeded with a cool $250 million by CalSTRS, the retirement fund for Californian teachers.

---

4   https://www.msci.com/esg-integration

ESG ETFS: THE LISTINGS.

We now turn to ETF listings themselves. Recent ESG ETFs have been a variegated lot, ranging from religious products concerned with gay rights to feminist ETFs wanting more gender diversity to fossil fuel divestment products. Rather than type out all the ESG ETFs listed this year we've taken a selection of those we've found most interesting.

Evangelical Christian ESG ETFs

One of the big media attention getters for ESG ETFs recently has been evangelical Christian ETFs. While it may be tempting to discard religiously motivated ETFs from the ESG pile, it is important to note the slipperiness of definitions discussed above as well as the fact that they're included in the ESG category by index providers. They also function in a manner more or less the same as other kinds of ETFs, bringing non-financial indicators to bear in screening through investments.

Evangelical Christian ETFs have mostly come from one issuer: Inspire Investing, which is based in San Benito, California. Inspire aim to promote "biblically responsible" investing and have released a line of ETFs this year that are in keeping with that mission. Products listed this year include:

- Inspire 100 ETF (BIBL), which invests in an index of 100 US large cap stocks.

- Inspire Global Hope ETF (BLES), which invests in 400 large cap stocks from around the world.

Both BLES and BIBL invest in companies that "align with biblical values" through an in-house index. Their indices remove companies that promote "the LGBT lifestyle", porn, abortion, tobacco, alcohol, gambling and do "business in terrorist-sponsoring countries", their prospectuses say. Companies they invest in do not have to be Christian at all. They only have to have products and services, work conditions and pay, community and environmental standards that are above their peers. Both products centralise corporate governance and doing good in a manner similar to more mainstream ESG ETFs.

Feminist ESG ETFs

Passive investing may seem like an unlikely place for gender politics. And weighting companies by how many women sit on their board may seem like an unusual asset allocation strategy. But recent years have seen a number of feminist ETFs. These products are quite like fossil free funds in that they're didactic and take much impetus from university campuses. This year's listings include:

- Lyxor Global Gender Equality UCITS ETF (ELLE), in France
- Daiwa ETF MSCI Japan Empowering Women Index WIN (1652), in Japan
- Mackenzie Global Leadership Impact ETF (MWMN), in Canada
- Evolve North American Gender Diversity Index ETF (HERS), again in Canada
- Impact Shares YWCA Women's Empowerment ETF (WOMN), in the US

What all these funds have in common, besides great tickers, is that they rank companies by commitment to gender diversity. Such commitment is gauged through workplace policies like family leave, flexible hours, gender diversity of companies' staff and pay disparity. This isn't completely new. As discussed above, it got going in 2016 with the State Street's SHE. But recently the listings turned up a gear and went global.

Fossil free ESG

Fossil free ETFs do what's on the tin: exclude fossil fuel companies from their indices. Like feminist ETFs, fossil free ETFs have their home base on university campuses, where they remain a subject of ongoing debate. And the debate has high stakes. According to a 2011 study, fossil fuel companies produced more money for US university endowments than any other asset class in the 2000s. This year's listings have been:

- Change Finance Diversified Impact US Large Cap Fossil Fuel Free ETF (CHGX), in the US

- BetaShares Australian Sustainability Leaders ETF (FAIR), in Australia

CHGX and FAIR weed out companies that are in the fossil fuel industry and score negatively companies with environmentally questionable records. But what's also interesting about these products is that they add further ESG screens on top of this, including treating employees well, having good human rights histories and being relatively scandal free. Fossil free ETFs existed before this year, of course (ETHO and SOYC were both listed in 2015), but what's new is how they've added more ESG screens on top of them and built out a wider audience.

DOES IT MAKE A DIFFERENCE TO THE WORLD?

The great promise of ESG is that it puts human affairs at the heart of finance and tries to bring the vast capital in financial markets to bear on what are, essentially, political issues. After all, if asset allocation can be used to support changes in racial law, as in South Africa, why not widen the net slightly and let it help change gender laws? Here, the question then becomes: does ESG work? And will ESG ETFs help change the world?

At the outset it is worth noting that very few ETFs claim that they change the world. Most ESG ETF providers claim only the more modest accomplishment: that they offer investment solutions for people with certain convictions or viewpoints. Other ESG providers claim that they offer outperformance, with some evidence (discussed below). And despite "do ESG ETFs help make the world ESG?" being an obvious question, within the ETF industry it is not so often asked or answered.

MOST EVIDENCE SAYS ESG MAKES NO DIFFERENCE

The efficacy of divestment has been a sticking point for ESG investing outside of the financial services industry. Among scholars the consensus is that divestment and ESG investing do not help make the world more environmentally friendly or better socially governed. Here one of the best examples is Sudan. Despite being boycotted by virtually the entire world in the early-2010s, oil remained flowing in Sudan providing profits to companies involved, thanks to the help of China and a few small Asian countries which ignored the international call. A study of the Sudanese boycott found that it simply gave China a fire-sale bargain on Sudanese oil wealth. Other studies have noted similar things on tobacco and gambling. Despite decades of stigmatisation, tobacco and gambling remain reliable investments because their 'sin stock' status means they have better price-to-earnings ratios.

Making matters worse, some critics allege that ESG investing can undermine the very causes it aims to help. As William MacAskill, a philosophy professor at Oxford University, wrote:

> [D]ivestment risks being harmful. Several studies have shown that, because of the pressure against investing in morally dubious companies, "unethical" investments (sometimes called "sin stocks") produce higher financial returns for the investor than their "ethical" alternatives.[5]

This then incentivises investing in unethical investments, Professor MacAskill notes.

On this score, fossil free funds like ETFs have come under fire. Critics allege that fossil fuel divestment has accomplished very little, otherwise oil majors would have seen declines in their valuations. Professor Nicholas Stern, the architect of the Stern Review on the UK's climate change policy, made exactly this point of government policy as well:

> There is therefore a profound contradiction between declared public policy and the valuations of these listed companies, based on their fossil fuel reserves, which appear to assume that the world will not get anywhere near its targets for managing climate change.

Critics also allege that targeting oil companies, as fossil free ETFs do, only hurts companies on the supply side. Oil majors and coal miners may extract fossil fuels, but they aren't the ones combusting them, which is ultimately what puts carbon dioxide in the atmosphere and causes global warming. As *Financial Times* columnist John Gapper noted:

> There is no logic to blaming the producers of energy raw materials, rather than the companies and people that consume energy. Why should Exxon be a divestment target while others such as Apple, which runs energy-sucking server farms and produces millions of electronic devices, escape?

---

5   https://www.newyorker.com/business/currency/does-divestment-work

Other criticism includes the fact that ESG ETFs can do almost nothing about companies that are privately held. Here it is worth remembering that only a minority of the world's companies are publicly listed, and only a minority therefore are susceptible to ESG ETF influence and the direct influence of indexing. Critics also point out that asset allocation and ESG ETFs do not directly affect state-owned enterprises – and for the same reason. Here, it can help to remember the majority of the world's untapped oil reserves are property of state-owned oil companies, not privately-owned businesses. It can also be worth remembering that governments are the world's largest polluters. The US military, for example, is the world's largest oil-consuming entity.

While examples here deal principally with fossil fuel free ETFs, the same can be said of Christian values and gender diversity ETFs. They too only target publicly listed companies and they too can create incentives to invest in companies deemed unethical.

Activists have replied that the point of ESG investing is not so much to inflict financial damage, but to remove 'social license' and promote stigma. Parallels are often drawn with the slave trade in the nineteenth century. While divestment did not end slavery, it helped mobilise political will and helped change Republican policy during the civil war. Nelson Mandela said himself that he believed the University of California boycott was helpful in changing US policy towards apartheid South Africa, which in turn helped twist the arm of South African elites.

On one point however, ESG ETFs are likely having an impact. Money managers have sometimes claimed that they will refrain from ESG investing because it adds unnecessary burdens on the investment process as well as costly restraints. And as there is mixed evidence on performance (discussed below), the costs outweigh the gains. ESG ETFs at the very least have taken this kind of argument off the table. ETFs require no active management and provide transparent asset allocation at low cost. They therefore significantly reduce the compliance and research burden on the asset allocation process. And this may well be ETFs' great contribution to ESG: they lower the barriers to entry, lower costs and heighten transparency. If nothing else, they've made ESG funds available to retail investors – and that in itself is an achievement.

DO ESG ETFS PERFORM?

Reasons for investing in ESG ETFs vary markedly. Some investors – if only a handful – invest in them purely for the returns. But every investor needs to know that their investments are making some returns, otherwise it's not an investment. And indeed, convincing university endowment managers or whoever else to dump fossil fuels or switch to companies with more women on their boards is made easier if activists can prove that it doesn't harm the bottom line. And this is where the tar sticks: what effect does ESG have on returns?

Commentary in the financial press recently has mostly painted ESG investing in a positive light. "The outperformance of ESG strategies is beyond doubt," declared a feature length piece in the *Financial Times*. The article takes index data from MSCI comparing the performance of "ESG leaders" in emerging markets with those dubbed less-than-leaders. These findings were backed up by a well-publicised study by consultancy Boston Consulting Group, which found that among the world's 300 largest companies those with more "ethical operations" tend to have larger profits and higher valuations, and that there was a correlation between doing good and making money.

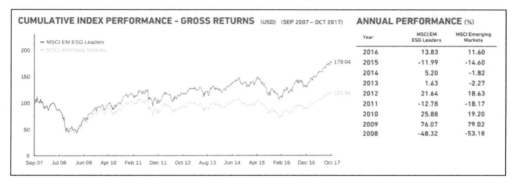

CUMULATIVE INDEX PERFORMANCE - GROSS RETURNS (USD) (SEP 2007 – OCT 2017)

— MSCI EM ESG Leaders
— MSCI Emerging Markets

ANNUAL PERFORMANCE (%)

Year	MSCI EM ESG Leaders	MSCI Emerging Markets
2016	13.83	11.60
2015	-11.99	-14.60
2014	5.20	-1.82
2013	1.63	-2.27
2012	21.64	18.63
2011	-12.78	-18.17
2010	25.88	19.20
2009	76.07	79.02
2008	-48.32	-53.18

Source: MSCI

This line of thinking tends to hook in with common sense. Most people think that companies that use resources more efficiently, don't need to keep firing and mistreating staff, and avoid the lawsuits and regulatory blowback that follow corporate malfeasance, will perform better. The notion gels with common sense.

But turning beyond industry thought pieces and commentary, the picture of ESG returns is quite different. Here an important place to start is just how extensively the correlation between performance and ESG has been studied. The biggest study to date, published in 2015 by the University of Hamburg with Deutsche Bank found that more than "2,250 academic studies have been published on the link between ESG and corporate financial performance 70% of which have been published during the last 15 years". Meaning that getting one's head around the literature is no mean feat.

This library of literature is bound up in inter- and intra-disciplinary disputes which has clouded any consensus on the topic. Nevertheless, according to the University of Hamburg report, which reviewed 60 reviews (that's how big the field is, that there are over 60 reviews of the field!), only 10% of studies found a negative relationship between ESG and corporate performance, with an "overwhelming" majority found there that incorporating ESG filters can boost performance. Based on this, they say there is "evidence for the business case for ESG investing". The study notes however, that this finding may not be true of portfolio studies, which is perhaps the most relevant to ETFs.

On the other hand, an October 2016 study in the *Journal of Business Ethics* by a group of Dutch academics looked at the academic literature and concluded the opposite. "The prevailing notion is that social[ly] responsible investing does not yield significant positive risk-adjusted returns. There is even evidence that investing in 'irresponsible' stocks (like tobacco, alcohol, and gambling) might result in extra-financial returns."

It might be due to the lack of consensus that advisory bodies steer clear of outright recommending ESG as a driver of outperformance. Boston College's prestigious Center for Retirement Research, which provides advice for hundreds of billions of dollars' worth of public pensions in the US, published a major study on ESG in November 2016. Its conclusion was blunt:

> Social investing is often not effective, as other investors step in to buy divested stocks, [it] can also produce lower investment returns… In short, public pension funds should not engage in social investing.

Part of the reason for the performance, as studies have noted, could well be fees. It seems that across the board, ESG funds cost more. A study of mutual funds in 2008 by German scholars published by the Leibniz Information Centre found that mutual funds that use SRI criteria are more expensive. This appears to hold true of ETFs as well. The top 10 sustainability impact ETFs as rated by ETF.com have an average expense ratio close to 50 basis points. This compares with the asset-weighted average of 21 for all US ETFs and an average of 9 basis points for the top 10 plain vanilla ETFs by assets managed.

Another vein in the literature on performance suggests that sin stocks like tobacco, weapons and gambling – the bane of many ESG ETFs – often trade at better value. They also tend to offer better dividends. Tobacco companies, for example, usually trade at price-to-earnings ratios of around 15, compared to the 20-plus we've seen tech stocks trade at recently.

If there is a silver lining in all this, it seems that there is little evidence that ESG investing undermines performance to any major degree. This is clearly true of the major ESG ETFs, which have performed more or less in line with their benchmarks this year.

LEVERAGED ETFS

L EVERAGED ETFs ARE kind of like a high stakes casino. They have potentially high rewards and always carry high risks. And like gambling, they've always been controversial.

Leveraged ETFs use derivatives to give a multiple – such as 2x or 3x – the performance of an index. So, for example, if the FTSE 100 goes up by 2% on some trading day, a 2x leveraged FTSE 100 ETF would go up by 4% on the same day – giving double the performance of the FTSE. This also works the other way: if the FTSE 100 drops -3%, the 2x leveraged ETF will drop -6% that same day.

The following graph compares the performance of the unleveraged iShares S&P 500 ETF (IVV) with the 2x leveraged ProShares Ultra S&P 500 (SSO) and 3x leveraged Direxion Daily S&P 500 Bull 3x Shares ETF (SPXL).

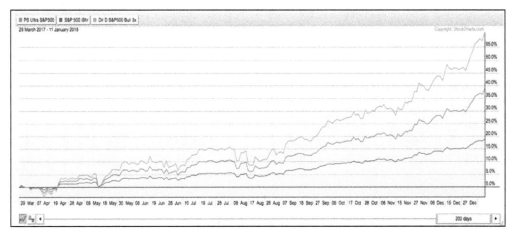

Source: StockCharts.com

Inverse

Inverse ETFs by contrast, try to give the opposite performance of an index on a daily basis. They offer ways for investors to profit from falling markets. So, for example, if the FTSE 100 falls -2% on some day, then the inverse ETF will increase in value by 2%. And vice versa.

Inverse ETFs offer a way for investors to express a view that a market will fall. They offer a one-stop-shop alternative to short selling, which comes with burdens like paying rental fees, returning borrowed stocks and meeting margin calls. In theory at least, inverse ETFs are less risky than their leveraged and ultra-short cousins (discussed below) as they do not give a multiple of the performance of any index – only the inverse.

Ultra-short

Ultra-short ETFs (sometimes called 'leveraged inverse') are for those who believe that some kind of major market downturn is on its way – and in the very near term. They work by putting together the dynamics of both leveraged and inverse ETFs, providing an inverse multiple of the daily performance of an index. So, for example, if the FTSE 100 falls by -3% on some day, then a FTSE 100 -2x leveraged ETF will rise 6% that same day. And vice versa.

Daily resets: investors need a rock-solid understanding

Leveraged ETFs might sound great and like an easy way to make money, after all, if the S&P 500 only ever seems to go up – as the experience of 2017 suggests – why not just buy a fund that gives double or triple the performance of that index?

But this is where daily rebalancing comes in. Leveraged ETFs are rebalanced every day at the end of trading, meaning they give double the *daily percentage movement* of a commodity. This means that their long-term performance is vastly different from the performance of their underlying index. The US Securities Exchange Commission gives the following warning on its website, which investors considering leveraged ETFs should read in full:

WARNING FROM THE SEC

"Let's say that on Day 1, an index starts with a value of 100 and a leveraged ETF that seeks to double the return of the index starts at $100. If the index drops by 10 points on Day 1, it has a 10 percent loss and a resulting value of 90. Assuming it achieved its stated objective, the leveraged ETF would therefore drop 20 percent on that day and have an ending value of $80. On Day 2, if the index rises 10 percent, the index value increases to 99. For the ETF, its value for Day 2 would rise by 20 percent, which means the ETF would have a value of $96. On both days, the leveraged ETF did exactly what it was supposed to do – it produced daily returns that were two times the daily index returns. But let's look at the results over the 2 day period: the index lost 1 percent (it fell from 100 to 99) while the 2x leveraged ETF lost 4 percent (it fell from $100 to $96). That means that over the two day period, the ETF's negative returns were 4 times as much as the two-day return of the index instead of 2 times the return."

This effect can be particularly acute in volatile markets. It is for this reason that most experts will warn that leveraged and ultra-short ETFs should not be held for much longer than a few weeks.

Costs and issuers

In addition to higher risks, leveraged and inverse ETFs also tend to carry higher fees. Most plain vanilla ETFs that track famous indices like the FTSE, S&P 500, EURO STOXX 50, have fees below 10 basis points – making them very cheap (and those fees continue to trend down). But leveraged and inverse ETFs tend to have higher fees. Among leveraged ETFs, Amundi provides some of the cheapest in Europe. Yet its 2x leveraged MSCI USA tracker charges 35 basis points, well beyond the pale for plain vanilla funds.

Investors considering leveraged funds should also be aware that the big three issuers – Vanguard, BlackRock, State Street – do not provide these types of fund. This too has implications for fees as these three issuers are key players in lowering fees across the board.

ROBO-ADVICE COMES OF AGE

FINANCIAL DISRUPTION: THE BACKGROUND TO A ROBO REVOLUTION

CCORDING TO HARVARD professor Clayton Christensen's classic book, *Disruptive Innovation*, technological change follows a remorseless logic. Small but disruptive innovators take the fish that John West rejects. They slowly but steadily figure out what to do with it. And once they've figured it out, they use their idea to wither away the competitive advantage of dominant players. With the disruption, prices fall, new services emerge, and the innovators turn into the new dominant players. Consumers benefit from increased choice, new ease of access and lower cost.

Disruptive innovation is all around us. The internet has disrupted and lowered the costs of media, music and retail. Apps and smartphones have disrupted the food, taxi and navigation and mapping industries. But financial services seems to have mostly escaped the pattern of disruptive change. In fact, evidence suggests that costs and fees in banking and finance have increased in the past several years.

According to Professor Thomas Philippon of New York University, the total compensation of financial institutions (profits, wages, salary and bonuses) as a fraction of US GDP is at an all-time high, around 9% of GDP. In his recent study, appropriately titled "Finance vs Wal-Mart: Why are Financial Services So Expensive?", Philippon suggests the costs of financial services has been somewhere between 1.3% and 2.3% of assets. Yet despite improving technology and heightened productivity, costs have been trending upwards since 1970 – or as Prof Philippon puts it:

> The finance industry of 1900 was just as able as the finance industry of 2010 to produce loans, bonds and stocks, and it was certainly doing it more cheaply. This is counterintuitive, to say the least.

There's no doubting that technology has had a major impact on financial services, as innovations like ATMs, banking apps and ETFs make clear. But for the poor old end user, their costs have remained much the same.

Yet there is reason to believe that now, finally, things are starting to change. Regulators have made it clear they want lower costs and more choice. And, crucially, ETFs have enabled upstart, purely digital investment platforms to flourish.

Enter robo-advice

The incentives for robo-advice driven disruption are huge. A 2015 report by consultancy McKinsey estimated the potential value of personal financial assets that could be served by robo-advice at $13.5 trillion, split into $6.4tn in North America, $3.4tn Asia, $3.3tn Europe, $0.4tn Australia and $0.1tn Latin America. This report assumed that 25% of rich households ($100k to $1m in financial assets) and 10% of high net worth households ($1m to $30m) are prime candidates for online advice.

These findings are echoed by Citigroup, whose analysts reckon that the total wealth held by robo-advisers' target market – 25–44 year olds with £40k–£250k total assets – sits at £983 billion. Of this, the bank reckons that the total addressable market is probably about £138 billion, representing 2.2% of the total industry AUM.

Disruption thus far

As with ETFs themselves, the most dramatic market disruption has been in the US where a host of new technologically savvy, digital-only investment platforms have emerged in the last decade with independent startups like Betterment, Personal Capital and Wealthfront coming to the fore. Their total AUM according to investment bank Numis is $19bn – against an industry holding $14,500bn. The growth rates of these startups (in the US at least) has been rapid. Wealthfront, the largest independent robo-adviser, reached its first billion AUM in 2.5 years, and its second billion in the 9 months after that. But these numbers need context. Charles Schwab, one of the largest brokerage houses in the world, has an average account size of $262,000. This is almost 30 times larger than Wealthfront's average account size of $9,000.

In the UK, we're seeing the green shoots of this disruption. Several young, internet-based platforms have sprung up to attack this potentially huge market led by industry pioneer in the UK Nutmeg – its rivals now include Money on Toast, Wealth Horizon, Moneyfarm, Strawberry Invest, Wealthify, Fiver a Day and newest player MoneyBox. We'll examine these platforms in a little more detail below.

WHAT IS ROBO-ADVICE?

Over the last few years the term robo-advice has emerged as the main catch all term for describing digital wealth products. It conjures up an image of a ghostly robot managing your portfolio using clever algorithms. The reality is very far from this.

Until recently most investors were faced with a choice: invest directly through a platform that deals in shares and funds or use a financial adviser, like an IFA. The former uses lots of digital technology (apps, web portfolios) while the latter involves more of the personal, face-to-face element. This contrast in models is reflected in the charges – direct online platforms charge a combination of low dealing fees and a small platform fee, while the adviser model rightly costs much more, either charged as an hourly fee or as a percentage of portfolio managed.

Robo-based products attempt to bridge this divide. Investors get all the benefits of the digital access – lower costs, clever technology – but with some of the portfolio building advice offered by advisers. In very simple terms, a robo platform involves the following elements:

- Your primary point of access is online.

- Your provider guides you through some questions about your attitude towards risk and reward.

- They then provide you either with a personalised or model portfolio.

- This portfolio can change and is probably fairly low-cost.

- The underlying funds will almost certainly be passive and mostly include ETFs.

- Some platforms will only review your portfolios infrequently (perhaps yearly) whereas other platforms will be much more active in moving funds around.

- The overall cost of ownership (fund fees, platform fees and any other charges) shouldn't exceed 1% per annum, with some offering much lower rates.

Notice, that in our very brief summary we've made no mention of robots: that's because they aren't present! There are some providers who will use big data and clever algorithms to build a bespoke portfolio, but by and large the classic robo-advice is basically an online portfolio platform stuffed full of cheap ETFs and smart customer-facing software and apps.

IS ROBO A THREAT TO TRADITIONAL WEALTH MANAGERS?

Whether robo-advice constitutes a threat – and if so, what kind – to traditional wealth managers has been widely discussed. Views differ from person to person and from study to study. Below are two arguments from each side.

Yes: Accenture	No: Christensen Institute
A major review by consultancy Accenture claimed that robo-advice could make active managers feel the sting. This is because robo-advice technology can be picked up by big players like insurance companies, who can offer it to existing clients. Accenture also notes that because robo-advice is so cheap, it can open up new markets.	On the negative side, the Christensen Institute, a Silicon Valley think tank founded by Prof Christensen who was mentioned above, put out a review claiming that robo-advice is somewhere between un-revolutionary and counterrevolutionary.
"Although robo-advice to date has gained only a miniscule share of assets under management (AUM), it presents investors with an interesting value proposition — with a price reduction of as much as 70 percent for some services — and its rate of growth is both rapid and accelerating... Overall, we believe robo-advice capabilities will effect profound and permanent changes in the way advice is delivered," Accenture said.	The think tank claimed that robo-advice only tweaks financial services by bringing software to investors rather than their advisors. Worse: because it can easily be adopted by incumbents, it may not just be un-revolutionary but actively counterrevolutionary.
	"Considering the function they provide, robo-advisors are more sustaining than disruptive. The process of investing has not changed; the current crop of robo-advisory solutions are built as an enabling interface on top of the existing methods of investing," it said.
	"All they have done is automated the process of onboarding to make it easier for individuals to avail wealth management services. Because incumbents are motivated to adopt robo-advisor technology, entrants are facing steep competition. Thus, we see a fierce response from incumbents including Charles Schwab, Vanguard and BlackRock who have made significant gains against startups."

IS IT A GOOD IDEA?

The best thing about robo-advice is that it fills the advice gap – at least partly, anyway. Since the Retail Distribution Review was implemented in 2013, financial advisers have to quote hourly fees for their services and that's put off a lot of consumers from using their services. Some have become DIY investors instead.

There's a decent chance that DIY investors will get the risk all wrong. They might leave too much money in cash and not get a big enough return to fund their retirement or they may take too much risk and be punished for that. With robo-advice, you should end up with a portfolio that is broadly in line with your risk profile. That said, most robo sites are not offering full financial advice. There's no face-to-face meeting with the customer, and there's no in-depth investigation of the customer's financial aims or circumstances. There's a risk that the customer *thinks* she's had proper financial advice when she hasn't.

Other advantages include transparency – investors can quickly find out what's in their portfolios – and rebalancing. That means that if your portfolio starts out with 10%

exposure to US stocks, and then US share prices rise much more quickly than other assets, some of your US shares will be sold to take the overall US exposure back down to 10%. If you don't rebalance your portfolio, your risk level can increase because your exposure to a particular asset class or region can become too large. The other issue with robo-advice is the fees. Most robo sites keep their costs down by using ETFs and other passive funds, but you can definitely save more money by taking the DIY approach, but we've already seen the potential downsides to that approach.

LEADING ROBO-ADVICE SITES

Let's now look at some of the leading UK robo-advice sites. This list is not exhaustive: new sites are being launched all the time. As more of the traditional financial services companies launch their own robo services, the number may well rise further. First, here's a table comparing the different fee structures:

Platform	Fees	Minimum investment
Nutmeg	Up to £100k: 0.45%/0.75% £100k+ 0.25%/0.35%	£500 + £100 a month
Wealthsimple	0.7% (up to £5000 is managed for free for first year)	Zero
Wealthify	£1k+: 0.7% £15k+: 0.6% £50k+: 0.5%	£1
Moneyfarm	0 to £20k: 0.7% £20k to £100k: 0.6% £100k-£500k: 0.5% £500k+ 0.4%	£1
Scalable Capital	0.75%	£10,000
Evestor	0.35%	Zero
IG Smart Portfolio	Up to £50k: 0.65% £50k to £250k: 0.35% £250k+: 0.1%	£500
ETFmatic	Up to £25k: 0.5% £25k+:0.3%	£100

NUTMEG

In addition to the above fees, you'll also have to pay fees for the underlying investments in your portfolio, which are normally ETFs. ETF charges often work out at around 0.13% on average. When the portfolio buys or sells the ETFs, there's a cost arising from the bid-offer spread.

Nutmeg was the first robo-advice platform in the UK and offers two different services: 'fully managed portfolios' and 'fixed allocation portfolios'. If you look at the charges in the above table, the fixed allocation portfolios are cheaper.

With the fully managed portfolios, the Nutmeg team can move in and make 'strategic interventions' when they see fit. For example, in the run-up to the Brexit referendum, the fully managed portfolios were no longer invested in UK small-cap stocks. There are ten possible portfolios within this service, you're allocated a portfolio once you've answered the questionnaire.

The fixed allocation portfolios are designed by the Nutmeg team and are automatically rebalanced to stay in line with the chosen risk level. Apart from that, the team keep their hands off their portfolios. There are only five available portfolios within this service.

WEALTHSIMPLE

Wealthsimple is a Canadian firm that launched in the UK in September 2017. The firm constructs a range of portfolios made up of ETFs which are then assigned to customers depending on their risk profile. Users can easily see how their portfolio is performing and drill down into the performance of the different assets.

WEALTHIFY

With its low minimum investment, Wealthify is aimed at the broad general market. Insurance giant Aviva bought a majority stake in the platform and this deal should give Wealthify the cash to become a major player in this market.

MONEYFARM

Moneyfarm was originally an Italian business but launched in the UK in 2016. It already has more than 10,000 customers in the UK.

SCALABLE CAPITAL

Scalable has higher charges than most of its rivals but perhaps can justify those higher fees with a particularly sophisticated investment process.

EVESTOR

This service launched this year and is co-founded by Duncan Cameron, one of the original founders of MoneySupermarket.

Unlike most of its rivals, it offers fully regulated financial advice, which should take account of all your circumstances and goals. You can speak to Evestor's financial advisers whenever you want. That said, the company's advisers are only going to recommend you solutions from a limited range of products.

ETFMATIC

ETFmatic makes a big play of being a European player and operates across 32 countries. Its fees are on the low side; the 0.3% fee for holdings above £25,000 is especially attractive. Although the service is a discretionary investment model, it does give the user more input than many rivals. That's because there are three types of portfolios for the user: starter portfolios, investment plans and custom portfolios.

The starter is the simplest offering – ETFmatic sets the asset allocation across bonds and equities according to your attitude to risk. The custom portfolios are similar but you set the initial allocation percentages, such as 20% in bonds or whatever. With the investment model, the asset allocation is constantly being updated by ETFmatic according to what's happening in markets at the time.

IG SMART PORTFOLIO

IG is one of several bigger financial services companies moving into the robo-advice arena. You can reduce your fees for Smart Portfolio by trading regularly on IG's spread betting or stockbroking services.

CHALLENGES: CUSTOMER ACQUISITIONS

Any new industry or startup faces challenges. One of the biggest ones facing robo-advisers – and other fintechs too, for that matter – is customer acquisition. Your average Englishman is more likely to leave his wife than leave his bank. Financial services is a very sticky industry: customers tend to be very loyal to the institutions they know and do not like change. This obviously poses a challenge for robo-advisers as they aim to shake things up and change loyalties.

Customer acquisition costs

On average, UK robo-advisers spend £200–£500 to acquire each new customer, according to a study from consumer website Boring Money. Considering that the average British robo-adviser charges only 50 basis points, this means they need more than £40,000 assets from each investor just to even out the costs of acquisition. "Low ongoing charges, combined with high upfront acquisition costs, mean that revenues might never cover the costs of acquisition," said Holly Mackay, the founder of Boring Money.

WHAT ARE THE RISKS FOR INVESTORS?

Many investors remain wary about allocating too much money to these online digital wealth solutions. This sensible caution unfortunately results in a rather worrying feedback loop. If potential investors only allocate a small amount of money to this radical new idea, most of the startups will have small amounts of capital invested with them. As they are low cost platforms that means that revenues will also be low. But you won't be surprised to discover that many of the big platforms have had countless tens of millions invested in them. At which point the challenge becomes obvious – the only way that many of these businesses will thrive is if they have huge amounts of assets under management. But if investors are cautious, revenues will be low and over time many upstart providers will go bust.

A US technology expert called Michael Kitces has written extensively – and enthusiastically – about the uses of technology for investment advice but he recently warned about an "inability to scale their robo advice platforms' marketing to sustain growth rates in the face of increasing competition and challenging client acquisition costs, coupled with a similar inability to grow their average account sizes". Kitces reports an average account size of $20,000, which, in turn, produces revenue of just $50 per year at a 0.25% fee schedule.

Over here in the UK, wealth adviser Gina Miller at SCM has echoed these concerns. She reckons that robo-advisers in the UK are wired to lose money, and most will go bust before acquiring the sizeable assets under management to ensure their sustainability. By her maths the average UK robo-adviser receives revenue of just £147.50 per annum per account, but the cost of acquisition is at least £180 per annum per account. She also reports on "one well known UK robo-adviser firm reported costs in its latest available accounts of £9.42 for every £1 of revenue".

A report a few years back from the Chartered Financial Analysts Institute echoed these fears – CFAs are the pre-eminent investment professionals. The CFA's main body the CFAI asked its members what they feared most about the rise of online, automated financial advice tools. 46% said they were concerned by flaws in the algorithms powering these solutions with another 30% worried about mis-selling of financial advice. Another 12% also said they were fearful about privacy issues.

These professional concerns about wonky algorithms and mis-selling reflect a deeper truth. Every investor is unique and many of us boast financial planning issues that are much more complicated than online tools currently allow. Algorithms and whizzy graphics are one thing, but many investors crave someone to talk to about key life choices.

Willingness to embrace online solutions also varies greatly by age group. A recent survey from UK provider IG revealed that in fact older, wealthier investor's might be more willing to sign up for DIY-based solutions especially if it cuts costs and improves transparency of returns. Equally the survey reveals that wealthier investors – usually older as well – might be receptive to the right online solution. A noticeably smaller percentage of earning more than £75,000 per annum think they receive value for money from their existing financial adviser (at 65% compared to 78% for investors with less than £50,000). Wealthier investors are also more worried about the lack of transparency about costs with traditional channels. The chart below from the CFAI looks at attitudes towards automated financial tools and reveals that mass affluent customers are much more likely to be interested in web-based solutions.

Investors affected by automated financial advice tools*

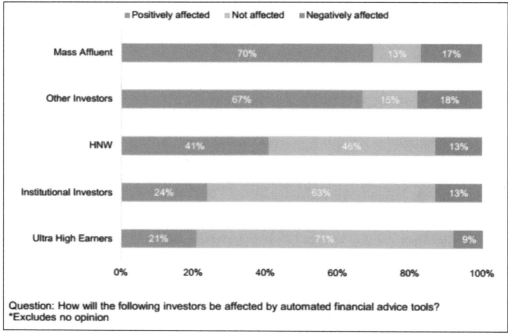

Question: How will the following investors be affected by automated financial advice tools?
*Excludes no opinion

Source: CFAI

But there may be one last rub. These older, wealthier investors might indeed start to try out automated and robo-based solutions, but they might be provided by big, well-known brand names – not the scrappy upstarts looking to redefine the market place. In the US for instance it's noticeable that one of the most successful robo-based platforms is provided by the huge stock broking service Schwab. Its robo-advice offering, Schwab Intelligent Portfolios or SIP, gathered over $3bn in AUM in just the first four months of existence – quickly overtaking much younger, arguably more tech-savvy peers. In sum, technological disruption might not actually work to the favour of the smaller players. More choice online and lower costs could, perversely, result in bigger, larger scale players with trusted brands dominating the markets of tomorrow.

ASSET CLASSES

GLOBAL EQUITIES

MAIN INDICES

- **MSCI World Index**
  Captures large and mid-cap representation across 23 Developed Markets (DM) countries. With 1,652 constituents, the index covers approximately 85% of the free float-adjusted market capitalisation in each country.

- **FTSE All-World Index**
  A market capitalisation-weighted index representing the performance of the large and mid-cap stocks from the FTSE Global Equity Index Series and covers 90–95% of the investable market capitalisation.

- **Dow Jones Global Titans 50 Index**
  Designed to measure multinational companies whose blue-chip stocks are traded on the major exchanges of countries covered by the Dow Jones Global Indices (DJGI) benchmark family.

DESCRIPTION AND COMPOSITION

Rather than buy lots of different developed world markets (the US, Europe, and Japan for instance) why not buy into one fund that tracks a big, well-known index of nearly all the developed world's stock markets? That's the idea behind a small band of comprehensive indices – and ETFs – which represent a compelling proposition for private investors. Within one ETF an investor can buy aggregate exposure to the major large caps in all the big developed world markets.

Two choices await. The first is the index you track – we've featured four global indices but most ETFs tend to track the MSCI version. The second choice is whether to buy into this index so that it includes the UK (the default choice for most) or excludes the UK market – if you decide the latter, you might then buy into a separate FTSE All-Share or FTSE 100 tracker. Note also that these global indices only track equities – not bonds – and are focused on developed world markets and blue-chips in particular.

Let's look at each of the major indices in turn.

MSCI WORLD INDEX

The most popular index is called the MSCI World Index. The name of this index is a little misleading because it doesn't include emerging market countries. It does, however, include around 1650 stocks drawn from 23 countries. Here's a table of the biggest constituents from 2017:

Percentage of index broken down by country and sector

Country or Region	Weight(%)	Sector	Weight(%)
US	59.9	Financial Services	17.9
Japan	9.1	Technology	17.6
UK	6.4	Consumer Discretionary	12.7
France	4.1	Health	11.7
Germany	3.6	Industrials	11.6

The table illustrates the big problem with global index investing. You end up with a large weighting towards US stocks. That reflects the reality that the US stock market is still by far the largest in the world by value.

The index is also biased towards large-caps. That said, investing in an ETF tracking this index would still diversify you away from the UK market, and most investors should have at least some exposure to US equities. So, we think backing this index might work for some people.

MSCI ACWI INDEX

Next up we have another index from the same company called the MSCI ACWI Index (All Country World Index). This index is similar to the MSCI World Index except it adds in around 850 extra stocks from 24 emerging market countries. Emerging market stocks account for around 12% of the value of the fund.

Percentage of index broken down by country and sector from 2017

Country or region	% of index	Sector	% of index
US	52.0	Financial Services	19.4
Eurozone	10.6	Technology	16.6
Japan	7.6	Consumer Cyclicals	11.3
UK	5.8	Healthcare	11.1
Asia – emerging	5.7	Industrials	11.0

Thanks to the 12% exposure to emerging markets, the index is a bit more diversified than the main MSCI World index. But the US still accounts for more than 50% of the index, which is probably too large a weighting if all your money was invested in this index. There's also an ex-UK version of this ACWI index.

FTSE ALL WORLD INDEX

Moving away from MSCI we also have the FTSE All World Index. This index covers both developed and emerging markets. It comprises around 2900 stocks from 47 different countries and represents over 90% of the global stock market.

Percentage of index broken down by country and sector from 2017

Country or region	% of index	Sector	% of index
US	51.1	Financial services	19.8
Eurozone	10.7	Technology	16.0
Japan	8.4	Health	11.2
UK	5.9	Consumer Cyclical	10.9
Asia – emerging	5.4	Industrials	10.8

DOW JONES TITANS 50

Finally, we have the Dow Jones Titans 50. This index comprises 50 of the largest global stocks. It's very heavily slanted towards the US.

Percentage of index broken down by country and sector from 2017

Country or region	% of index	Sector	% of index
US	76.0	Technology	30.8
UK	6.1	Financial Services	15.8
Europe – ex eurozone	6.1	Health	14.5
Eurozone	6.1	Consumer Defensive	11.3
Asia – developed	3.8	Energy	9.7

WHAT TO WATCH OUT FOR

Our general preference is to buy an ETF that invests globally but which avoids the UK – we suspect that most investors are already rather too biased towards UK stocks and so a World ex-UK index should fit the bill.

What's even better in our view is that all of these indices are very diversified – you're buying into a portfolio of companies where the top 3 companies usually only comprise between 5 and 9% of the total holdings. There is one downside though – you are buying a heavy mix of US stocks which comprise between 40 and 50% of total holdings. This may worry some UK investors concerned about exposure to the US although we'd say it's simply a reflection of what actually happens on the global equity markets. If you want to buy exposure in a slightly more balanced way, you could assemble an ETF portfolio that included a FTSE All UK tracker, a Eurozone tracker (the EURO STOXX 50) and a US benchmark index such as the S&P 500 – all in equal portions.

Alternatively, if you're looking for a little more diversification you could build a very simple four index portfolio tracking say the MSCI World, a FTSE tracker, an MSCI Emerging Markets Index fund and a global government bonds fund. Bundle up these four funds and you'd have a diversified multi-asset, international portfolio on the cheap – the combined expense shouldn't be more than 0.4% per annum.

Finally in terms of valuations, it's worth observing that the MSCI World Index doesn't look like very reasonable value – at the end of 2017 it was trading at around 20.8 times earnings with a dividend yield of 2.4%. That's not expensive by historic standards but it certainly isn't cheap. The chart below is from the excellent Yardeni Research Group[6] in the US and shows the forward price-to-earnings ratio for the All Country World version of the MSCI Index. Current valuations are close to decade highs.

---

6   https://www.yardeni.com/pub/mscipe.pdf

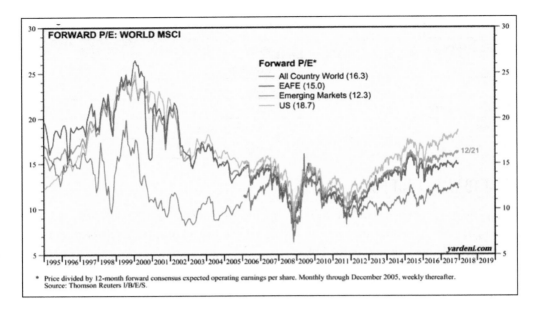

* Price divided by 12-month forward consensus expected operating earnings per share. Monthly through December 2005, weekly thereafter.
  Source: Thomson Reuters I/B/E/S.

Returns for the MSCI World Index

2017	20.11%
2016	8.15%
2015	-0.37%
3 yrs	7.15%
5 yrs	9.46%
Volatility	5.52%
Correlation with S&P 500	0.7351

GLOBAL EMERGING MARKETS

MAIN INDEX

MSCI Emerging Markets Index

This index captures large and mid-cap representation across 24 Emerging Markets (EM) countries. With 837 constituents, the index covers approximately 85% of the free float-adjusted market capitalisation in each country. From just ten countries in 1988 representing less than 1% of world market capitalisation to 24 countries representing 13% of world market capitalisation, today the MSCI Emerging Markets Index can be segmented by regions and market segments/sizes.

DESCRIPTION

Emerging market economies now account for almost 40% of global GDP. That's a pretty striking figure, and it means that most investors should at least consider investing in emerging markets. But before we go any further, we should clarify what the term 'emerging markets' actually means. The best known emerging economies are probably China, India and Brazil, but many other countries fall into the bracket. Emerging markets are countries that have many of the characteristics of a developed economy such as the US and Europe, but don't yet meet all of the standards expected in a developed market.

Countries that haven't developed as far yet – for example, Zambia or Pakistan – are often described as 'frontier' markets, not emerging. The main argument for investing in emerging markets is pretty obvious. Economies such as China and India have grown very quickly over the last 20 years, and there's a good chance that these economies will continue to outpace the US and Europe.

Emerging markets tend to have young populations which means there's plenty of cheap labour, and productivity is rising fast too. Even better, the new emerging market middle classes are boosting consumption significantly – this is especially true in China. But investing in emerging markets comes with risks and drawbacks – not least that economic growth isn't always reflected in stock market growth.

Political instability is another risk. So, in 2017 we saw corruption scandals in Brazil and moves by President Erdogan in Turkey to seize power from traditional democratic institutions. These developments fuelled sell-offs of both these countries in 2018. For investors, the worry is that some governments might decide to hit successful businesses with big tax raids or even nationalisation. With some authoritarian governments, you may find that businesses are run more in the interests of the government than shareholders – this is an oft-cited worry with larger Chinese companies.

Another problem is that emerging stock markets tend not to be as liquid as the S&P 500 or the Footsie which can lead to more volatility and is also a problem for institutional investors when they want to sell out.

Inflation tends to be higher in emerging markets which increases the risk of dramatic currency moves. A big fall can destroy any profits you may have made once your investments are converted from an emerging market currency back into base currency.

There are also significant country-specific risks. Many commentators worry about levels of debt in China, and the country's population is now ageing quickly. If the Chinese economy did get into trouble, a fall in demand for commodities could hit producers such as South Africa.

It's also worth noting that the performance of emerging market share prices over the last five years and ten years has been disappointing. However, emerging markets have done better since early 2016.

The MSCI Emerging Markets Index or MSCI EM for short is widely used by the institutions as a benchmark index and comprises 837 businesses from around the global emerging markets. In essence the index consists of the world's main emerging stock markets in one composite index, although it's worth adding that you can also buy into the various different components (regional or national) on an individual basis if you so choose.

Before we look at the various funds that track this investment space, let's look at the index in a little more detail first. According to index builders MSCI, the MSCI Emerging Markets Index is a free float-adjusted market capitalisation index that is designed to measure equity market performance of emerging markets.

As of November 2017, the countries in the list include Brazil, Chile, China, Colombia, Czech Republic, Egypt, Greece, Hungary, India, Indonesia, Korea, Malaysia, Mexico, Pakistan, Peru, Philippines, Poland, Russia, Qatar, South Africa, Taiwan, Thailand, Turkey and United Arab Emirates. Returns from these vastly varying nations is shown in the following table.

Regional Performance through to 31 December 2017	1 Yr	3 Yr	5 Yr	10 Yr
BRIC	38 .5%	8.5%	2.4%	-2.8%
EM (EMERGING MARKETS)	34.2%	6.6%	1.9%	-0.7%
EM (EMERGING MARKETS)+CHINA A	29.6%	4.3%	2.5%	-1.1%
CHINA	51.1%	10.2%	7.1%	0.4%
INDIA	35.7%	6.9%	6.9%	-1.0%
INDONESIA	22.0%	3.4%	0.6%	3.0%
KOREA	45.5%	12.7%	5.2%	2.4%
MALAYSIA	21.1%	-4.3%	-4.6%	-0.6%
PHILIPPINES	23.3%	1.5%	4.4%	5.2%
TAIWAN	23.8%	6.8%	6.8%	2.5%
THAILAND	30.9%	6.2%	2.5%	5.9%
EM ASIA	39.9%	8.6%	5.5%	1.3%
EM FAR EAST	40.7%	8.9%	5.4%	1.7%
BRAZIL ADR	24.2%	2.8%	-7.8%	-7.6%
BRAZIL	21.0%	3.4%	-5.8%	-6.3%
CHILE	39.8%	8.7%	-3.3%	1.2%
COLOMBIA	13.8%	-7.5%	-14.0%	0.3%
MEXICO	13.6%	-5.2%	-5.6%	-1.2%
CZECH REPUBLIC	29.4%	-3.0%	-6.5%	-9.4%
GREECE	27.1%	-25.3%	-18.3%	-29.9%
HUNGARY	36.9%	34.1%	9.1%	-3.5%
POLAND	52.3%	2.7%	-2.4%	-6.1%
RUSSIA ADR/GDR	3.2%	13.4%	-5.2%	
RUSSIA	0.3%	14.3%	-5.6%	-8.9%
TURKEY	34.3%	-7.2%	-7.7%	-5.5%
SOUTH AFRICA	33.1%	3.7%	0.8%	1.8%
QATAR	-15.0%	-12.4%	-1.4%	-1.9%
UNITED ARAB EMIRATES	-1.3%	-5.1%	12.0%	-5.0%

There are also a number of related smaller indices that don't quite fit inside the MSCI Emerging Markets mother ship but overlap – chief amongst them is the MSCI AC (All Country) Far East ex Japan Index which is a free float-adjusted market capitalisation-weighted index that is " designed to measure the equity market performance of the Far East, excluding Japan and comprises China, Hong Kong, Indonesia, Korea, Malaysia, Philippines, Singapore, Taiwan, and Thailand" i.e. the emerging Asia. You might also notice MSCI AC Far East Ex-Japan SmallCap which is a variation of the Emerging Asia index and tracks small cap stocks.

The most obvious choice for mainstream investors looking to buy into the emerging markets investment space is to start with the mother ship index, namely the MSCI EM Index, tracked by a long list of EM issuers. All these global EM ETFs are cheap, fairly diversified across different countries and biased towards the biggest and best companies in the global emerging markets space. By contrast we'd worry that country specific index tracking funds in the developing world are just too risky and specialised for the ordinary investor. Your best bet with specific countries might be to either use a specialised active fund manager who can take those judgement calls for you or stick with a global EM index fund.

A final observation – one alternative to a global emerging markets tracker fund is to prioritise a bunch of countries known as the BRICs. Most of the big index developers have an index which allows you to invest in the top companies (50 of them) of Brazil, Russia, India and China specifically, otherwise known as the BRIC countries.

COMPOSITION

Looking at the MSCI Emerging Markets Index, the top three businesses by market capitalisation are all tech businesses, at the end of 2017 at least – Chinese outfit Tencent Holdings tops the list with a weighting of 5.5%, followed by South Korean giant Samsung at 4.4% and Chinese rival to Tencent, Alibaba at 3.88%. Information technology businesses not unsurprisingly dominate in sector terms, with a 28% weighting, followed by financials at 23% with consumer discretionary businesses lagging far behind at a weighting of just 10%. In term of country weights four countries dominate: China at 30%, South Korea at 15%, Taiwan at 11%, and India at 8%.

WHAT TO WATCH OUT FOR

The first thing to say is that traditionally emerging markets have been seen as expensive, growth stocks i.e. valuation multiples have been stretched. That's certainly true for some of the Chinese tech stocks but paradoxically as a whole EM stocks trade at a big discount to developed world stocks. The current aggregate dividend yield is running at 2.25% and the price-to-earnings multiple for the entire universe is at 15 times earnings. These aren't particularly expensive in aggregate terms. But the reality is that most of the recent gains in the EM index have been driven by expensive Chinese tech stocks – and these could be vulnerable to profit taking.

A broader concern with global EM index funds is whether a passive fund is necessarily the best approach to investing? Many EM investors worry that these broad indices are just too... global and broad! These critics worry that the indices are structurally biased towards larger markets and larger companies which means that you might be missing out on some of the best investment opportunities in this asset class, which are often in smaller countries and the small and mid-cap space. Many critics also argue that these more niche opportunities are best exploited by good, specialist and active stock pickers.

Supporters of ETFs by contrast point out that specialist, active fund managers may be able to provide market timing and risk management skills, but that their expertise comes at a cost. Most actively managed, diversified emerging markets funds charge at least 1.5–2% a year in management fees plus an initial charge that can amount to 5%. ETFs from the major issuers should cost less than 0.50%, a huge saving. ETF supporters also argue that index funds are simpler and cleaner – they claim that most active fund managers fail to hit their benchmark returns whereas with an ETF you're simply buying the market.

Performance analysis of MSCI EM index

2017	34.0%
2016	11.0%
2015	-2.2%
3 yrs	6.6%
5 yrs	1.8%
Volatility	9.5%
Correlation with S&P 500	0.81

US EQUITIES

MAIN INDICES

- **S&P 500**

  The major US benchmark – and our preferred index – is the S&P 500 which is a value-weighted index published since 1957 of the prices of 500 large cap liquid stocks actively traded in the USA. The stocks included in the S&P 500 are those of large publicly held companies that trade on either of the two largest American stock markets, the New York Stock Exchange and NASDAQ. Almost all of the stocks included in the index are among the 500 American stocks with the largest market values or capitalisations.

- **Dow Jones Industrial Average**

  The Dow Jones Industrial Average is a price-weighted average of blue-chip stocks and the oldest index by far. The index covers all industries with the exception of transportation and utilities. The index has been a widely followed indicator of the stock market since 1st October 1928.

- **Russell 1000®**

  The Russell 1000® Index measures the performance of the large-cap segment of the US equity universe. It is a subset of the Russell 3000® Index and includes approximately 1000 of the largest US securities. The Russell 1000® represents approximately 92% of the US equity market vs. only 66% for the S&P 500. Russell Indices are used by more US institutional investors than all other index providers combined.

- **Russell 2000®**

  The Russell 2000 Index measures the performance of the small-cap segment of the US equity universe. The Russell 2000® Index measures the performance of the 2000 smallest companies in the Russell 3000® Index, which represents approximately 8% of the total market capitalisation of the US equity market vs. 3-4% for the S&P 600.

- **MSCI USA Index**

  The MSCI USA Index is based around the hugely popular MSCI World Developed Markets Index and covers almost 98% of all the stocks – large and small – listed on the US stock markets (including the NASDAQ and the NYSE).

DESCRIPTION

The US stock market is huge, by far the largest global market. It comprises just a bit less than 40% of the total world stock market. The US also delivered healthy profits for investors. Over the last 25 years, the flagship S&P 500 Index has delivered a return of 9% a year (dividends reinvested, to July 2017.) If you had invested £1 at the start of this period, it would have grown to £853 by the end.

The US market also comprises a wide variety of companies across all the sectors. Whereas the FTSE 100 is overly concentrated in a few sectors, the S&P has a better spread. But even with that spread, the US market is particularly strong in technology with world famous companies like Facebook, Amazon and Apple. If you want to get exposure to the giants of the technology industry, you're going to have to buy some US-listed shares.

On top of that, many of the world's leading consumer companies are also listed in the US – for example, Coca-Cola, McDonald's, and Procter & Gamble. We'd suggest that any internationally diversified portfolio should have some exposure, no matter how small, to the US market – that could be done indirectly through a World Developed Markets index which would have a heavy US weighting or directly through a fund that tracks a major US index. If you decide to track a major US index you'll be spoilt for choice. There's an almost bewildering array of ETFs that are based on major US indices – both large cap and small cap.

Which index to use?

Given this huge range we'd initially stick with perhaps the best known of the large cap indices namely the S&P 500 Index which is tracked by all manner of ETF issuers with very low TERs – you really shouldn't ever have to pay more than 0.20% per annum to track this deep and liquid US equities index. If you're looking for a slightly more comprehensive index that includes small caps we'd suggest looking at the MSCI USA Index while the Russell 2000® is our preferred index for capturing the vibrant small cap segment in the US markets.

COMPOSITION

Focusing on the S&P 500 benchmark blue-chip index, the top five holdings at the end of 2017 consisted of Apple at 3.82%, Microsoft at 2.88%, Amazon at 2.06%, Facebook at 1.85% and Berkshire Hathaway at 1.67%. In sector terms, tech stocks are dominant with a 23.5% weighting in the index followed by financials at 14.78% and healthcare at 13.84%. At current levels, valuations look a tad rich with the PE ratio at the end of 2017 at 23 times earnings and the yield at just 1.45%.

WHAT TO WATCH OUT FOR

The S&P 500 is heavily impacted by global trends, and as with the FTSE 100, is not necessarily a straight read through to the US economy. The S&P 500 has also been influenced by the boom in tech stocks, with four of the top five stocks in weighting terms, comprising technology leviathans. Investing in US stocks also opens the investor up to currency risks – the dollar could move sharply in one direction or another hitting returns. It's also worth noting that the US central bank, the Federal Reserve, is likely to be the most aggressive proponent of raising interest rates – which might have a knock-on impact on FX rates, the stock market and the domestic economy.

Performance analysis of the S&P 500

2017	19.4%
2016	9.5%
2015	-0.7%
3 yrs	8.5%
5 yrs	13.8%
Volatility	5.1%
Correlation with S&P 500	1

What the experts say

Peter Sleep, Senior Investment Manager at Seven Investment Management, says when it comes to investing in US ETFs, it's essential that UK investors go for ETFs that are domiciled in Dublin. That's because the Republic of Ireland has a double taxation treaty with the US, so that dividends paid by US companies are only taxed at a 15% rate. The tax rate would be 30% on any US ETF domiciled in Luxembourg as there's no double taxation treaty between the US and Luxembourg. (The vast majority of London-listed ETFs are domiciled in either Dublin or Luxembourg.)

EUROPEAN EQUITIES

MAIN INDICES

- **EURO STOXX 50 Index**
  Europe's leading blue-chip index for the Eurozone, provides a blue-chip representation of supersector leaders in the Eurozone. The index covers 50 stocks from 11 Eurozone countries: Austria, Belgium, Finland, France, Germany, Ireland, Italy, Luxembourg, the Netherlands, Portugal and Spain.

- **MSCI Europe Index**
  Captures large and mid-cap representation across 15 Developed Markets (DM) countries in Europe. With 445 constituents, the index covers approximately 85% of the free float-adjusted market capitalisation across the European Developed Markets equity universe.

- **FTSEurofirst 80 Index**
  Comprises the 60 largest companies ranked by market capitalisation in the FTSE Eurozone Index and 20 additional companies selected for their size and sector representation.

- **FTSEurofirst 100 Index**
  Comprises the 60 largest companies ranked by market capitalisation in the FTSE Developed Europe Index and 40 additional companies selected for their size and sector representation.

DESCRIPTION

The EURO STOXX 50 is the bellwether index for Eurozone equities. It is the biggest, and probably the most tracked European index for Eurozone blue-chip outfits such as Total or Siemens.

Before working out whether you should buy (or short) this index as part of your portfolio, it's important to understand that the EURO STOXX 50 is one of many popular blue-chip indices on offer, with rival indices (and accompanying index tracking funds) from both the FTSE Russell Group and MSCI. The first key distinction is between those like the MSCI Europe index and the FTSEurofirst 100 Index that include countries such as the UK and

Switzerland which sit outside of the Eurozone. The EURO STOXX 50 (alongside the FTSEurofirst 80 Index) by contrast only includes companies from inside the Eurozone and excludes all UK and Swiss stocks (as well as nearly all Nordic companies). Just to confuse matters, the MSCI Europe excluding the UK index, obviously excludes the UK but includes all the other European markets including those outside the Eurozone such as the Swiss market. Our advice for most UK based investors is to avoid any fund that is European by title but still invests in UK companies – you'll probably already have a bias towards UK stocks in your portfolio and indices like the FTSEurofirst 100 will simply increase that bias.

The next key distinction is in number of shares listed – the DJ EURO STOXX 50 is by definition focussed on just the top 50 companies, the FTSE Eurofirst on the top 80 and the FTSEurofirst 100 on the top 100. That concentration on top companies matters because the top three stocks in the EURO STOXX index account for just under 13% of the fund whereas in the MSCI Europe ex-UK index they account for less than 10%.

So, if you're after an index that only tracks Eurozone blue-chips – and only the biggest – the EURO STOXX 50 is probably the index for you.

COMPOSITION

We'll focus on the EURO STOXX 50 here, as its likely to be the main index used for tracking the Eurozone blue-chips. Top three stocks include oil giant Total (with 4.84% by market cap), Siemens (4.11%) and SAP (3.88%). Financials account for 22% of the total value of the index followed by industrials at 13.6% and consumer discretionary stocks (11.70%).

WHAT TO WATCH OUT FOR

The EURO STOXX 50 is very much a play on the Eurozone, which introduces some political risk. There's also a very strong correlation between returns from this index and the German DAX and French CAC 40 indices. French and German stocks account for 70% of the market value of the index with Spain and Netherlands accounting for 10% each.

Performance analysis of the EURO STOXX 50 (in Euros)

2017	6.5%
2016	3.7%
2015	6.8%
3 yrs	6.6%
5 yrs	9.7%
Volatility	8.9%
Correlation with S&P 500	0.6291

EUROPEAN EQUITY SECTORS

MAIN INDEX

STOXX Europe 600 Index

Derived from the STOXX Europe Total Market Index (TMI) this is a subset of the STOXX Global 1800 Index. With a fixed number of 600 components, the STOXX Europe 600 Index represents large, mid and small capitalisation companies across 18 countries of the European region: Austria, Belgium, Denmark, Finland, France, Germany, Greece, Iceland, Ireland, Italy, Luxembourg, the Netherlands, Norway, Portugal, Spain, Sweden, Switzerland and the United Kingdom.

DESCRIPTION

The broad STOXX 600 index comprises all of the main European markets including non-Eurozone indices such as the FTSE 100 from the UK. The EURO STOXX 50 index and its accompanying series focuses by contrast exclusively on the Eurozone markets. The STOXX 600 index is widely used by investors looking to play a particular sector within the European region. It's a market cap weighted series which means that the biggest companies by market capitalisation have the highest weighting. It's also worth noting that the underlying index series is denominated in Euros, and most ETF trackers are also quoted in Euros. The sectors covered include all the major sectors tracked by global indices such as the MSCI Sector series. The sectors within the series include all the usual candidates (financials, oil and gas, and technology) plus a smattering of more specialised sectors including construction and materials, chemicals and retail. These sectors included are listed below.

- STOXX Europe 600 Banks (SX7P)

- STOXX Europe 600 Health Care (SXDP)

- STOXX Europe 600 Industrial Goods & Services (SXNP)

- STOXX Europe 600 Personal & Household Goods (SXQP)

- STOXX Europe 600 Insurance (SXIP)

- STOXX Europe 600 Food & Beverage (SX3P)

- STOXX Europe 600 Oil & Gas (SXEP)

- STOXX Europe 600 Chemicals (SX4P)

- STOXX Europe 600 Telecommunications (SXKP)

- STOXX Europe 600 Utilities (SX6P)

- STOXX Europe 600 Technology (SX8P)

- STOXX Europe 600 Retail (SXRP)

- STOXX Europe 600 Automobiles & Parts (SXAP)

- STOXX Europe 600 Media (SXMP)

- STOXX Europe 600 Basic Resources (SXPP)

- STOXX Europe 600 Construction & Materials (SXOP)

- STOXX Europe 600 Real Estate (SX86P)

- STOXX Europe 600 Travel & Leisure (SXTP)

- STOXX Europe 600 Financial Services (SXFP)

COMPOSITION

The overall STOXX 600 index, comprising all the sectors, is comprised of banks for 13% of its value, industrial goods and services for 11.8% and healthcare for 11.5%. In terms of geographical mix, UK stocks comprise 27%, French stocks 16.7% and German stocks 15.2%. Switzerland also comprises 12.9% with Swedish stocks representing 4.4% of the market cap. The top three holdings are Nestle with 2.7%, Novartis at 2.16% and HSBC at 2.06%.

WHAT TO WATCH OUT FOR

The STOXX 600 is a very diversified index and at the aggregate level represents all the major European blue-chips. But the index does include UK, Swiss and Swedish stocks although most ETFs tracking individual sectors report in Euros. The sector indices are especially useful for investors looking to express a tactical view on equities.

Performance analysis of the STOXX Europe 600 Index

2017	15.3%
2016	18.5%
2015	3.4%
3 yrs	11.7%
5 yrs	11.9%
Volatility	5.8%
Correlation with S&P 500	0.75

UK EQUITIES

MAIN INDICES

- **FTSE 100 Index** (UKX) – comprises the 100 most highly capitalised blue-chip companies listed on the London Stock Exchange.

- **FTSE 250 Index** – comprises mid-capitalised companies not covered by the FTSE 100, and represents approximately 15% of UK market capitalisation.

- **FTSE All-Share Index** – representing 98–99% of UK market capitalisation, the FTSE All-Share Index is the aggregation of the FTSE 100, FTSE 250 and FTSE Small Cap Indices.

DESCRIPTION

The main catch all index is the FTSE All-Share Index. It's a market capitalisation-weighted index representing the performance of all eligible companies listed on the London Stock Exchange's main market, which pass a screening for size and liquidity. In total the FTSE All-Share Index covers 641 companies – approximately 98% of the UK's market capitalisation. Many investors are confused by the FTSE 100 and the FTSE All-Share Index – they presume that the best way to track the broad market is via the FTSE 100 (the better-known index) whereas in fact the FTSE 100 Index tracks the large caps in the UK market. Which is not to say that the FTSE All-Share Index doesn't also capture those large caps as well – its composition is still weighted by the size of the market cap and the top 10 companies in the FTSE All-Share comprise 35% of the index as opposed to 46.5% with the FTSE 100. So although the FTSE All-Share casts a wider net, it's still very focussed on mega-cap blue-chips.

But that said, the FTSE All-Share Index does capture a much broader range of companies and comprises the FTSE 100, the FTSE 250 and the members of the FTSE Small Cap Index, but all weighted by market cap (which means that it's still dominated by the biggest FTSE 100 companies).

But there's another crucial point – the FTSE All-Share is not actually *all* the market as the title implies. It doesn't include some really tiny companies that comprise the fag end of the market, namely micro-caps in the FTSE Fledgling Index i.e. really tiny companies valued at less than £10m. There are actually many, many of these very small companies but they don't really amount to much in economic size or footprint so they're not covered by the FTSE All-Share. So, when you buy this index don't think you're actually buying all the UK market – no one index captures that.

So FTSE 100 or FTSE All-Share – which one should you invest in?

If you want a broader market use the FTSE All-Share whereas if you want a more focused large-cap index go for the FTSE 100, but be aware that even the FTSE All-Share is still, in practice, a large-cap index. Also, whatever you do *don't buy both* – you'll be effectively duplicating a lot of the holdings and the FTSE All-Share Index tends to move in the same direction as the FTSE 100 and so you won't get much diversification benefit.

Much the most common index for ETFs is the FTSE 100 Index which consists of the 100 largest companies by market capitalisation. This blue-chip index is the equivalent of the S&P 500 index but has a very heavy international bias with well over 50% of the aggregate earnings for the businesses in the index sourced from abroad.

The FTSE 250 Index is the main mid-cap index and has a much more UK bias. Investors may also encounter an index called the FTSE Small Cap Index which tracks much smaller businesses alongside the micro-cap focused FTSE Fledgling Index.

COMPOSITION

The FTSE 100 Index primarily comprises blue-chip, very internationally-focused businesses. Major sectors include financials at 22% of the index at the end of 2017 (at 27% combined), resources (energy and mining) and consumer stocks/staples (16.8%). The index is also regarded as a reliable source of dividend income with a year-end dividend yield of around 4%

WHAT TO WATCH OUT FOR

The FTSE 100 is very internationally focused, and large-cap based. It also has a high concentration of cyclical resource and financial services firms. The FTSE 100 space is very competitive for ETF issuers, so make sure you don't overpay in terms of the TER. UK equities are very closely correlated with developed world equities and especially the S&P 500.

Performance analysis of the FTSE 100 Index

2017	7.6%
2016	14.4%
2015	-4.9%
3 yrs	5.0%
5 yrs	5.3%
Volatility	5.5%
Correlation with S&P 500	0.83

GERMAN EQUITIES

MAIN INDICES

DAX

Exposure to 30 companies that are either domiciled in Germany or a minimum of 33% of their stock turnover is traded on the Frankfurt Stock Exchange and they are domiciled in an EU or EFTA country.

DESCRIPTION

Although the DAX index is very far from being the only German equity index, it is overwhelmingly the major index used for tracking blue-chip German stocks – although a few ETFs also track the Kursindex and there is also a TecDAX (comprising tech stocks). The DAX is also very widely used by options and leveraged-based investors, which means liquidity is very high and spreads tight. Crucially the DAX is a focused play on a) the German economy, b) the Eurozone's premier economy and c) export-orientated businesses boasting global brands.

COMPOSITION

In sector terms the top three constituents in weighting terms at the end of 2017 are consumer discretionary stocks (18%), financials (16%) and industrials (14%). The top three stocks, by market cap, are tech giant SAP (9.38%), industrial giant Siemens (9%) and Bayer (8.23%), a major player in the healthcare space.

WHAT TO WATCH OUT FOR

The DAX index is very concentrated with just 30 stocks which can make it very volatile and closely correlated with the Eurozone. The focus on export orientated businesses also makes the DAX closely correlated with the state of the global economy – and increasingly the Chinese economy! The DAX has been something of a star performer over the last few years but that's come at the risk of higher levels of volatility.

Performance analysis of the DAX

2017	11.6%
2016	6.9%
2015	9.6%
3 yrs	9.2%
5 yrs	-
Volatility	10%
Correlation with S&P 500	0.64

FRENCH EQUITIES

MAIN INDEX

CAC 40

A free float market capitalisation-weighted index that reflects the performance of the 40 largest and most actively traded shares listed on Euronext Paris and is the most widely used indicator of the Paris stock market.

DESCRIPTION

The CAC 40 is the main index for tracking French stocks, with a total market capitalisation of 1.5 billion euros. The CAC 40 started at the end of December 1987 with a base value of 1,000. Its nearest equivalent is the German DAX index, which is also fairly concentrated in a small number of stocks. The CAC 40 has been heavily impacted by events in the Eurozone and largely comprises internationally-focused businesses. Compared to some peers, the French blue-chip market isn't egregiously expensive – at the end of 2017 it traded at around 20 times price to earnings and yielded 3.11% in dividends. That slightly below average rating is perhaps a legacy of the perceived political risks with France, which under President Macron seem to be ebbing away.

COMPOSITION

The CAC 40 is like many of its peers, a blue-chip index with some powerful international businesses dominating in terms of market capitalisation. Consumer discretionary businesses have the heaviest weighting with 19.3%, followed by industrials at 18% and financials (mainly banks) at 14.2%. The top three holdings at the end of 2017 were global oil giant Total with a 9.44% weighting, medical giant Sanofi at 7% and bank BNP Paribas at 6%.

WHAT TO WATCH OUT FOR

The CAC 40 is like the DAX, and the FTSE 100, a blue-chip index with mega large cap businesses dominating the list. It's also very international in terms of revenues and profits. But the CAC 40 isn't as widely used as say the DAX for options trading, largely because

France isn't traditionally seen as the strongest economy in Europe. Also, investors need to be aware that French stocks have a huge impact on the mainstream European, and especially Eurozone indices, such as the EURO STOXX 50. Unless you have a specific conviction trade about France and its prospects, it's probably best to stay more diversified with one of the broader Eurozone equity indices.

Performance analysis of the CAC 40 Index

2017	9.1%
2016	4.9%
2015	8.5%
3 yrs	7.2%
5 yrs	8.0%
Volatility	8.2%
Correlation with S&P 500	0.56

JAPANESE EQUITIES

MAIN INDICES

Nikkei Stock Average

The Nikkei 225 is used around the globe as the premier index of Japanese stocks. More than 60 years have passed since the commencement of its calculation, which represents the history of the Japanese economy after World War II. Because of the prominent nature of the index, many financial products linked to the Nikkei 225 that have been created are traded worldwide while the index has been sufficiently used as the indicator of the movement of Japanese stock markets. The Nikkei 225 is a price-weighted equity index, which consists of 225 stocks in the first section of the Tokyo Stock Exchange.

TOPIX

The TOPIX is a free float-adjusted market capitalisation-weighted index that is calculated based on all the domestic common stocks listed on the TSE First Section. TOPIX shows the measure of current market capitalisation assuming that market capitalisation as of the base date (January 4 ,1968) is 100 points. This is a measure of the overall trend in the stock market and is used as a benchmark for investment in Japanese stocks.

JPX-Nikkei Index 400

Composed of companies with high appeal for investors, which meet requirements of global investment standards, such as efficient use of capital and investor-focused management perspectives. The index was jointly developed by Nikkei, Japan Exchange Group and Tokyo Stock Exchange. The JPX-Nikkei 400 comprises common stocks whose main market is the TSE first section, second section, Mothers or JASDAQ market.

MSCI Japan Index

Designed to measure the performance of the large and mid-cap segments of the Japanese market. With 321 constituents, the index covers approximately 85% of the free float-adjusted market capitalisation in Japan.

DESCRIPTION

It's often said that stock markets always rise over the long-term; investors just have to be patient to make money. However, there is one massive exception to this rule – Japan. Japan's flagship index, the Nikkei 225, hit its all-time peak of 38,916 back in 1989, and there's no sign of it going back to its former peak any time soon. Granted, the Japanese market had a strong run between 2012 and 2015, but long-term investors who entered the market in 1989 will still have been caned. On top of that, economic performance since the early 90s has been pretty sluggish too. That said, Japan has its plus points. The country is still a leader in technological innovation, and the government's economic reforms, known as 'Abenomics' have delivered a modest boost to economic growth. The Bank of Japan's QE programme has also boosted asset prices.

A passive strategy makes a lot of sense for anyone who wishes to invest in Japan. That's because most academic studies suggest that the Japanese market is pretty efficient. In other words, share prices across the market accurately and quickly reflect all the information available at the time. The more efficient a market, the harder it is for traditional active fund managers to deliver a market-beating return, so anyone investing in Japan should at the very least consider using passive ETFs.

When most investors hear about Japan they usually hear about the price movements in something called the Nikkei 225 index – it's the most widely used measure of the Japanese stock market used by the global media but bizarrely it's not actually tracked by that many major ETFs in the UK. The most widely used index is a subset of the MSCI World index and is called the MSCI Japan Index, although some issuers also use another locally developed index – operated by the Tokyo Stock Exchange – called the TOPIX. This latter index is also known as the Tokyo Stock Price Index, and it's a fairly conventional capitalisation weighted index of all companies listed on the First Section of the Tokyo Stock Exchange. The index is supplemented by the sub-indices of the 33 industry sectors. The TOPIX Index is widely used by institutional investors and is also popular with structured product providers. It covers much the same kind of companies as the Nikkei but with a wider spread of companies and sectors i.e. it's slightly less concentrated than the Nikkei.

The MSCI Index is also a market capitalisation basis index comprising 85% of the constituents of the Tokyo Stock Exchange. The small cap variation of the MSCI Index comprises the smallest 40% of that index group with market cap in the range of $200 to $1500 million. The MSCI Index doesn't track an actual market by the same name as such – it's actually an institutional construct based on the widely used MSCI Index series and includes virtually all the companies that are found on the TOPIX Index.

Finally, investors might also want to look closely at the JPX-Nikkei 400 Index which is a relatively new, government approved index, which only selects those listed businesses with high levels of corporate governance – traditionally an air of great concern for foreign investors.

COMPOSITION

The most widely followed index is the Nikkei 225, where industrials dominate the index with a 22.6% weighting followed by consumer businesses at 19.77% and IT businesses at 17%. In terms of individual businesses, Fast Retailing is the biggest weighting at 7.29% in the Nikkei followed by robotics business Fanuc at 4.39% and tech giant Softbank at 4.35%. In valuation terms, the Nikkei was valued at around 19.8 times earnings at the end of 2017. The MSCI Japan Index is also widely used by ETF issuers and has a subtly different profile – top two businesses in terms of weighting in this index are Toyota at 3.77% and Mitsubishi UFJ Financial at 1.97%. Honda, Sony and Sumitomo are also in the top ten. Industrials comprise 22% of the value of this index.

WHAT TO WATCH OUT FOR

There's a great deal of choice when it comes to indices to track in Japan, but they all contain hidden dangers with the most obvious being FX. It's all very well if your chosen Japanese index rises 30% over two years, but if the yen falls 20% against the pound over the same period, you'll only make a 10% return rather than 30%. And this isn't a hypothetical issue. Between January 2012 and August 2015, the Nikkei 225 rose 147% while the yen fell 35% against the pound. So, a sterling investor would have seen their profits cut back to something like 110% thanks to the falling yen. But an investor who put their money into a hedged ETF would have done much better and got closer to 147%. On the downside though, hedged ETFs normally have higher management charges, and you shouldn't assume that the yen will necessarily go against you over the next few years.

Investors also need to be aware that the Japanese central bank has been aggressively buying local ETFs, especially those in the JPX 400 – it's all part of a determined effort to change the corporate culture of Japan. Many investors also worry about the huge quantitative easing engaged in by the central bank, and the vast levels of national debt. That said, Japanese businesses have thrived by selling internationally, and especially into China. And last but by no means least, valuations don't appear stretched with the MSCI Japan Index for instance trading at just 17.44 times earnings.

Performance analysis of the Nikkei 225

2017	19.1%
2016	0.4%
2015	9.1%
3 yrs	8.7%
5 yrs	16.9%
Volatility	9.8%
Correlation with S&P 500	0.66

CHINESE EQUITIES

MAIN INDICES

MSCI China Index

Captures large and mid-cap representation across China H shares, B shares, Red chips, P chips and foreign listings (e.g. ADRs). With 149 constituents, the index covers about 85% of this China equity universe.

Hang Seng China Enterprises Index (HSCEI)

The major index that tracks the performance of China enterprises listed in Hong Kong in the form of H-shares. The index comprises the largest and most liquid H-shares. It has high market value coverage over all H-shares and 10% capping is applied to avoid single stock domination.

CSI 300 Index

Consists of the 300 largest and most liquid A-share stocks. The Index aims to reflect the overall performance of China A-share market.

DESCRIPTION

Investing in China is tempting. The economy has grown at a stunning rate since the 80s and plenty of pundits think China can maintain strong growth in the medium term. What's more, Chinese firms like Baidu, Alibaba and JD.com have been strong stock market performers in recent years.

China isn't a one-way bet, however. The country's stock market had a major wobble in 2015 over concerns about debt and those concerns haven't completely gone away. By the end of 2016, China's total debt had grown to $28 trillion, up from $6 trillion at the end of the financial crisis, according to the Bank of International Settlements. That's a fast growth rate for debt.

There are also worries about a large shadow banking sector which is at least partly supported by retail investment products offered by banks and large internet companies. Bears worry that Chinese savers and investors wrongly see these products as risk-free.

Corporate governance is another issue – it's relatively weak, and you might also be put off by the fact that the government is communist, at least in name, and certainly isn't democratic. Remember also that China's demographics aren't good. A big part of the initial China growth story in the 90s was that there was plenty of cheap labour for manufacturers. However, the 'one child' policy means that the population is now ageing. If you're looking for cheap labour, India is a more attractive country to set up shop in.

On the other hand, the government is very focused on keeping the growth story going and also seems very aware of the debt situation. Overseas investors seem happy to buy Chinese debt. And don't forget China now has a growing middle class which should support consumption and growth. What's more, MSCI is also set to include some mainland China shares in its emerging markets and global indices. This should lead to share purchases by passive investors and may provide a price floor for some of the largest mainland shares.

If you do decide to invest directly in China, the big issue is which index to actually focus on – there are a number of different ways of buying into big Chinese mega-caps plus the odd few small cap options. Our preference is for an index called the Hang Seng China Enterprises Index which is, according to its developers "a free-float capitalisation-weighted index comprised of H-Shares listed on the Hong Kong Stock Exchange and included in the Hang Seng Mainland Composite Index". As of November 2017, the constituents comprised 40 H-shares.

All this jargon about H-shares needs some explaining as evidenced in the box below – the key principle to grasp is that China is not really like other countries. On paper it's a capitalist's paradise but in practice, most of the very big companies are largely owned – and certainly controlled through their management – by the state, aka the Chinese Communist Party. One of the ways that the state/the CCP exercises control is via different classes of equity, with some only available for local Chinese nationals and quoted on the local Chinese exchanges (Shanghai principally), alongside other classes (H-shares) that are available to foreigners through well-established exchanges such as the Hong Kong market. This Hong Kong dimension adds another complication – there are some very successful Chinese companies that are based on the Hong Kong exchange, which have nearly all their operations in China, but are not in practice properly Chinese companies. Confused? So are most institutional investors!

Share classes according to FTSE Russell

"A" Shares – Securities of Chinese incorporated companies that trade on either the Shanghai or Shenzhen stock exchanges. They are quoted in Chinese Yuan (CNY). They can only be traded by residents of the People's Republic of China (PRC) or under the Qualified Foreign Institutional Investor (QFII) and Renminbi Qualified Foreign Institutional Investor (RQFII) schemes.

"B" Shares – Securities of Chinese incorporated companies that trade on either the Shanghai or Shenzhen stock exchanges. They are quoted in U.S. dollars on the Shanghai Stock Exchange and Hong Kong dollars on the Shenzhen Stock Exchange. They can be traded by non-residents of the PRC and also by retail investors of the PRC with appropriate foreign currency dealing accounts.

"H" Shares – Securities of Chinese incorporated companies and nominated by the Central Government for listing and trading on the Stock Exchange of Hong Kong. They are quoted and traded in Hong Kong dollars. Like other securities trading on the Stock Exchange of Hong Kong, there are no restrictions on who can trade "H" shares.

"N" Shares – Companies controlled by Mainland Chinese entities, companies or individuals. They must be incorporated outside the PRC and traded on the New York Stock Exchange, the NASDAQ exchange, or the NYSE MKT with a majority of its revenue or assets derived from PRC.

"Red Chip" Shares – Securities of companies incorporated outside the PRC that trade on the Stock Exchange of Hong Kong. They are quoted in Hong Kong dollars. A Red Chip is a company that is substantially owned directly or indirectly by Mainland China state entities and has the majority of its revenue or assets derived from Mainland China.

"P Chip" Shares – Securities of companies incorporated outside the PRC that trade on the Stock Exchange of Hong Kong. A P Chip is a company that is controlled by Mainland China individuals, with the establishment and origin of the company in Mainland China and has the majority of its revenue or assets derived from the Mainland China.

"S Chip" Shares – Companies controlled by Mainland Chinese entities, companies or individuals. It must be incorporated outside the PRC and traded on the Singapore Exchange with a majority of its revenue or assets derived from PRC.

To make matters even worse, you'll also encounter many rival indices, chief among them the FTSE China 50 Index which tracks shares of the most widely followed 50 Mainland enterprises available to offshore investors, which are traded on the Stock Exchange of Hong Kong Limited (SEHK). On paper it's very similar to the HSCEI but it tracks a smaller number of companies and is much less diversified. The Shanghai Shenzhen CSI 300 Index includes the 300 A-share stocks traded on the Shanghai and Shenzhen stock exchanges and is taken as indicative of trends in both of those markets. The Shenzhen SE Composite Index is an index weighted by market capitalisation that tracks the performance of both A-share and B-share stocks traded on the Shenzhen Stock Exchange. The index and its selection criteria are designed to represent the overall performance of A-shares that are traded on either the Shenzhen or Shanghai stock exchanges.

COMPOSITION

Starting with the MSCI China Index, technology stocks are the biggest in terms of market cap with a 41% weighting, followed by financials at 22% and consumer discretionary stocks at 9.5%. The three biggest holdings within the index are Tencent at 18.5%, Alibaba at 12.89% and China Construction Bank at 4.69%. In terms of valuations, the current PE is 17 times earnings (at the end of November 2017) with dividend yield of just 1.65%.

The Hang Seng Index looks very different, with insurance business Ping An the biggest weighting at 12%, followed by banks ICBC at 10.07% and CCB at 9.6%. Financials amount to 73% of the total value of this index.

Finally, the CSI 300 index comprises 31% based in the Shenzhen Index and 68% in Shanghai. Financials amount to 41% of the value of the index, followed by industrials at 13.8% and consumer businesses at 11.5%. The top three holdings in this index are Ping An (at 6.6%), Kweichow Moutai at 2.79% and China Merchants Bank at 2.63%. As for valuations the CSI 300 is currently valued at just 14.9 times earnings and a yield of 1.81% while the Hang Seng is valued at 9.8 times earnings on a yield of 3.48%.

WHAT TO WATCH OUT FOR

Investors need to be aware that the underlying shares owned by the main ETFs are usually classes exclusively for foreigners and do not grant ultimate power or control over the companies concerned. Private investors looking to invest in any of these ETFs also need to be aware of the much broader risks of investing in China – apart from that political control we mentioned above, Chinese equities are enormously volatile and liable to fluctuate madly with many frequent busts. Also, compared to many emerging markets, Chinese shares are comparatively highly rated – although valuations depend hugely on which index you use. The MSCI China Index looks highly priced whereas the Hang Seng for instance is much better value.

The high ratings attached to businesses such as Alibaba and Tencent might perhaps be deserved given the phenomenal growth prospects of the Chinese economy, but investors need to be aware that this potential high growth comes at the cost of high volatility and high valuations compared to peer markets.

Performance analysis of the FTSE China 50 Index

2017	32.9%
2016	0.7%
2015	-13.0%
3 yrs	4.7%
5 yrs	3.7%
Volatility	11.0%
Correlation with S&P 500	0.78

INDIAN EQUITIES

MAIN INDICES

S&P BSE SENSEX

India's most tracked bellwether index. It is designed to measure the performance of the 30 largest, most liquid and financially sound companies across key sectors of the Indian economy that are listed at BSE Ltd. The Sensex index has a long history of more than 30 years and covers more than 50% of the total market cap of the listed universe at BSE Ltd.

NIFTY 50

A diversified 50 stock index accounting for 12 sectors of the economy. The NIFTY 50 Index represents about 62.9% of the free float market capitalisation of the stocks listed on NSE as at March 31, 2017. The total traded value of NIFTY 50 Index constituents for the last six months ending March 2017 is approximately 43.8% of the traded value of all stocks on the NSE.

DESCRIPTION

India has traditionally played second fiddle to China in terms of emerging markets in Asia but ever since Prime Minister Modi has come to power, at the head of the BJP, Indian equities have been on a tear. It helps that India has a big, vocal private investor community, many of whom are embracing ETFs locally. There's also a large diaspora of Indian investors, many of whom are bringing money back to their homeland to invest in notoriously inefficient sectors such as banks and transportation. The BJP government has also been making all the right noises about liberalisation and privatisation although actual progress to date has been patchy to say the least. The other good bit of news is that there are only two major indices worth tracking, both of which are widely used by fund managers. In practice there's not a lot of difference between the two indices, as both are heavily reliant on a small number of big blue-chip businesses, many with extensive international operations.

COMPOSITION

Starting with the NIFTY 50 Index, at the end of 2017, the top three sectors in terms of market weightings comprise financials at 35%, Energy at 15% and IT at 11%. Top three individual stocks within this index include HDFC at 9.41%, Reliance Industries at 7.8% and Housing Development Finance Corp at 6.71%. Over at the BSE Sensex index, the top three holdings are the same: HDFC Holdings Bank, Reliance Industries and Housing Development Finance.

WHAT TO WATCH OUT FOR

Investors really need to watch out for valuations when it comes to Indian equities. The Sensex index currently trades at a price to earnings ratio of 24 earnings while the NIFTY 50 trades at 27 times earnings, on a yield of just 1%. These valuations are well in excess of other peers within the BRIC community as well as other emerging markets. Arguably these prices are valued if India lives up to its growth potential, but a lot depends on the ability of the Indian government to boost the comparatively low rates of economic growth over the last few decades.

Performance analysis of the S&P BSE SENSEX

2017	27.9%
2016	3.5%
2015	-3.7%
3 yrs	7.5%
5 yrs	11.8%
Volatility	6.3%
Correlation with S&P 500	0.56

LATIN AMERICAN EQUITIES

MAIN INDICES

Bovespa Index

Tracks the Brazilian stock market in Sao Paulo. It is the largest stock exchange in Latin America that accounts for some 75% of the volume of shares traded in the region.

MSCI Emerging Markets (EM) Latin America Index

Captures large and mid-cap representation across 5 Emerging Markets (EM) countries in Latin America. With 113 constituents, the index covers approximately 85% of the free float-adjusted market capitalisation in each country.

DESCRIPTION

Our advice is for the general investor to be cautious about investing in ETFs for specific countries and region, especially within the fast-expanding Emerging Markets investment universe. We sense that the risks are just too great even though some countries such as India or even Russia do present enormous opportunity. For many investors the best way of accessing the emerging markets story is probably through a cheap, liquid, MSCI Emerging Markets Index tracker. But there are two notable exceptions to this rule – China and Latin America.

The sudden emergence of Latin America and especially Brazil onto the investment landscape in this century is nothing short of extraordinary. Growth in countries like Brazil and Mexico and even Chile and Peru have been translated into some astonishing stock market gains and a number of world-beating, mega-corporations have emerged – names like Petrobas from Brazil (a massive oil company) and America Movil (a Mexican mobile phone giant) are increasingly forces to be reckoned with.

We think adventurous investors should seriously consider some sort of investment in this region – although we'd caution that its heightened volatility and bias towards the resource sector will probably put off more conservative investors who are risk averse. Also, we'd recommend exposure to the whole region and not just to Brazil – most Latin American funds tend to have massive exposure to Brazil anyway, thus a LatAm fund will give investor's the benefit of some diversification into interesting economies such as Mexico and Chile.

Until just a few years ago, any investors wanting to invest in Latin America as a specific region would have had very few choices – basically only a few specialist investment trusts operated in this new investment space. Now we see a growing number of ETFs all tracking the same regional index which includes massive outfits like Petrobas as well as minnows from countries like Colombia and Peru plus the odd outfit from once mighty markets like Argentina.

The truly adventurous investor could of course just go straight to the source of much of the biggest returns of recent years and invest directly in a Brazilian index tracking fund. There are two main indices worth following in Brazil – the most common comes from the ubiquitous MSCI which tracks nearly all the most liquid stocks on the Brazilian market and is a subset of the wider MSCI EM Latin American Index. The other main choice is based on the main local market and is called the Bovespa Index which is an index of about 50 stocks that are traded on the Sao Paulo Stock Exchange (Bolsa de Valores do Estado de São Paulo). In effect this index is the local, smaller equivalent of our FTSE 100.

COMPOSITION

The MSCI Latin America Index is dominated by Brazilian stocks, which represent 57% of the total value of the index at the end of 2017. Mexico is next up with 24% and Chile comes in third with 10.5% exposure – Colombia and Peru amount to less than 7% of the value of the index. Financials (banks) dominate the index with 30% exposure followed by consumer staples at 16.7% and mining at 16.5% (energy is at 8.7%). The three biggest individual stocks within the LatAm index are Brazilian – Itau Unibanco at 6.57%, Vale at 6.13% and Banco Bradesco at 4.90%.

WHAT TO WATCH OUT FOR

Looking at Brazilian equities in particular, investors need to be aware of a strong bias towards resource stocks – just over a quarter of the Bovespa Index for instance is invested in mining and oil companies, notably Petrobas and Vale. But there's also a huge reliance on financials such as Itau Unibanco and Banco Bradesco.

Latin American equities can also be very volatile, with politics a major factor – the ongoing investigation into corruption at Brazilian oil giant Petrobas has badly hit investor confidence. Latin American economies can also be vulnerable to sudden changes in the currency markets, much of the time influenced by strong local inflation. Last but by no means least, state expropriation is a real risk with Venezuela the prime example. But Argentina has also had its run-in with the global financial markets, repudiating its debts before electing a more business-friendly President who is looking to attract inward foreign investment.

Performance analysis of the Bovespa

2017	7.6%
2016	14.4%
2015	-4.9%
3 yrs	6.9%
5 yrs	3.8%
Volatility	-
Correlation with S&P 500	-

GOVERNMENT BONDS

MAIN INDICES

FTSE Actuaries UK Gilts

Consist of all securities from the conventional index family of the FTSE Actuaries UK Gilts Index Series, which includes all British Government Securities quoted on the London Stock Exchange.

Citigroup of Seven Index or (G7) Index

Measures the performance of fixed-rate, local currency, investment grade sovereign bonds. The index comprises sovereign debt from seven countries: Canada, France, Germany, Italy, Japan, the United Kingdom and the United States. It is a subindex of the World Government Bond Index (WGBI), a broad benchmark for the global sovereign fixed income market.

Bloomberg Barclays Global Aggregate Index

A flagship measure of global investment grade debt from 24 currency markets. This multi currency benchmark includes treasury (government), corporate and securitised fixed rate bonds from both developing and emerging market issuers.

ICE US Treasury Index Series

Developed as a broad representation of the US Treasury market and includes a number of maturity subindices ranging from one month to 30 years. All ICE U.S. Treasury Indices are market value weighted and designed to measure the performance of the US dollar-denominated, fixed and floating rate US Treasury market. As of December 31, 2015 the ICE US Treasury Index Series consists of:

- ICE US Treasury Bond Index
- ICE US Treasury 1 – 3 Year Bond Index
- ICE US Treasury 3 – 7 Year Bond Index
- ICE US Treasury 7 – 10 Year Bond Index
- ICE US Treasury 10 – 20 Year Bond Index
- ICE US Treasury 20+ Year Bond Index

- ICE US Treasury Short Bond Index
- ICE US Treasury Floating Rate Note (FRN) Index
- ICE US Treasury Inflation Linked Bond Index
- ICE US Treasury 0 – 5 Year Inflation Linked Bond Index

DESCRIPTION

Bonds issued by governments, especially in the developed world, are generally regarded as low-risk investments. Government's such as the UK and the US have never defaulted on their debts although the market price of govies (government securities) and gilts (UK government securities) can rise above the redemption price, and thus produce losses for investors over the long term. Most governments can issue bonds with a AA rating attached, which in turn allows them to pay a relatively low yield when compared to corporate securities.

The key issue for investors in deciding which government bonds to track is geography. For global bonds the best bet is probably the Bloomberg Barclays Bond series which is an aggregate bond index comprising government and government-backed issuers but also some corporates.

For the US market there's a range of indices tracking the rates available on US Treasuries. These are obviously denominated in dollars and investors can in addition choose which maturities to invest in. In the UK, the main benchmark index comes from FTSE and is known as the All Stocks Gilt. This index's full title is actually the FTSE Actuaries Government Securities UK Gilts All Stock Index and it gives exposure to a diversified basket of UK government bonds, across all maturities – all in the conventional space i.e. there are no index linked holdings within this exclusively sterling-denominated fund. At any one time there are roughly 43 individual gilts in this basket, with a combined market cap of £144bn, with the largest individual holding rarely worth more than 3.5 to 4% of the total value of the index. That diversification makes this index a brilliant tool for buying into a diversified basket of what are called conventional government securities, otherwise known as gilts.

The UK Gilts Index isn't well known among private investors but there are a growing number of ETFs which do track this home-grown index – which we view as an absolutely core holding for all but the most adventurous investor. Why? If you want government bonds exposure, your safest bet is probably gilts and if you want the best basket of sterling gilts this index gives you that in spades. What's even better is that most ETFs tracking this index are very cost-effective – don't expect to pay much more than 0.20% in TER.

COMPOSITION

The FTSE Index comprises only UK government securities, all AA rated. Around 33% of the value of the holdings in the index is 0 to 5 years in duration, 16% 5 to 10 years and 50% 10 years or more. For the Bloomberg Barclays Aggregate index approximately 65% to 70% of the historical composition of the index has been direct government securities or government related, with around 55% AAA or AA rated. Fixed minimum issue sizes at $300m for US assets or £200m for sterling assets. In terms of national issuers, US bonds are just under 40%, Japanese at 16% and France at 6% (the UK comprises 5.6% of the index).

WHAT TO WATCH OUT FOR

Government securities are seen as boring and dull but that doesn't mean that investors haven't made bumper profits over the last decade of low interest rates. As rates have collapsed close to zero, prices for bonds have shot up giving investors big profits from boring bonds. But the flipside of this boom in bonds is that yields are now currently very low. For the Bloomberg index the weighted average yield to maturity at the end of 2017 was a measly 1.66%. For the FTSE All Stock Gilt it is 1.20% – the average coupon on the FTSE product is around 3.5%. The upside of these low yields is that the return is pretty much guaranteed!

Crucially all these indices – including the FTSE All Stocks Gilt – track fixed-rate securities i.e. they pay a fixed yield that does not vary with inflation. You shouldn't buy into these indices if you think inflation is all set to shoot up – in that case the UK index linked variant is probably a better idea.

In terms of maturities – a key question if you want to invest in US Treasuries – generally shorter durations of 1 to 3 years are seen as very safe but also very low yielding. Longer maturities of over 10 years throw out a higher yield but there's also a greater risk attached to these securities i.e. prices can be more volatile.

Performance analysis of the UK Gilts Index

2017	2.1%
2016	9.9%
2015	0.4%
3 yrs	4.0%
5 yrs	3.7%
Volatility	7.4%
Correlation with S&P 500	0.31

CORPORATE BONDS

MAIN INDICES

Bloomberg Barclays Bond Indices

The family of Bloomberg Barclays Bond indices (formerly the Barclays indices) are the best known indices in this area. The Bloomberg Barclays Global Aggregate Corporate Bond Index comprises investment grade corporate bonds issued by companies in developed and emerging markets. The minimum maturity is one year and the index is market-cap weighted. Around 66% of the fund is made up of dollar-denominated bonds with 23% being euro-denominated bonds.

The Bloomberg Barclays Euro Corporate Bond Index

Comprised of European investment grade corporate bonds. These bonds are mainly issued by industrial, financial and utility companies. This is also a market-cap weighted index. Only bonds with a minimum remaining time to maturity of one year are included in the index. There also needs to be a minimum amount outstanding of 300 million euros.

The Bloomberg Barclays US Aggregate Bond Index

A broader US index. It's composed of dollar-denominated investment grade bonds and includes US Treasuries (US government bonds) as well as corporate bonds. It's market-cap weighted.

DESCRIPTION

Traditional investment theory suggests that just about everyone should have some exposure to bonds in their portfolio. That's because bonds should provide a low-risk and reliable income stream. The problem has been that in recent years the returns have been very low. And that's why some investors have moved away from the ultra-safe government bonds towards corporate bonds. Investors have taken on more risk to get a higher return.

Investing in corporate bonds, however, isn't always easy. You can invest in some corporate bonds directly via the London Stock Exchange's ORB (Order book for Retail Bonds), but the range isn't that wide and retail investors can feel intimidated. Although the bond issuer must provide information for prospective investors, there isn't much commentary or guidance available for private investors.

So, funds, including ETFs, can offer an attractive and simple way to invest in corporate bonds. Of course, the corporate bond market is very diverse – some corporate bonds are 'investment grade' which means the chances of default are low whereas others are 'high yield' or 'junk' which means there is a greater risk of default. Junk bonds offer a higher return to investors in return for higher risk. Most mainstream UK corporate bond trackers though are focused on lower risk, sterling-based, large borrowers with yields in excess of those available on government securities.

COMPOSITION

The best aggregate way of understanding the global corporate bond landscape is to look at the Bloomberg Global Corp Bond Index. This is dominated by US issues at 53%, followed by the UK at 8.54% and France at 6.45%. In currency terms US dollar assets are even more important at 65% of the total value of the index – many non-US issuers still choose to issue US dollar bonds. Euro based assets are at 23% with sterling assets at 5.4%. In terms of credit quality only 1.4% is AAA rated, 9% AA rated and 40% A rated. BBB rated is the single biggest exposure at just under 50%. Crucially over 25% of the total outstanding debt is from banks with telecoms businesses at 8.5%. Last, but by no means least, the average weighted maturity of the bonds is around nine years although around 43% of the bonds in the index have a maturity of five years or less.

WHAT TO WATCH OUT FOR

Duration is an important consideration for bond investors. If a bond won't mature for, say, ten years, it's riskier than one with just a year to go. If interest rates rise significantly from here, the value of a one-year bond won't fall that much, but it would be a different story for a bond with a longer duration. And if you invest in overseas corporate bonds, you also have to think about currency risk.

Critics of passive bond investing also focus on the fact that the major bond indices are all market-cap weighted. That means these indices are weighted towards larger borrowers who may be higher risk than smaller borrowers simply because they've taken on too much debt.

Performance analysis of the Bloomberg Global Corporate Bond Index

2017	6.0%
2016	4.3%
2015	-3.6%
3 yrs	2.6%
5 yrs	2.3%
Volatility	2.4%
Correlation with S&P 500	0.05

FEATURED ETFS

Let's now turn to some of the leading corporate bond ETFs. These are all UCITS regulated and listed in London.

1. BIGGEST: ISHARES CORE EURO CORPORATE BOND UCITS ETF EUR (GBP) (LSE:IEBC)

This ETF tracks the Bloomberg Barclays Euro Corporate Bond Index and has 8.5 billion euros under management – that's if you include all the different currency versions of this ETF. The ETF invests in the underlying bonds in the index so it's a physical fund. The ongoing charge of the fund is 0.2% and it's fairly well distributed across different maturities. Here is the maturity distribution:

1 to 3 years	18.8%
3 to 5 years	25.4%
5 to 7 years	20.5%
7 to 10 years	20.5%
10 to 15 years	6.7%
15 to 20 years	1.9%
20 to 30 years	2.4%
Over 30 years	3.8%

Source: Morningstar

2. JOINT CHEAPEST: ISHARES $ ULTRASHORT BOND UCITS ETF GBP (LSE:ERNU)

This ETF has a super-low ongoing charge of 0.09% a year. So if the value of your investment in the fund is £1000, you'll pay just 90p in charges for the year.

The ETF invests in dollar-denominated investment-grade corporate bonds. The fixed rate bonds must have a duration of no longer than a year, and the fund also invests in floating rate securities that can have a duration of up to three years. The ETF tracks the Markit iBoxx USD Liquid Investment Grade Ultrashort Index and is a physical fund.

3. JOINT CHEAPEST: LYXOR IBOXX GBP LIQUID CORPORATES LONG DATED UCITS ETF (LSE:COUK)

This ETF also has an ongoing charge of 0.09% a year. It tracks the Markit iBoxx GBP Liquid Corporates Long Dated Mid Price TCA Index and as the names suggests, the vast majority of bonds in the portfolio have a maturity of over 10 years.

1 to 3 years	4.6 %
3 to 5 years	5.5 %
5 to 7 years	1.3%
7 to 10 years	3.7%
10 to 15 years	25.3%
15 to 20 years	30.3%
20 to 30 years	23.7%
Over 30 years	5.7%

Source: Morningstar

This isn't a pure corporate bond fund, it includes some UK government bonds (gilts) as well. It's a synthetic fund that uses swaps to track the index.

4. BIGGEST HEDGED: ISHARES EURO CORPORATE BOND INTEREST RATE HEDGED UCITS ETF EUR (LSE:IRCP)

This ETF invests in the Eurozone corporate bond market and is hedged. The hedge is against interest rate risk rather than currency risk. The fund achieves this partial hedge by selling German government bond futures. The size of the fund is 1.5 billion euros and the ongoing charge is 0.25% a year.

HIGH-YIELD BONDS

MAIN INDICES

Unlike many asset classes discussed so far, there's a growing multitude of indices tracking this space.

Markit iBoxx USD Liquid High Yield Index

Designed to reflect the performance of USD-denominated high-yield corporate debt. The index rules aim to offer a broad coverage of the USD high-yield liquid bond universe. The indices are an integral part of the global Markit iBoxx index families, which provide the marketplace with accurate and objective indices by which to assess the performance of bond markets and investments. The index is market-value weighted with an issuer cap of 3%. The Markit iBoxx USD Liquid High-Yield Index is rebalanced once a month at the month-end (the 'rebalancing date') and consists of sub-investment grade USD-denominated bonds issued by corporate issuers from developed countries and rated by at least one of three rating services: Fitch Ratings, Moody's Investors Service, or S&P Global Ratings. All bonds in this index need to have an average rating of sub-investment grade. Ratings from Fitch Ratings, Moody's Investor Service and Standard & Poor's Rating Services are considered. If more than one agency provides a rating, the average rating is attached to the bond.

Barclays Capital High-Yield Very Liquid Index

Includes publicly issued US dollar-denominated, non-investment grade, fixed-rate, taxable corporate bonds that have a remaining maturity of at least one year, regardless of optionality, are rated high-yield (Ba1/BB+/BB+ or below) using the middle rating of Moody's, S&P and Fitch respectively (before July 1, 2005, the lower of Moody's and S&P was used), and have $600 million or more of outstanding face value.

BofA Merrill Lynch 0–5 Year US High Yield Constrained Index

Tracks the performance of short-term US dollar-denominated below investment grade corporate debt issued in the US domestic market with less than five years remaining term to final maturity, a fixed coupon schedule and a minimum amount outstanding of $250 million, issued publicly. Prior to September 30, 2016, securities with a minimum amount outstanding of $100 million qualified. Allocations to an individual issuer will not exceed 2%.

ICE BofAML US High Yield Index

Tracks the performance of US dollar-denominated below investment grade corporate debt publicly issued in the US domestic market. Qualifying securities must have a below investment grade rating (based on an average of Moody's, S&P and Fitch), at least 18 months to final maturity at the time of issuance, at least one year remaining term to final maturity as of the rebalancing date, a fixed coupon schedule and a minimum amount outstanding of $250 million. The ICE BofAML US Fallen Angel High Yield Index is a subset of ICE BofAML US High Yield Index including securities that were rated investment grade at the point of issuance. Inception date: December 31, 1996.

Barclays Global Corporate ex EM Fallen Angels 3% Issuer Capped Index

Designed to track the performance of corporate fallen angel bonds issued by developed market issuers. To be included in the index, securities must currently be rated high yield, while having been assigned an investment grade index rating either at issuance or at some point since its issuance.

DESCRIPTION

High-yield bonds are arguably better known amongst many investors as *junk bonds* – they are corporate bonds with a credit rating well below investment grade. A junk bond refers to high-yield or non-investment grade bonds. Junk bonds are fixed-income instruments that carry a credit rating of BB or lower by Standard and Poor's or Ba or below by Moody's Investors Service.

The extra risk of default is compensated for by a higher yield. But junk also conjures images of distressed debt, which is an entirely different category. Most junk or high-yield bonds are actually entirely mainstream and predictable. High yields can thus be a great addition to a yield-starved portfolio, as they can offer yields into the double digits for those willing to take on the risks that come along with it. The high returns come from riskier bond choices who have to pay out higher ratios to compensate investors for high risks. this means that the holdings of these ETFs will have higher chances of defaults and could potentially leave investors out to dry. Because most broad-based bond ETFs focus only on the investment grade side of the market, junk bond ETFs can be useful for rounding out the fixed income side of a long-term portfolio.

COMPOSITION

What's inside the various high-yield indices varies greatly between the different indices, but if we focus on just two competing indices we see some common themes: a focus on US issuers, from a very wide range of sectors but with media and telecoms businesses near the top of any list of constituents. The Markit iBoxx US Liquid High Yield Index for instance is tracked by iShares in Europe and has a weighted average yield to maturity of 5.27%. Top individual bonds in this index at the end of 2017 include Sprint, Western Digital and Reynolds Group. In terms of sector mix, communications, telecoms and consumer businesses dominate the list. In terms of credit quality, BB rated represents the biggest slug of bonds with a 50% plus share followed by B rated at just over one-third of the value of the index. Maturities tend to be focused around the two to seven-year time span – nearly two-thirds of the index.

WHAT TO WATCH OUT FOR

Investors have swarmed into high-yield credit for one simple reason – in a time of near zero interest rates, yields of 5% or more have proved very attractive. But the lower credit ratings for these bonds tells you everything you need to know – defaults can shoot up in a recession as heavily leveraged businesses (many owned by private equity firms) start to experience sharply reduced cash inflows. It's also worth noting that junk bonds as an asset class have historically tended to produce equity-like returns with relatively low volatility.

In terms of investment choices, as you'd expect there are some variations on the theme. Short-term high yield can be attractive for some investors especially if they are concerned about rising interest rates: the lower the effective duration, the lower the impact of rate changes on the value of the related fixed income securities. The downside though is the elimination of some interest rate risk may also translate into a reduction of yields as well.

More adventurous bond investors have also focused on a category called Fallen Angels, a subcategory of the very broad (and US-focused) high-yield space which focuses on bonds from issuers that were once investment grade but have seen their credit rating downgraded.

Performance analysis of the iBoxx Markit index

2017	7.4%
2016	-5.6%
2015	2.0%
3 yrs	7.3%
5 yrs	8.0%
Volatility	NA
Correlation with S&P 500	NA

EMERGING MARKET BONDS

MAIN INDICES

J.P. Morgan Emerging Markets Bond Index Plus

A market-capitalisation weighted index based on bonds in emerging markets. The EMBI series covers all of the external currency denomination debt of the emerging markets and is constructed with well-defined liquidity criteria to ensure that the index provides a fair and replicable benchmark. There are currently 31 instruments from 21 countries.

There are three different EMBI indices produced by J.P. Morgan's Global Index Research group: EMBI+, EMBI Global and EMBI Global Diversified. The indices are rule-based with specific liquidity, maturity and structural constraints.

- **EMBI+**: This tracks total returns for traded external debt instruments (external meaning foreign currency-denominated fixed income) in the emerging markets. EMBI+ covers US dollar-denominated Brady bonds, loans and Eurobonds.

- **EMBI Global**: The J.P. Morgan Emerging Markets Bond Index Global ('EMBI Global') tracks total returns for traded external debt instruments in the emerging markets, and is an expanded version of the EMBI+. As with the EMBI+, the EMBI Global includes US dollar-denominated Brady bonds, loans, and Eurobonds with an outstanding face value of at least $500 million.

- **EMBI Global Diversified**: takes the same global index but puts weight limits on countries with more debts to ensure better diversification. This tends to mean that larger EM countries get less weighting in this index.

The EMBI family of indices was launched in the summer of 1999 and historical daily data has been backfilled to December 1993.

DESCRIPTION

Emerging market or EM bonds have become one of the hottest asset classes of the last decade. Traditionally most investors have approached emerging markets through equities – using benchmarks such as the MSCI EM. But bond investors have also woken up to the opportunities presented by emerging markets – they may typically be higher risk, but their yields are usually much more generous when compared to developed world bonds. In fact, at the tail end of 2017 the gap between the average EM bond (tracked by the EMBI+) yield versus 10-year US government debt) narrowed to just 278 basis points. This implies that either US govies haven't budged much in price or that EM bonds have shot up in price, pushing down yields – arguably both have been at work.

One of the reasons why this asset class has proved popular is that the main indices (tracked by the J.P. Morgan series) have provided a deep, liquid pool of income paying securities, all denominated in dollars. This removes the currency risk for most global investors – they only need worry then about repayment risk.

The main index used by most ETFs comes from US investment bank J.P. Morgan. J.P. Morgan's initial EMBI was launched in 1992 covering so-called Brady bonds, which are dollar-denominated bonds issued primarily by Latin American countries but was later expanded to also include dollar-denominated loans and Eurobonds. The principal and interest payments on these bonds are made in US dollars rather than a foreign currency, which eliminates currency risks for most international investors who use dollars. The EMBI+ was subsequently introduced to also track total returns for external debt instruments in emerging markets around the world.

The good news is that investors have many different options when selecting emerging market bond indices. While the J.P. Morgan EMBI, EMBI+ and EMBIG indices may be the most popular, there are other popular indices available including:

- DB Emerging Market USD Liquid Balanced Index

- Bloomberg USD Emerging Market Sovereign Bond Index

- Barclays USD Emerging Market GovRIC Cap Index

COMPOSITION

If we look at the main J.P. Morgan EMBI index we find that at the end of 2017 it had 390 individual holdings of bonds – all dollar-denominated. In country terms the top three weightings are in Mexico at 6%, Indonesia 5% and Turkey at 4.35%. Crucially over 80% of the value of the index is based on issues from sovereigns (governments). In terms of aggregate maturities, 0 to 5 years consists of 25% of the value of the index, 5 to 10-year maturities around 45%, while another third of the value of the index comprises maturities of 10 years or more. As for credit risk – around 35% is BBB rated, 25% B rated and only 10–12% A rated.

WHAT TO WATCH OUT FOR

Looking at the J.P. Morgan Index, yields are appreciably higher than for developed world bonds. At the end of 2017, the distribution yield for this index was just over 4.5% with weighted average yield to maturity of 5%. This yield is hugely attractive to many investors but be aware that these bonds can also be very volatile in terms of price – in a recession, emerging market economies frequently suffer greatly, forcing up defaults or prompting extensive restructuring. That means that investors need to be aware how any ETFs tracking these indices fit into their overall portfolio. Older investors may want lower exposure to these bonds than younger investors that have a longer time horizon due to their higher volatility than US or developed market bonds.

Dollar-based assets are probably the most popular way to buy into this asset class, but investors also need to be aware that there are bond indices which track EM bonds in the local currency. In this case, the investor will have to convert dollars to the foreign currency, such as the Mexican peso, prior to buying the bond. The result is that in addition to the price movement of the underlying bond, the value of the investment is affected by currency fluctuations – the rise or fall of the foreign currency/US or UK dollar exchange rate. The potential benefit of local currency funds is two-fold – it allows investors to diversify their holdings away from the US dollar but also allows investors to benefit from the cumulative positive effect of emerging market nations with stronger economic growth. At the same time, it's worth noting that currency exposure adds another layer of volatility – EM currencies are notoriously volatile when compared to their developed world peers.

Last but by no means least, investors might also want to have specific exposure to certain regions or countries – there are a much smaller number of country and region-specific EM bonds ETFs. One word of caution though for those seeking a more specific way of playing EM bonds – the EMBIG index has become so popular that many of the largest and most liquid ETFs and mutual funds use it as a basis, which means that choosing a less popular index's funds could lead to higher liquidity risk and potentially higher fees.

Performance analysis of the J.P. Morgan EMBI Index

2017	4.5%
2016	9.6%
2015	0.5%
3 yrs	5.9%
5 yrs	4.3%
Volatility	2.9%
Correlation with S&P 500	0.28

FLOATING RATE AND INFLATION-LINKED SECURITIES

MAIN INDICES

Barclays World Government Inflation-Linked Bond Index

Measures the performance of the major government inflation-linked bond markets. The index is designed to include only those markets in which a global government linker fund is likely to invest. To be included a market must have aggregate issuance of $4bn or more and have minimum rating of A3/A- for G7 and Eurozone issuers, Aa3/AA- otherwise. Markets currently included in the index, in the order of inclusion, are the UK, Australia, Canada, Sweden, the US, France, Italy, Japan, Germany and Greece.

Bloomberg Barclays US Corporate FRN 2-7 Yr Index

Tracks only investment-grade bonds with at least $500 million outstanding. The index is representative of the performance of US dollar-denominated, investment-grade, floating-rate notes issued by US and non-US corporates from the industrial, utility and financial sectors, with maturities from two to seven years. Bonds issued more than two years ago, or from emerging market companies are excluded from the index universe.

DESCRIPTION

Most bonds are what are called fixed-interest securities i.e. they pay a fixed annual income coupon. This certainty of regular interest payments is arguably the greatest attraction of bonds – as well as the likely certainty of getting repaid at maturity. But the certainty of regular payments comes with a catch. If inflation eats into the real value of those payments, investor's effectively have to put up with the pain. Also, if interest rates rise as a result of increasing inflation, fixed income investors also have to lump it – by definition they have a fixed payment.

Inflation-linked securities offer extra protection in these circumstances. They in effect link the regular interest payment (and final repayment at maturity) to the prevailing inflation rate. Floating rate bonds and loans are another innovation. They are in effect variable rate loans and bonds – their interest rate moves up and down with interest rates (usually connected to the well-known LIBOR rate).

The vast majority of inflation-linked securities are issued by governments whereas most floating-rate securities are from corporate issuers. The biggest market by far though is for inflation-linked government securities. In the UK, these bonds were first issued back in 1981 and these 'linkers' as they're popularly called now account for just under 25% of the Government's gilt portfolio. Index-linked gilts are still bonds issued by the government to pay for spending but their structure of payouts is very different from that of conventional gilts – with linkers the semi-annual coupon payments and the principal (the final payout) are adjusted in line with a measure of inflation called General Index of Retail Prices (also known as the RPI).

This means that both the coupons (the cash flows paid out) and the principal paid on redemption are adjusted to take account of *accrued* inflation since the gilt was first issued – note though that the redemption price may be many years away, so prices may fluctuate on a day-to-day basis, reflecting investors' changing yield expectations.

The idea behind these innovative instruments is to protect the real value of investors' savings against the menace of inflation which is especially dangerous for investors in securities with a fixed income. Many investors buy conventional bonds for the stable and predictable income stream, which comes in the form of interest, or coupon, payments. However, because the rate of interest, or coupon, on the vast majority of fixed-income securities remains the same until maturity, the purchasing power of those interest payments falls as inflation rises. Economists even have a measure for this called the *real interest rate* which is the normal or nominal rate minus that of inflation. So, if a bond has a nominal interest rate of 5% and inflation is 2%, the real interest rate is 3%.

Index linked bonds or gilts – linkers – help to address this (largely hidden) inflation menace. Rather than pay a fixed interest rate (or coupon) and principal/par on redemption, index linked gilts set the coupon and the principal repayment based around an index which measures inflation (either the CPI or the RPI, depending on the government). In essence with an inflation-linked bond, the interest and/or principal is adjusted on a regular basis to reflect changes in the rate of inflation, thus providing a 'real', or inflation-adjusted, return. But that inflation-adjusted return needs to be put into some perspective – in practice there's always a lag between the relevant time period for which an index value is worked out and the date on which that number is published. Here in the UK all new index-linked gilts are issued with a three-month indexation lag (as opposed to the eight-month lag used for earlier issues).

A floating-rate loan or bond, also known as a *floater*, is an investment with interest payments that float or adjust periodically based upon a pre-determined benchmark. While floaters may be linked to almost any benchmark and pay interest based on a variety of formulas, the most basic type pays a coupon equal to some widely followed interest rate plus a fixed spread usually LIBOR. This last term refers to the 'London Interbank Offered Rate,' which is a benchmark rate used by banks making short-term loans to other banks. For instance, a rate could be quoted as 'LIBOR + 0.50%;' if LIBOR stood at 1.00%, the rate would be 1.50%. While the yield changes throughout the life of the security as prevailing interest rates fluctuate, the spread (the '+0.50' in the example above) typically stays the same.

The frequency at which the yield of a floating rate note resets can be daily, weekly, monthly, or every three, six, or 12 months. Corporations, municipalities, and some foreign governments typically offer floating rate notes – which are sometimes called 'FRNs'. The US Treasury now issues floating rate notes as well.

COMPOSITION

Inflation-linked securities come in two main varieties – via a global index or just sterling-denominated UK gilts. For the Barclays World Government Inflation-Linked Bond Index, the weighted average yield to maturity is a lowly 1.75% per annum, with a flat yield of under 1%. US issues account for over 40% of the value of the index followed by the UK at just under 30%. France is around 10% of the value of the index. The single largest maturity is for 20 plus years although there's also a heavy weighting towards 7 to 10-year maturities. Credit quality is overwhelmingly AA or AA rated as you'd expect from an index tracking government securities.

For UK index linkers, the underlying yield to maturity is also low at around 1.5% with a flat yield of just 0.6%. More than 50% of the value of the main UK index comprises linkers with a maturity of over 20 years.

Looking at the main index used for floating rate ETFs, the Bloomberg Barclays index currently consists of 438 individual components within the index. Due to the floating-rate nature of the securities, the index's modified duration is close to zero (0.17 years), highlighting the ability to protect portfolio value from changes in interest rates.

The US represents the largest country exposure in the index at 53% followed by Canada at 9%, Japan at 5% and Australia at 5%. Banks are by far the biggest issuer of the floaters, accounting for more than 50% of the value of the index, with most common maturity at 3 to 65 years. Around 80 to 85% of the index is in AA to A rated bonds with the average yield to maturity at 2% per annum.

WHAT TO WATCH OUT FOR

Yields on inflation linkers are very low, as you'd expect for a low-risk investment choice. Some inflation linkers trade at negative yields, such has been the demand. If inflation fails to increase markedly, many linkers might represent poor value. On the plus side, these linkers are a great diversifier for investors with a negative correlation to equities.

One small additional caution on floaters – many are issued with either a *cap*, a *floor* or both. A cap is the maximum interest rate the issuer will pay regardless of how high the reference rate may go, and it protects the issuer from escalating interest costs. Conversely, a floor sets the minimum rate that will be paid even if the coupon determined by the reference rate were lower, and it partially protects the investor from declining income.

Performance analysis of the Barclays World Government Inflation-Linked Index

2017	-4.7%
2016	7.0%
2015	5.7%
3 yrs	2.8%
5 yrs	3.0%
Volatility	4.4%
Correlation with S&P 500	-0.08

CASH

MAIN INDEX (UK)

Sterling Overnight Index Average

Introduced in March 1997, SONIA is the Sterling Overnight Index Average. It is a widely used benchmark, including as the reference rate for the sterling Overnight Indexed Swap (OIS) market. It reflects bank and building societies' overnight funding rates in the sterling unsecured market.

DESCRIPTION

SONIA, a widely followed benchmark, is the rate at which the biggest banks in the UK lend money to each other on an overnight basis (the euro equivalent is EONIA). SONIA is very often used by financial institutions as a benchmark against which to price things, usually debts. It is administered by the Bank of England, which uses an algorithm to calculate the average of all overnight transactions.

COMPOSITION

The index is the aggregate of all overnight transactions in UK interbank lending, capturing almost £40bn worth of transactions every day. Unlike indices more commonly tracked by ETFs, such as the FTSE 100, the composition of this index changes daily, meaning that SONIA cannot be tracked by full physical replication.

WHAT TO WATCH OUT FOR

Many investors have worried that the QE punchbowl will run dry sometime soon, leaving interest rates floating north. For this reason, short-term bond ETFs have become popular as they are least susceptible to interest rate movements. But cash indices like SONIA and funds that track them are the shortest of all short-term bonds, as they are – literally – issued overnight. While the low risk profile of this index may prove attractive for some, investors should be aware that returns historically have been very similar to what term deposits and savings accounts generate.

COMMODITIES

MAIN INDEX

Bloomberg Commodity Index Total Return (BCOMTR)

Tracks futures contracts on a basket of 26 commodities including energy, agriculture, livestock, industrial and precious metals. The index combines the performance of this basket of commodities with the returns on three-month US Treasuries.

DESCRIPTION

The index has had many owners and managers the past 20 years. It began in 1998 as the Dow Jones-AIG Commodity Index. After AIG hit strife in the 2008 financial crisis the index was sold to UBS and became the Dow Jones-UBS Commodity Index. The index was then bought out by Bloomberg in 2014, hence its current name.

BCOMTR has three sources of return. First, the spot prices of commodities futures contracts. Second, the roll yield when old futures contracts are sold and new ones are bought. Third, the yield from US Treasuries (hence it is a 'total return' commodities index). The index builds in treasury yields to reflect the fact that when investors buy commodity futures, they do not buy them outright. Rather, they pay a margin and put the rest in T-bill collateral.

BCOMTR has 22 commodities in six sectors. The index rules make every commodity weigh between 2% and 15% of the index, and prevent any sector taking more than 33% of the index. The weightings of each commodity are intended to reflect their significance in the global economy. As an example, because oil is judged to be more important than zinc, it holds a higher weighting in the index. The index is rebalanced annually.

COMPOSITION

BCOMTR breaks commodities down into six sectors: energy, grain, industrial metals, precious metals, softs and livestock. While energy receives the biggest weighting at 30%, BCOMTR differs from the S&P GSCI, the other major global commodity index, in that it has a smaller energy concentration (GSCI has historically weighted energy over 55%).

	Target Weight		
Energy	Natural Gas	8.01%	30.43%
	Brent Crude Oil	7.68%	
	WTI Crude Oil	7.31%	
	RBOB Gasoline	3.75%	
	ULS Diesel	3.66%	
Grains	Corn	6.13%	22.44%
	Soybeans	5.95%	
	Wheat	3.25%	
	Soybean Meal	3.03%	
	Soybean Oil	2.74%	
	HRW Wheat	1.30%	
Industrial Metals	Copper	7.15%	17.53%
	Aluminum	4.50%	
	Zinc	3.09%	
	Nickel	2.76%	
Precious Metals	Gold	11.94%	15.62%
	Silver	3.67%	
Softs	Sugar	3.53%	7.60%
	Coffee	2.60%	
	Cotton	1.45%	
Livestock	Live Cattle	4.31%	6.39%
	Lean Hogs	2.07%	

WHAT TO WATCH OUT FOR

Commodities tend to give the inverse performance of the US dollar. This is well known for oil and gold. But scholars have found other commodities also tend to give the inverse of the US dollar. Why? Mostly because commodities futures are listed in dollars. This means that if the value of a commodity stays the same, while the value of the dollar increases, the dollar will get more of that commodity. Investors looking to diversify against the dollar or simply bet on commodities cannot go wrong with this index.

Performance analysis of the Bloomberg Commodity Index Total Return Index

2017	1.7%
2016	11.8%
2015	-24.0%
3 yrs	-8.4%
5 yrs	-9.5%
Volatility	-
Correlation with S&P 500	-

COMMODITIES BREAK OUT ON CONTANGO

When investing in commodity ETFs, watch the futures curve

In the land of commodity investing, not all commodities are equal. Before investing in commodities, there are some things investors ought to know. Like while pigs cannot fly they can contango. This term may sound like a Latin dance, but if you're investing in ETCs, it can kill you.

When issuers of ETCs track commodities, they do not go out and actually buy the commodity, except for precious metals which are easily stored. Investors do not want to buy a sty full of pigs and put them in a pen somewhere. It's impractical. With other commodities, like oil, governments will intervene to stop investors stockpiling them.

So, if investors want commodities exposure, it often has to be through ETC issuers buying futures contracts, which are bought and sold on exchanges.

But futures contracts are an imperfect way to invest. Unlike shares, futures contracts cannot be held indefinitely. Futures contracts have delivery dates. And if you're left holding the can on the delivery date, the commodity – be it pigs or oil – could be delivered to your front door!

To avoid this, ETC issuers sell futures before delivery and buy new ones with more distant delivery dates. This process of selling near dated futures and buying further-dated futures is called 'rolling'. It allows investors to stay exposed to a commodity via futures, without having to hold or store the commodity in question.

Rolling contracts adds another dimension – and another chance for loss or gain – to commodity investing. Thus, whenever investors are looking to buy commodities, they must take into account how much the commodity costs ('the spot price' in the jargon) but also how much it will cost to roll futures contracts before they decide to sell. This is where contango and backwardation come in. So, what is contango? As said above, futures contracts have to be rolled. Otherwise they'll be delivered. When they're rolled, the two futures contracts – i.e. the near-dated one being sold and the further-dated one being bought – are rarely the same price.

Contango is when you're the loser in this exchange. It is when your near-dated Pig Futures Contract sells for $50, and your further-dated Pig Futures Contract costs $52 (as an example), so you lose $2 when rolling so you need the pig price to increase by $2 just to break even. In the jargon, contango is when the futures curve slopes upwards.

Contango is a problem because if you keep rolling your futures contracts in a contango market, it will whittle away any potential returns. Worse, a long contango market can undermine all the gains made from rising spot prices.

Sticking with the example, say the first Pig Futures Contract cost $47, which then rose to $50 and was rolled. That is a $3 profit. But here's the thing: the second Pig Futures Contract cost $52 – $2 more than the first Pig Futures Contract. Contango will cost you $2, which will eat away at the $3 you made from the rising spot price, leaving you a profit of just $1 rather than $3.

Fortunately for investors, commodity markets are not always in contango. They are often in backwardation. Backwardation is the opposite of contango. It is when investors win. It is when the first Pig Futures Contract is sold for $52 when rolling into a second Pig Futures Contract costing only $50, meaning you make a $2 profit from the roll. This is called 'the roll yield'.

As a rule of thumb, if you're investing in commodities ETFs, backwardation is good and contango is bad. Investors can never be certain which way the market will go. Some futures, like pigs, wheat and natural gas, are almost always in contango. Others, such as soybeans and gasoline, are often in backwardation. But as the disclaimers always say: past performance is no indication of the future.

Overcoming contango

ETCs that invest in futures cannot overcome contango. If a fund buys futures, the fund has to roll them to prevent delivery. And when the futures are rolled, the prices will usually be different. There is no escaping this.

There are, however, alternatives and ways to mitigate this.

1. PHYSICAL ETCS

One alternative – the most popular one – is to avoid futures altogether and leave contango at the bus stop. This can be done by buying ETCs that physically hold the actual commodity: 'physical ETCs'. This is only feasible and economic for certain commodities, such as precious metals, where holding the commodity is common place and governments do not mind investors hoarding it.

With gold, silver, platinum and palladium, investors overwhelmingly prefer physical ETCs. ETCs holding physical bullion are among the most popular in the world. State Street's GLD in the US and ETF Securities' PHAU in Europe, ETFs that stores gold bullion in vaults, are two of the top ETCs worldwide by assets. Other physical metals ETCs such as those storing palladium, (like ETFS Physical Palladium PHPD, which trades in London, for example), are also popular.

2. ROLLING STRATEGIES

If futures contracts are the only way to get exposure to a commodity, there are ways to mitigate the roll costs. One such strategy is to buy ETCs with longer futures contracts. That way there is less rolling. "Rolling less usually improves returns," explains James Butterfill, head of research at commodities issuer ETF Securities. "Instead of rolling every one month, there are longer roll strategies that usually reduce volatility and therefore give better risk-adjust returns. An index tracking futures with longer maturities can minimise the number of occasions it is exposed to a roll." The downside of this strategy is that the longer dated price tends not to fluctuate as much as the spot price because the futures are not set to be delivered for some time. This can reduce returns expected when the spot price increase quickly.

3. LADDERING

Another, less common, strategy is called laddering. Laddering is, in effect, a kind of hedging, but for futures. It's where an ETC will buy several differently dated futures contracts, selling the most expensive and buying the cheapest. While this kind of strategy reduces the losses of contango, but the cost of hedging also means it reduces any upside from backwardation.

PRECIOUS METALS

MAIN INDEX

None. Most precious metals ETFs do not use indices. Rather, they physically hold the metals they track in vaults, meaning that no index is necessary. (They will track the spot price of metals, which can be reflected in an index however.)

DESCRIPTION

The majority of money invested in precious metals is invested in gold – in ETFs as elsewhere. But investors can often be interested in other precious metals, most often silver, platinum and palladium. While some ETF providers do use indices to track precious metals futures contracts, investors almost always prefer physically backed precious metals ETFs. This is because they are guaranteed to track their underlying, avoid problems of futures indices like contango, and tend to be cheaper and simpler.

COMPOSITION

Gold is by far and away the most popular precious metal among investors. Its sources of appeal are well known: it provides a crucial hedge against the dollar and is one of the only assets known to appreciate during financial crises and political turmoil. Gold's status as a safe haven asset has been rock solid for centuries.

Silver tends to correlate with gold, but not perfectly. Silver has more demand for industrial use than gold, meaning that it can be more affected by the business cycle. Silver-backed ETFs are less liquid than gold ETFs and for whatever reason their storage costs tend to be higher. Silver ETFs also do not allow for the physical delivery of the commodity like gold products do.

Platinum is the most expensive and strictly speaking the most precious of the precious metals, costing the most per ounce. A considerable fraction of platinum's pricing is determined by industrial demand and jewellery. A small percentage of platinum is held by investors, but that fraction is rising.

Palladium is the most obscure of the precious metals and many investors do not know what it is. The silvery white metal is the 46th element in the periodic table. Like gold, silver and platinum, palladium is a noble metal, meaning it does not corrode or react easily. Most demand for palladium comes from car catalysts. And with increased use in China many investors have spotted an opportunity.

WHAT TO WATCH OUT FOR

The watchword for any gold investment is disaster. When bad luck strikes – be it a financial crisis or inflation – investors have a habit of running back to gold. When gold goes up, silver tends to follow. For this reason, many large financial institutions often hold gold and silver, awaiting the rainy day. Platinum and palladium pose more interesting investment propositions as their prices are still mostly driven by demand from industry. Palladium has had a promising two years, owing to increased car demand in China. Whether this continues though is anyone's guess.

Performance analysis of the Physical Gold spot prices ($)

2017	12.0%
2016	9.2%
2015	-11.5%
3 yrs	2.7%
5 yrs	-4.7%
Volatility	6.3%
Correlation with S&P 500	0.53

ALTERNATIVES – INFRASTRUCTURE EQUITIES

MAIN INDICES

FTSE Infrastructure Index series

Constituents are selected from the FTSE Global All Cap Index using FTSE's definition of infrastructure. FTSE applies minimum infrastructure revenue thresholds of 65% for constituents of the Core Infrastructure indices and 20% for constituents of the Infrastructure Opportunities indices. This series also incorporates the old Macquarie Infrastructure indices.

S&P Global Infrastructure Index

Designed to track 75 companies from around the world chosen to represent the listed infrastructure industry while maintaining liquidity and tradability. To create diversified exposure, the index includes three distinct infrastructure clusters: energy, transportation, and utilities.

DESCRIPTION

The infrastructure space has been one of the fastest-growing bits of the investment universe over the last decade. According to the FTSE Russell Group, "infrastructure and utility assets are an essential for all investors". The index firm cites the following positives for the investment space:

- Essential and irreplaceable services with inelastic demand means exposure to infrastructure provides adequate gearing for growth in portfolio.

- Global trend towards PPPs and privatisation of traditionally public funded assets is driving rapid growth of infrastructure with expectations for continued development in the three diverse areas of roads, airports and telecommunications.

- Strong cash flows characterised by low volatility and average correlation with other asset classes make infrastructure an excellent toll for properly diversifying a portfolio.

- Strong record of market index outperformance.

Many investors are attracted to this relatively new alternative asset class by the relatively steady flow of income – yields of between 3 and 6% are common – and the subdued volatility (at least in recent years). As an asset class, infrastructure will never deliver huge returns, but it does offer the hope of relatively low correlations with mainstream equities.

The two big global indices come courtesy of the FTSE Group and rivals S&P. The S&P Global Infrastructure Index series includes 75 large, liquid infrastructure stocks from around the world with one-fifth of the constituents emerging market stocks with a liquid, developed market listing (NYSE ADRs, LSE GDRs or Hong Kong listings of Chinese stocks). To ensure diversified exposure across different infrastructure clusters, S&P makes sure that the 75 constituents are distributed at each rebalancing as follows:

*   Energy: 15–20%

*   Transportation: 30–40%

*   Utilities: 30–40%

The other main index comes from rival outfit FTSE, namely their FTSE Global Infrastructure series.

But beyond these two global, broad indices you'll also see some indices focused on just energy infrastructure and master limited partnerships – very popular in the US as a source of steady income. Both ETF Securities and Invesco Source offer products in this specialist space. There are also a small but growing number of ETFs which track both infrastructure equities *and* bonds issued by infrastructure businesses – State Street in Europe offers one such ETF.

COMPOSITION

Both the FTSE and S&P global indices have a very strong US bias. The FTSE Global Infrastructure index has 51% exposure to the US with Canada at 10% and Japan at 9% – the S&P index has US exposure at 35% with Spain at 12% and Canada also at 10%. In terms of the kinds of businesses within the index (sector mix), in the FTSE index electricity businesses amount to 30% of the value of the index followed by railroads at 12% and multi utilities (which could include some power generation assets) at 9%. In the S&P series industrials account for 41%, utilities 39% and energy businesses 19%. Largest individual stocks within the FTSE index are Union Pacific at 4.18%, NextEra Energy at 2.89% and Enbridge at 2.5%. Enbridge is also a major holding in the S&P index alongside Transurban Group and Abertis, the giant Spanish transport infrastructure operator.

WHAT TO WATCH OUT FOR

The focus on US assets is an obvious risk as is the exposure to regulatory changes/rethinks in just a few key markets – the US, Spain, Canada, Japan and the UK. Big changes can happen, with a devastating impact on share prices. In Spain for instance, subsidies to solar were drastically scaled back a few years ago during the recession, causing a sudden slump in profits for some utilities. An incoming Labour government in the UK might also nationalise key assets.

Another big risk is that some individual utility stocks can be surprisingly volatile – arguably the main direction of travel for some utilities has been downwards over time. As leverage at the corporate level has increased and dividend payouts ramped up, share prices in some key utilities have tended to deflate.

This cyclicality is also obvious in the energy infrastructure space, tracked by MLP indices and ETFs. The collapse in the price of oil badly hit investor confidence and the share price of supposedly safe pipeline and storage operators fell sharply. Combining equity with debt-based opportunities – the focus of a State Street SPDR ETF – might help dampen down the volatility of returns and also increase the income potential. But total upside returns might also end up being much more muted in the long term.

Performance analysis of the FTSE Global Infrastructure Index

2017	16.9%
2016	12.1%
2015	-9.3%
3 yrs	6.0%
5 yrs	12.0%
Volatility	4.7%
Correlation with S&P 500	0.47

ALTERNATIVES – GLOBAL PROPERTY

MAIN INDICES

FTSE EPRA/NAREIT Global Real Estate Index Series

Designed to represent general trends in eligible real estate equities worldwide. Relevant activities are defined as the ownership, disposal and development of income-producing real estate. The index series now covers Global, Developed and Emerging indices, as well the UK's AIM market.

FTSE EPRA/NAREIT Developed Dividend+ Index

Represents stocks that have a one-year forecast dividend yield of 2% or greater. The index is then weighted by market capitalisation in line with the free float-adjusted EPRA/NAREIT Developed Index.

DESCRIPTION

Property and especially commercial property has emerged over the last decade as perhaps the single most important alternative asset class, helped in part by the boom (until recently) in capital prices and the increasing number of specialist, tax-efficient real estate investment trusts (REITs).

What are these REITs? A REIT is a type of company that specialises in property, usually commercial property that generates income. To classify as a REIT, regulations have to be met. The most important is that a certain amount of a company's assets must be in real estate. Most major REITs trade on exchanges and buying shares in a REIT gives investors a chance to get some of the rents that tenants pay. Property ETFs take an index of REITs and buy all the companies in the index – as they do with any other kind of equity ETF. Properties REITs often own:

- shopping centres
- office space
- hospitals

- apartments

- warehouses

- hotels

Global REIT indices track property investments around the world, not just their home country. It should be noted that REITs, like trusts themselves, are mostly an Anglo-Saxon thing. Thus, every major Anglo economy – the US, Canada, the UK and Australia – has a home market REIT ETF that's highly liquid and cheap. Outside the Anglosphere, REIT ETFs do exist, but they tend not to have the depth or liquidity. REITs offer a number of not insubstantial advantages for the private investor:

- They allow you to diversify across national and regional markets.

- They allow access to global commercial property markets – from offices through to industrial estates.

- They're usually invested in core REIT holdings which are tax efficient – REITs must pay most of their income stream as a dividend to investors (free of tax).

- They produce a useful dividend yield.

- They also offer investors a way of diversifying risk against core equity holdings. Most of the funds on offer boast correlations with the FTSE All Share of less than 0.5 while the US version is also fairly lowly correlated with the US equity markets.

COMPOSITION

As we've already observed, the most common index series from FTSE is heavily dominated by Anglo-Saxon nations – and especially the US. The Global FTSE EPRA/NAREIT Dividend+ index for instance has 54% exposure to the US, with Australia at 6.3% and the UK at 4.90%. Hong Kong and Japan are also hugely important with 9% and 6% exposure respectively. In terms of property types, retail-based assets account for 23%, residential at 14.5% and offices at 3.11%. Top individual businesses within the index include Simon Property Group at 3.89%, Prologis at 2.48% and Public Storage at 2.26% – all US-based businesses.

WHAT TO WATCH OUT FOR

As with every investment, property ETFs have risks. These include the fact that prices can go down as well as up. This was demonstrated in dramatic effect during the 2008 property bubble in the US, during which some REIT ETFs lost 75% of their value, compared with the 50% drop experienced by the S&P 500.

One key risk that differs slightly from a regular equity ETF is REIT's geographic concentration. Property prices across a country tend to correlate over the long-term, but there can be important differences between different parts of that country, especially in the short-term. This can be an issue for ETFs as the largest REITs by market capitalisation also tend to focus on the same major cities within a country.

Another potential risk for property ETFs is sectoral. This has been highlighted by the rise of online shopping. Online shopping has powered a rally for warehouse REITs, which provide the facilities that online shops depend on. But many retail REITs, which depend on shopping centres and malls for their income, have found the rise of ecommerce an unwelcome disruption.

Investors considering property ETFs should look at which sectors their ETF focusses on, as well as which geographies. And as with any investment, investors considering property ETFs should always do their research.

The bottom lines? We do have some concerns with these funds, but we nevertheless think they really do deserve a place in most long-term portfolios. They're still a cheap and easy way of buying access to the best commercial real estate companies and they also pay out a cracking yield. So, these are a great series of products to buy if you want to access the global commercial property markets.

Performance analysis of the FTSE EPRA/NAREIT Developed Dividend+ Index

2017	11.7%
2016	6.5%
2015	0.3%
3 yrs	6.4%
5 yrs	9%
Volatility	7.5%
Correlation with S&P 500	-

ALTERNATIVES — AGRICULTURE

MAIN INDEX

Bloomberg Agriculture Subindex (BCOMAGTR)

DESCRIPTION

This is the subindex of Bloomberg's famous and widely used commodity index BCOMTR. It follows some of the most-used agricultural goods, such as wheat, corn (called maize in the UK), soybean varietals, coffee and sugar. In other words, everything you see at a good breakfast table. Investors considering this index may want to get familiar with what Chicago and Kansas wheats are and how they're different (they trade on different exchanges, Kansas tends to trade at a premium). And what's so special about soybean products (soybean meal tends to be a protein supplement and is common in animal feed; soybean oil is often called vegetable oil).

COMPOSITION

The exact composition of the index will vary from day to day as futures prices rise and fall. As of January 2018, the composition is as follows:

Chicago Wheat	11.5%
Coffee	7.3%
Corn	24.90%
Cotton	4.80%
Kansas City Wheat	4.0%
Soybean Meal	10.3%
Soybean Oil	9.2%
Soybeans	19.6%
Sugar	8.4%

WHAT TO WATCH OUT FOR

While energy companies and precious metals like gold are common in portfolios, soft commodities like agriculture are harder to find. Yet agriculture can make for a great hedging tool as major indices – like Nikkei, the S&P 500 and FTSE – all have less than 5% exposure to agricultural companies. The world will never run out of demand for agriculture and with unusually favourable growing conditions, which have driven down agriculture prices in recent years, potentially coming to an end, agriculture could well have a good upside in the mid-term.

ALTERNATIVES — ENERGY

MAIN INDEX

Bloomberg Energy Subindex (BCOMENTR)

The index reflects the returns that are potentially available through an unleveraged investment in the futures contracts on energy commodities. The index currently consists of five energy-related commodities futures contracts (Natural Gas, WTI Crude Oil, Brent Crude Oil, Heating Oil and Unleaded Gasoline) which are included in the Bloomberg Commodity Index Total Return.

Brent crude is the most traded of all of the oil benchmarks, and is defined as crude mostly drilled from the North Sea oilfields: Brent, Forties, Oseberg and Ekofisk (collectively known as BFOE). This oil type is widely used as it is both sweet and light, making it easy to refine into diesel fuel and gasoline. That, and its relative ease of transporting being produced at sea, make it so widely traded.

West Texas Intermediate (WTI) crude oil is of very high quality and is excellent for refining a larger portion of gasoline. Its API gravity is 39.6 degrees (making it a light crude oil), and it contains only about 0.24% of sulfur (making a 'sweet' crude oil). This combination of characteristics, together with its location, makes it an ideal crude oil to be refined in the United States, the largest gasoline-consuming country in the world. Most WTI crude oil gets refined in the Midwest region of the country, with some more refined within the Gulf Coast region. Although the production of WTI crude oil is on the decline, it still is the major benchmark of crude oil in the Americas. WTI is generally priced at about a $5 to $6 per-barrel premium to the OPEC Basket price and about $1 to $2 per-barrel premium to Brent, although on a daily basis the pricing relationships between these can vary greatly.

DESCRIPTION

Our sense is that if you really must buy access to an individual commodity in your portfolio, you're probably best off focussing on just two – oil and gold. The trickier question is how to buy that access – do you invest in a fund that tracks something called WTI or Brent. But this distinction between Brent and WTI is just the start of the process of working out how to invest – your next challenge is to work out whether you want to invest in a broad crude oil index, a specific Brent/WTI fund and whether you want to track futures prices. Just to add to the confusion you can also make money on price falls in oil – by investing in an inverse short ETC – or gear up your exposure to oil increases by investing in a leveraged oil ETC.

If we had a preference we'd suggest the Brent Oil 1-month futures ETC – sterling-based – which, as the name suggests, invests in one month futures-based contracts based on spot Brent Oil prices.

Arguably the best idea though is to invest in an index which tracks a broad basket of energy prices, which includes crude oil but also derivatives such as heating oil as well as natural gas. That implies using a broad commodities index, but with a focus on the subindex – the Bloomberg index series is probably the most widely used. Bloomberg has taken over UBS' title as the major provider of commodity indices. BCOMENTR is a subindex of BCOMTR, Bloomberg's overarching commodities index. It measures the performance of energy commodities futures contracts (including roll yield and collateral yield – hence total return). It weighs oil heavily, using both WTI and Brent benchmarks, which is intended to reflect the importance of oil in global commerce. It does not use alternative energy sources like ethanol or hydrogen. Nor does it use green energy infrastructure like wind turbines and solar panels.

COMPOSITION

The index is made up entirely of fossil fuels – tracking prices for Natural Gas, WTI Crude Oil, Brent Crude Oil, Heating Oil and Unleaded Gasoline.

Brent Crude Oil	27.1%
ULS Diesel	13.4%
Natural Gas	23.3%
RBOB Gasoline	12.40%
WTI Crude Oil	23.80%

WHAT TO WATCH OUT FOR

Many investors wanting exposure to energy buy shares in energy companies like Exxon and Schlumberger as they produce dividends and don't suffer the drawbacks of commodity futures indices (like contango) – and the valuations and profits of energy companies tend to correlate with energy prices anyway. Investors gunning for energy commodities directly have had a disappointing several years, as the US shale revolution has driven down prices across the globe. Most experts are expecting energy commodities to stagnate in 2019. But if the shale revolutions stalls energy commodity prices will only go one way. One last factor to watch out for – energy prices are staggeringly volatile.

Performance analysis for Brent Oil

2017	17.4%
2016	51.0%
2015	-34.0%
3 yrs	11.3%
5 yrs	-9.2%
Volatility	18.1%
Correlation with S&P 500	0.78

Section 4

PORTFOLIOS

MINIMISING RISK

I N THIS CHAPTER we're going to try to draw together many of the varied discussions in this book and focus on portfolio strategies; i.e. turning all these ideas about smart beta, bond ETFs and varying asset classes into sensible, practical portfolio principles. Over the following pages we'll explore various strategies for putting together different asset classes and ETFs into one portfolio. Varying from long-term ideas which echo the work of the big university endowment funds, through to market-timing strategies which use key macro-economic signals. At the end we'll draw together all these ideas and discussions and suggest a shortlist of model portfolios that can be put together using mainstream, cheap, easy-to-buy ETFs. We also include a shortlist of the top ETFs from varying asset classes.

But first we need to make some very obvious observations – call them our version of investing common sense. We'll explore each in more detail in this chapter.

Every individual has their own attitude towards risk and they should carefully understand and weight each asset class based on that appreciation of risk. Equities are risky and volatile and in the past have produced superior returns – are you happy to weight your portfolio towards those risky assets, knowing that you could suffer losses of 30% in some bear markets? If you are, consider a more adventurous bias towards risky assets like equities.

Diversifying between assets also still makes absolute sense, especially if those building blocks consist of gold, government securities, equities, commodities and corporate bonds. Many risky assets are increasingly moving as one (they're correlated) but gold and gilts in particular still have great value in diversification terms.

Every investor will also probably have their own attitude towards the different styles of investing. Some will be defensive, value-orientated and happy to avoid surging markets. Other investors, by contrast, will be happy to flow with the tide, and follow what are called momentum trades where positive sentiment is pushing up the value of shares. Neither style is right or wrong, and both can be very successful over different parts of a financial cycle.

One last observation – more adventurous investors willing to pay close attention to the ebb and flow of markets should also consider tracking the volatility of markets. In particular they might want to keep a reserve of cash to invest in the market during peaks in volatility

– in these circumstances where fear is dominating most trades, bargains abound and many structures become very attractively priced.

So, assuming that all the above strikes the reader as eminently sensible, let's start developing some ideas about sensible portfolio construction using ETFs.

Arguably the best place to start is with a discussion not of opportunity and upside but with a definition of risk. A sensible investor starts by controlling downside risk, which involves sensibly diversifying their portfolio of ETFs as well as thinking about how different asset classes move over time.

MINIMISING THE DOWNSIDE: CONTROLLING RISK

Unlike returns (which can be measured in a relatively simple fashion), risk is a more slippery customer. Risk comes in lots of different shapes and guises. Most private investors look at risk in a very simplistic way; they might ask "how much of my initial capital might I lose if I invest in an asset?". Risk in this sense is thus measured by the *potential drawdown*, i.e. loss in value.

This way of measuring risk has been taken to the extreme by academic economists who've constructed a pantheon of risk metrics that look at returns data (i.e. how much in percentage terms an asset has lost in value). These analyses can bring out exotic sounding terms like VaR, value at risk, a statistical term which puts actual numbers on the possible risk levels of an asset. Many smart investors do use measures like this, but investors need to think about risk in a much more holistic sense.

Risk could mean any or all of the following:

- **Volatility**. How much does the value of a share, bond or commodity vary on a daily basis? For many, high volatility implies higher potential risk.

- **Maximum Drawdown**. This simply means the potential maximum loss over a period of time that could hit my financial asset. Many stock markets can easily lose 20% or even 30% in a year whereas most bonds rarely lose more than 10% in any one year.

- **Systematic Risk**. This risk measure looks at how an asset might respond to risks within the system i.e. how closely correlated the asset is with wider financial assets. If the US economy nose dives, will my asset also crash in value as well?

- **Idiosyncratic Risk**. If I employ a manager to manage my money, what risk am I taking if they make a bad decision? The best way of controlling this is to use a passive, index tracking fund where the risk of poor manager decisions is greatly reduced.

- **Currency Risk**. My investment in a foreign asset might increase in value but the currency it's denominated in might move in the opposite direction? One way of controlling this is to think about hedging over the currency risk over the short to medium term.

- **Credit Risk**. If I buy a bond, what's the chance of the issuer defaulting on the final payment (or the regular interest payments)?

- **Legal Risk**. Will the regulators decide to change the rules governing my investment?

- **Liquidity Risk.** My asset might increase in value but become increasingly difficult to sell i.e. it might become more illiquid which could be a risk if I need to access that investment immediately to raise some hard-needed cash!

- **Leverage Risk**. What happens if I borrow too much money and the cost of leverage starts to work against my investment?

- **Political Risk**. If I look for investment opportunities overseas, I should always be mindful of the political climate. Not every government creates favourable climates for foreign investment and some are actively hostile to foreign money.

Now that we've opened up the Pandora's box that is risk, let's explore some uncomfortable home truths, especially about investing in equities. We will look at three such home truths:

1. Equity premiums are more risky than you think

2. Value unlocks equity

3. Tortoise beats the hare

Let's look at each of these in turn.

1. Equity premiums are more risky than you think

Our first home truth is that equities are even more volatile than you imagine – remember that many investors regard volatility as the text book definition of risk.

Analysis by academics has consistently proved one simple truth about investing in equities over the long term – if the past is anything to go by, equities as an asset class outperform everything from cash and commodities through to bonds. Equities produced an average compound return of anything between 6 and 7% per annum – compound up that real return over the very long term and you could end with a very successful investment portfolio.

How does this past rate of return compare with other, less risky financial assets?

The answer lies in a relatively simple concept known as the *equity risk premium*, which is perhaps better understood as the extra profits (over safe bonds) to be had from investing in risky stuff like equities. According to academics at the London Business School this still looks like it's about 3 to 3.5% per annum although they also note that "the equity premium is smaller than was once thought".

On paper the case for investing a large chunk of portfolio money in risky equities looks incredibly compelling, until that is you examine the next three charts. They are all the work of SG quantitative analyst Andrew Lapthorne, and each graphic in turn reminds us that equities are very, very volatile.

The first chart examines the 20-year average real (after inflation) returns from holding the S&P 500 (the benchmark US blue-chip index) – the grey straight line in the middle shows the average return while the jagged lines show actual rolling returns from holding this index. Over the 90 years of different 20-year rolling periods, just 12 actually produced the average return of around 7% per annum – many decades produced returns in the double digits per annum while the last five twenty-year periods produced returns of close to zero (per annum, on average). This graphic reminds us that equities are incredibly volatile and that that volatility can hugely impact your expected 20-year returns.

20-year average real returns for the S&P 500

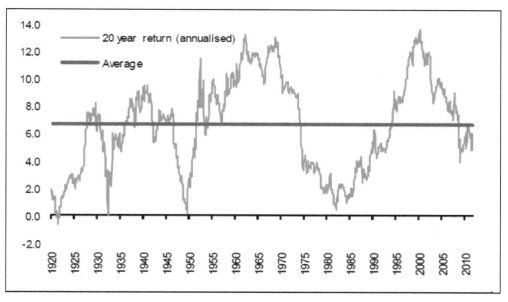

Source: SG Cross Asset Research, GFD

But how does that volatility compare with the next best alternative, less risky government bonds?

The next chart looks at the maximum capital loss over a number of five-year holding periods for both bonds (red, usually at the bottom) and equities (grey, usually on top). In nearly every period, equities produce much higher maximum losses than bonds – there are in fact many five-year periods where equities can produce a maximum capital loss of 10% or more whereas with bonds such losses are uncommon.

Rolling five-year maximum drawdown of US bonds and US equities (Nominal total returns)

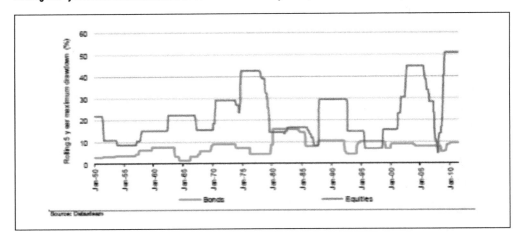

The final graphic from Lapthorne fleshes out the relative likelihood of big losses from bonds and equities. It breaks down those five-year holding periods and looks at the probability in percentage terms of different capital losses since 1950.

When investing on a five-year basis, what kind of drawdown you would have experienced (percentage of months seeing various levels of drawdown since 1950 – real returns)

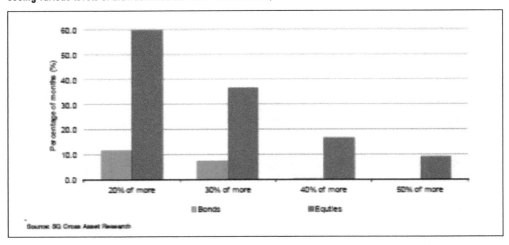

According to Lapthorne, this analysis suggests:

> The bond investor could have bought bonds 90% of the months since 1950 and avoided having a 20% drawdown or more, whilst the equity investor could have only invested in 40% of months to avoid such losses. Extreme drawdown of 40% or more, even on a real basis, is almost unheard of in the bond market, but seen 17% of the time in equities. Yes, bonds at sub 2% offer miserable returns, but equities will always offer a higher probability of major losses.

These statistics should not come as a surprise to any investor – the extra reward from holding equities over the long term comes with an obvious price, which is that equities are volatile and can fall very substantially in price during volatile years.

If you are willing to invest over the very long term and accept a window of opportunity that stretches out for 30 years or more, then you should perhaps be willing to embrace that volatility – if the future is anything like the past, equities could make you a compound return of nearly 7% per annum in real terms over the next few decades. Such an impressive return probably implies adopting a buy-and-hold strategy where you sit tight in terms of portfolio allocations and don't trade in the short term based on market cycles.

For investors with shorter time horizons, a number of alternatives suggest themselves:

1. If are not willing to suffer losses of more than 10% per annum, you should avoid equities entirely and stick to bonds – but be prepared to suffer in bullish years when equities shoot ahead.

2. Invest in volatility itself and carefully time investments so that they sync with increases in volatility. Investors can consider using structured investments to lock in spikes in volatility.

3. Don't try to second guess every bullish and bearish swing in sentiment and focus instead on buying quality assets (such as the S&P 500) when they are cheap.

2. The importance of value

Our next simple truth is based on a very established idea – that *the price at which an investor buys a financial asset matters greatly*. This doesn't sound uncomfortable on initial inspection but counterintuitively most investors run a mile from cheap stocks. If I were to give you the choice of a sexy, expensive but hugely popular option (a fast car or a highly rated tech stock growing in leaps and bounds) and a cheap, slightly tawdry alternative that has seen better days and is probably a tad unloved, which would you choose? The work of a small army of behavioural economist has proved beyond doubt that many will choose the shiny, new, expensive option – and not the cheap, unloved one. The sexiness helps but what is probably more powerful is the affirmation of others – as a crowd we feel safety in numbers, and if the crowd loves a hugely popular product, we feel safe in going with the flow. Our worry is that the cheaper option might be cheaper because it is less reliable, or more likely to prove problematic. Shares and bonds though are not like every other consumer product. As we've already discovered in our discussion on smart beta, copious amounts of evidence show that buying cheap shares – using valuation metrics – is actually the smart thing to do long term.

In sum, the cheaper you buy any financial asset, the greater your probability of making a big return. American stock market historian and strategist Ed Easterling[7] has mined huge amounts of historical equity market data to produce the next graphic. This chart shows

---

7   http://www.crestmontresearch.com/

a massive series of individual 20-year periods from 1919 through to 2011 and attempts to link equity returns to the change in the price earnings ratio of the benchmark S&P 500 Index.

The PE ratio is a very widely understood tool and simply measures the relationship between the aggregate profits of all the companies in the benchmark index versus the cost of buying the aggregate index through something like an ETF. A PE ratio of 15 for the S&P 500 Index implies that the combined companies in the index trade at an aggregate 15 times their total earnings or profits.

Easterling then makes one small change to this measure – instead of looking at simple year-based PE ratios, he averages out the PE ratio over the 10 years of a business cycle. The change in this cyclically adjusted PE ratio for the S&P 500 is then measured – over some 20-year periods the PE ratio starts at a very low level, and then finishes at a very high measure after a bullish rally, whilst in other years the exact reverse happens (a bear market). As you can see there is a relatively straightforward relationship between 20-year returns and the waxing and waning of the PE ratio.

20-year rolling stock market return (blue/left) and change in PE ratio (red/right) 1919–2011

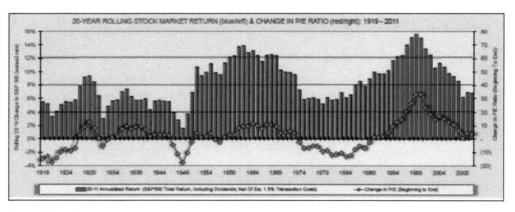

Source: Crestmont Research

The next table puts some more flesh on the bones of this argument – it looks at all these 20-year periods and then breaks them down into decile groups through to 2011. Easterling then looks at the range of stock market returns and compares them to changes in the PE ratio. In simple terms the bottom decile of 20-year periods boasted a PE which started at 19 and ended up with a PE ratio at the end of the period of nine – these 20-year periods produced net returns of between 1.2% to 4.5% per annum, on average.

If by contrast you'd have picked those 20-year periods where the PE started at say 10 or 12 (the top two deciles), and then sat tight as that PE ratio expanded to 29 or 22 times profits, you'd have made a huge annual average return. According to Easterling these 20-year periods produced net annual returns of anything between 12 and 15% per annum, on average over the full 20 years. This value-based idea of buying an asset (share, bond or even ETF) when it's cheap, based on fundamental measures, is one of the strongest and most powerful principles in investing. The only downside is that financial assets such as equities remain expensive for many years – this means that their share price trades at a level which is above the 'cheap' price, implying that investors either stay in cash or be willing to accept smaller returns.

20-year periods ending 1919 – 2011 (93 periods in all)

Decile	Net total returns by decile range			S&P 500 decile average	Average beginning PE ratio	Average ending PE ratio
	From		To			
1	1.2%		4.5%	3.2%	19	9
2	4.5%		5.2%	4.9%	18	9
3	5.2%		5.4%	5.3%	12	12
4	5.4%		6%	5.6%	14	12
5	6.2%		7.9%	6.9%	16	16
6	8.6%		9.6%	9.2%	16	19
7	9.7%		9.6%	9.4%	15	19
8	9.7%		11%	10.4%	11	20
9	11.5%		11.9%	11.7%	12	22
10	12.1%		15%	13.4%	10	29

Note: PE ratio based upon average 10-year real EPS

3. Tortoise beats the hare

The last idea is perhaps the most counterintuitive – it suggests that there is in fact no relationship between top-line GDP growth of regions such as the emerging markets and bottom-line equity returns. Again, we're back with the discussion of behavioural economics – and our preference for shiny, sexy, new things that are growing fast. The core idea here is that a fast-growing asset – probably measured by something like profits – is a better bet. This last statement sounds eminently sensible. Buy an asset where the cash flows are growing. What's not to like about this idea? In fact, quite a lot as it happens. Fast earnings growth is *not* necessarily a good guide to future capital gains. In sum, don't be seduced by good looks and a fast growth rate – focus on the fundamentals!

The graphic below is from Paul Marson who a few years ago was chief investment officer at Swiss Bank Lombard Odier and it looks at the relationship (correlation) between two sets of variables – the horizontal axis looks at GDP growth for a combined group of developed and emerging economies (as measured by the IMF) while the vertical axis looks at returns. The straight line plots the relationship between GDP growth and investor returns – it shows that as GPD growth rates increase, returns to investors actually start to *decline*. Paul Marson's analysis is backed up by academic research, which agrees on the idea that there is in fact a negative correlation between GDP growth and investor returns. For Marson and others, the moral of the story is that investors should ignore sexy, growth economies such as China and instead embrace boring, slower-growth economies such as Belgium.

What makes low growth attractive?

Two factors would seem to be at work, both related to the fundamental measures mentioned earlier. The first is that faster-growing economies do see an increase in the value of their local stock markets, especially as investors chase up PE ratios. But this mania inevitably results in speculative bubbles, and massive volatility in local share prices – most investors fail to get into local markets when they are cheap but buy as those PE multiples hit their highs.

The other key factor is the boring dividend cheque. Companies in fast-growing countries tend to ignore boring dividends in favour of reinvesting profits back into business expansion and new capacity – which sounds perfectly reasonable. But there is a slight hitch: the law of diminishing returns. This law suggests that over time, those returns from each extra dollar of new investment will diminish. In the cut-throat world of emerging market businesses, price competition eats into net margins – eventually it becomes obvious to all and sundry that a better alternative is to hand the money back to shareholders via dividends, rather like those boring Belgians! Sadly, in the meantime a vast amount of money has been wasted on unwise new investments, money which could have been handed back to shareholders to produce a greater total return.

Emerging and Developing Economies GDP Growth (IMF Data % y/y HORIZ AXIS) vs MSCI Emerging Markets Index Total Return (%y/y, VERT AXIS): 1988–2011

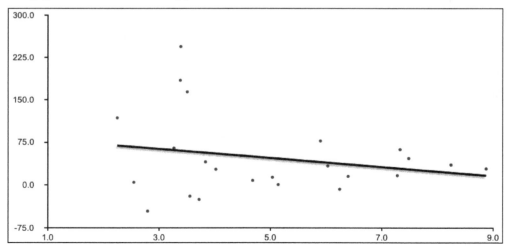

For investors a number of strategic ideas emerge from this important home truth. The first is that rather than modishly chase after global regions such as emerging markets, investors should actually focus on individual national markets and only buy those countries where the fundamentals look strong. The next idea is that investors should look to invest in faster-growing markets but look to take advantage of those swings in market sentiment and thus multiples. In simple terms, investors can buy faster-growing assets when they are cheap. Last but by no means least, investors should also stay focused on that dividend income, especially from emerging markets.

DIVERSIFICATION IS THE ONLY FREE LUNCH

So, armed with our home truths and an appreciation of risk in its many shapes and guises, what's a practical first step towards controlling the downside of investment? Our home truths reinforced the importance of buying cheap, even low-growth assets. They also reminded us that to reap the extra reward from holding risky equities, we need to be patient and wait for the long term.

Arguably though we have got ahead of the discussion.

A simpler truth needs repeating first – that diversifying between different asset classes can massively reduce potential portfolio risk. In simple terms why bet everything on a small number of investments or asset classes – broad clusters of investment types such as bonds or precious metals. The most robust proof of this finding came in a study of what's called *asset allocation* – a process where investors decide on the mix of different asset classes. A study by researchers at consulting firm Ibbotson Associates back in 2000 for instance showed that over 90% of the variance in investment outcomes from a wide range of large institutional pension funds could be explained by reference to their asset allocation ideas – the importance of individual stock selection or timing the exact ins and outs of a market position were found to be of minimal importance.

The Ibbotson Associates study showed the following relative importance of different factors for portfolio managers:

- asset allocation: 91%

- stock selection: 5%

- market timing: 2%

- other factors: 2%

On paper this analysis backs up the common-sense idea that sensibly diversifying between asset classes is a productive and worthwhile pursuit. The key to this process of diversification is to look at the returns characteristics of different markets and assets – this requires the investor to look at past relative returns compared to the accompanying risks, as measured by variance around a mean. Some assets are inherently riskier than others, but over time that extra possibility of a larger than average loss might be worth it, given the potential upside.

This thinking has spawned a veritable industry of research-based ideas such as modern portfolio theory and the elusive efficient frontier, yet one key insight remains – that a robust portfolio should contain different types of assets with different risk/return measures, preferably with assets that are relatively lowly correlated with each other. In fact, the ideal portfolio might have assets that are negatively correlated with each other i.e. that as one asset goes down in value, the other increases in worth. The key for the investor is to work out their own time horizon, and then look at the sensible mix of assets given their own tolerance of risk.

Yet this common-sense approach to investing has become incredibly difficult in recent years, as more and more assets move in the same direction. In previous decades we might have expected emerging markets equities and currencies for instance to move in a different way than developed blue-chip equities – that lack of correlation was a good thing, and a sensible investor mixed and matched different risky assets including racy small caps and emerging markets stocks as well as boring blue-chips. But in the last few years, global fear of a financial meltdown has changed everything, with correlations between risky assets increasing rapidly.

The next graphic is from analysts at J.P. Morgan and shows the average correlation between 45 different equity country benchmarks through to 2010. The message from this chart is obvious – the correlation of assets has increased over the last few decades. We don't have an updated chart for the period through to 2017, but rest assured the upwards trajectory of the chart wouldn't have changed much.

Globalization – rise of correlation between equity market benchmarks for 45 emerging and developed economies

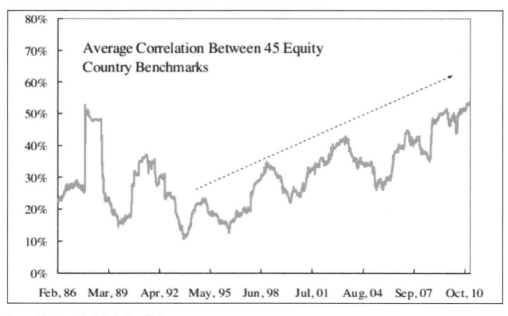

Source: J.P. Morgan Equity Derivatives Strategy.

This worrying trend has encouraged many investors to follow two simple strategies – the first is to use risk-based measures to suggest a simple switch between risky assets (equities and a mixed bag of other assets) and less risky assets (government bonds). In this strategy, your portfolio decisions are based on what is in effect market timing.

The second big switch is that rather than buy a diversified set of assets, investors might buy just a few simple proxies for each risk on/off theme. If risk is on, the investor buys US blue-chip equities through the S&P 500 Index. If risk is off, you buy US Treasury bills and bonds.

This simple idea has enormous appeal in volatile and difficult markets and is nothing if not simple to manage. But any investor who follows it faces two big risks – the first is that they are engaging in a form of market timing, which isn't generally a good idea for most investors. The second and more important criticism is that this elevated correlation is only true of certain markets, where volatility is high and fear rampant. As soon as markets normalise (volatility starts to decline) different asset classes start to behave in very different ways – in effect normalised markets encourage a dispersion of outcomes, which in turn benefits those investors with a more diversified portfolio.

The table below looks at returns from holding a very wide range of different indices over the last 12 months – notice the wide difference in returns from varying equity markets. In sum, diversification still works, as long as investors don't think the financial heavens are about to fall in!

Price returns from various indices

Index	Mid/Close	2017 price return (%)	Correlation (to S&P 500 last quarter)
NASDAQ Computer Index	4060.12	38.8	0.88
Hang Seng (Hong Kong)	29919.25	36.0	0.75
FTSE BRIC 50	1260.18	33.3	0.79
FTSE AIM 100	5408.23	32.9	0.63
NASDAQ 100	6396.42	31.5	0.90
FTSE Asia Pacific ex Japan	588.56	31.2	0.79
NASDAQ Composite	6903.39	28.2	0.92
S&P BSE India Sensex Index	34056.83	28.1	0.57
FTSE Asia Pacific	340.09	27.7	0.80
Dow Jones Industrial Average	24719.25	25.1	0.95
FTSE AIM All-Share	1049.63	24.3	0.59
FTSE All-World	340.29	22.0	0.95
S&P 500 – Total Return	5212.76	21.8	1.00
CSI 300 Index	4030.85	21.8	0.74

DJ Bric 50 (Eur) Index	593.25	21.6	0.80
Tokyo Stock Price Index	1817.56	19.7	0.66
S&P 500 GBP Hedged – Total Return	4505.99	19.6	1.00
S&P 500	2673.61	19.4	1.00
Nikkei 225	22764.94	19.1	0.66
Dow Jones Global Titans 50 Index (USD)	300.75	19.1	0.99
FTSE 250 Index – Total Return	15239.6	17.8	0.67
S&P 500 Equal Weighted Index	4092.21	16.7	0.98
FTSE 250	20726.3	14.7	0.67
FTSE All-Share – Total Return	7272.19	13.2	0.82
AEX Index (Amsterdam)	546.15	12.3	0.69
Macquarie Global Infrastructure 100	8816.38	12.1	0.48
FTSE 100 Index – Total Return	6519.85	12.0	0.83
DAX Xetra (Germany)	12938.7	11.6	0.64
Euronext 100	1034.59	10.2	0.61
BEL 20 (Brussels)	3978.22	9.6	0.66
FTSEurofirst 80	4912.78	9.5	0.63
FTSE All-Share	4225.61	9.1	0.83
CAC 40 (Paris)	5324.97	9.1	0.57
FTSE 350	4277.03	8.8	0.83
FTSE 100	7687.77	7.6	0.84
FTSEurofirst 300	1532.29	7.3	0.64
IBEX 35 (Spain)	10043.9	6.6	0.65
FTSEurofirst 100	4325.04	5.8	0.68
FTSE UK Dividend Plus	2895.05	1.6	0.63

Source: Sharescope

Diversifying between assets sounds sensible on paper, but how do we apply it in practice?

Academics at the London Business School, led by Professors Elroy Dimson and Paul Marsh have been mining long-term data from financial markets for many years now, and their recent conclusions repeat a number of common-sense ideas that are enormously useful for long-term investors looking to build a robust portfolio.

Bonds for instance are still a great diversifier (as is cash). Over varying years and even some decades, bonds can produce a better return than equities. That means that in years when shares fall in price, one might reasonably expect bonds to increase in price and vice versa. Many investors mock the simple notion of a 40/60 split in portfolio terms between equities and bonds but this a perfectly sensible idea as it diversifies a portfolio and hopefully makes it more robust in terms of susceptibility to different risks. Crucially there's some evidence that the negative correlation between bonds and equities has grown stronger over time.

But which bonds should investors opt for?

According to Dimson and Marsh there would appear to be what's called a maturity premium i.e. you receive a greater return for investing in a bond with a long maturity date of more than 10 or 20 years. The professors estimate that the return is likely to be a reward for the greater volatility and inflation risk of investing in long dated bonds and probably amounts to about 1% per year. There's also some evidence that investors demand what's called a 'credit risk premium' for investing in bonds which could in principle default i.e. corporate bonds. They reckon that this amounts to an extra 0.60% per annum.

Sticking with the income theme, **inflation-linked bonds** are also effective as a means of reducing real risk. In today's market however, they can make little contribution to achieving a positive real return over the period from investment to maturity i.e. inflation bonds will protect you against inflation, just don't expect to make anything more than inflation as a long-term real return.

Turning to equities, the long-term analysis of stock markets shows that stocks have still produced superior returns when compared to bonds – which is why analysts and academics suggest a weighting towards riskier assets (say 60%) for those with a long-time horizon. Other studies suggest that investors over the long term can hope to benefit from a 3 to 4% equity risk premium over bonds i.e. gain an extra 3 to 4% extra return over the very long term for taking on the greater risk of investing in equities.

But the London Business School researchers have also examined which particular types of equities outperform. One of their most surprising conclusions is that domestic equities usually perform best after periods of **currency weakness** – a positive portend for the UK market. They also suggest that shares generally regarded as risky, tend to outperform over the long term – especially **smaller cap stocks**. According to the researchers "there is therefore good reason to expect illiquid, smaller companies to generate larger returns over the long run". They also suggest that investors can expect to pick up some extra returns for a focused strategy of investing in cheaper, **value stocks** as well as chasing those stocks which display strong relative strength when compared to the wider market over a 3 to 12-month period – this is also known as the *momentum effect*. The researchers conclude that this **momentum strategy** has been powerful over the long term though it is volatile and costly to implement.

All of these observations back up the promise of smart beta investing, discussed earlier in this book.

Looking beyond equities, stock market analysts have concluded that **gold** is still useful as a diversifier especially for what is called volatility risk – this suggests that as markets become much more volatile, gold rises in price as fear drives assets' prices. Crucially the LBS academics suggest that gold is the only asset that does not have its real value reduced by inflation. But the bitter truth is that during periods of heightened inflation most assets perform poorly, even equities, though they are probably the least impacted. The researchers suggest that neither commercial property nor conventional bonds are a good hedge against inflation, with only gold a proper hedge. They also note that bonds come into their own (versus equities) during periods of disinflation and deflation but can be dangerous during inflationary bursts.

A diversification checklist

This long list of research findings from the various London Business School studies suggests that investors should focus on some basic ideas about robust portfolio construction – summed up in our seven simple ideas below.

1. Diversify between bonds and equities.

2. Within bonds diversify between those that will protect you in an inflationary environment (inflation-linked bonds) and their more conventional siblings. Crucially also diversify your durations (invest in short and long dated) and credit risk (low risk governments and higher risk corporate).

3. Within equities, those investors willing to stick with equities over the long term should consider investing in certain riskier types of shares – small caps – as well as value stocks and momentum-based strategies

4. Gold is a useful diversifier and a sensible way of insuring against sudden increases in volatility but over the very long term, it hasn't been a great investment – both bonds and equities have easily outpaced returns from gold over the last hundred years, although gold has had a very impressive last decade.

5. Investors worried about a sudden increase in inflation should probably weight their portfolios towards gold, inflation-linked bonds and equities. Those investors worried by deflation are probably best off in government bonds.

6. Currency is a risk for investors over the short to medium-term, but markets usually correct over the long term. Higher inflation rates (produced by faster GDP growth) usually result in a weaker exchange rate, so investors 'real' exposure should balance out i.e. what they gain on inflation, they lose via currency depreciation. Hedging your equity exposure does make some sense over the short to medium term but is difficult to achieve cost effectively over the longer term and of dubious benefit. This implies that international diversification is still useful and that investors shouldn't overly worry about currency risk.

All of these investing truths are hugely impacted by your time horizon and can vary between decades – for instance the last decade has been awful for equities but very positive for bonds and gold. That may change in the next decade but over the very long term, if you are willing to sit tight for 20 to 40 years, taking greater risk through equities could well make sense. Investors with a shorter-term time horizon might be less suited to equities and should carefully consider their exposure to interest rates, capital losses and inflation.

A TACTICAL APPROACH TO BUILDING AN ETF PORTFOLIO

CYCLES AND RATES

The core ideas of diversification outlined above should be easy to implement using ETFs – they certainly inform of model portfolios towards the end of this chapter. They suggest a patient, long-term approach to investing, ignoring the noise of modern markets and sticking with tried and trusted ideas.

But for many investors this approach seems strangely inadequate. Strange, because these more opportunistic types look at the ups and downs of markets and see opportunity. In a positive sense, they suggest buying when the market is at maximum distress and selling when the market is at maximum irrational over-exuberance. Call it market timing if you like – and ignore the evidence that it is only partially successful – but it can work if used selectively. By focusing on key signals from the wider national and global economy, we can aim to maximise upside opportunity and minimise downside risk. More practically deciding when to take the risk out of your portfolio (sell risky assets) can easily be managed by looking at how markets interact with the wider economy. i.e. how economic cycles affect the pricing of shares and bonds.

We start this journey around economic indicators by looking at three simple rates and their impact on the wider economy and thus financial markets: the inflation rate, the interest rate and the exchange rate. We then investigate the importance of four crucial cycles.

Inflation

The inflation rate, usually measured via an index such as the retail prices or consumer prices index, simply measures the change in prices of a basket of goods, services and in some limited cases assets. In incredibly simple terms a sharp increase in inflation rates generally tends to indicate that an economy is operating near its current capacity. That spike in prices is usually very bad news for investors in conventional bonds including government securities. As these have a fixed rate of interest, any increase in inflation rates blunts that income, putting off potential buyers and generally lowering the real, inflation-adjusted price of the financial asset. For equities the picture is slightly muddier as some equity sectors tend to benefit from rising prices (especially those based around resources) while most other sectors tend eventually to be hurt badly in terms of profits by rising inflation.

Interest rates and FX rates

But a sharp rise in inflation rates usually also has two distinct knock-on effects on our two other economic rates: the interest rate and the currency rate. As central bankers become more worried about rising prices they push up interest rates, forcing a slowdown in the economy, and a sudden collapse in the price of equities. This sudden spike in interest rates is better news for bond investors as there's a general scramble to move into safer government securities that pay a pre-determined interest rate.

Increasing inflation is also bad news for the foreign exchange rates of a country. Increasing prices tend to put off outside, foreign investors who worry that they are invested in a veritable basket case. They start selling, pushing down the external value of the local currency, increasing local inflation rates even more (although exports become cheaper), and trapping a country into a fast-deteriorating situation.

The growth cycle

The three rates all have a direct and sometimes immediate impact on a much longer cycle of economic activity, the ebb and flow of growth within an economy. The most commonly used way of measuring this cycle is to look at GDP or its growth rate. Crucially this growth rate also fits into a longer, trend pattern which indicates what the long-term growth rate for an economy is. Many developed world economies have been trending in a range of between 1 and 3% annualised GDP growth.

These trend GDP growth rates have a direct effect on two key financial variables – the earnings or profits of a company and the dividends it pays out. In very simplistic terms economists have discovered that the big companies within a broad index such as the S&P 500 tend to increase their profits at a rate which is roughly 1 to 2% above trend GDP growth rates. Dividends have also shown a remarkably steady pattern, growing at a rate of about 1.4% per annum above and beyond both the GDP growth rate and the annual inflation rate.

The business cycle

How does this longer-term GDP growth rate interact with the shorter-term rates such as interest rates and inflation? Step forward something called the *business cycle*. There is a mountain of research which looks at how this cycle works in practice but for our purposes we can recognise three distinct phases – growth, followed by a slowdown into recession, which can sometimes result in a deep depression.

This phasing of growth and recession (accompanied sometimes by the less frequent depression) can be attributed to all manner of underlying causes. The three rates encountered earlier on have a direct and immediate impact. If interest rates increase sharply following a surge in inflation, we would expect to move from heightened economic growth to a sudden and sharp recession.

But there are other factors at work as well. Many economists brought up on a particularly free market version of history (they are called the Austrians after their Austrian-born founding fathers) believe that the ebb and flow of the credit cycle (lending) has a massive impact. This group in particular pay close attention to the boom/bust cycle of bubbles. Whatever the exact cause of this ebb and flow within the economic cycle, we can definitively say that a business cycle exists and that economists have minutely detailed every up and down of this cycle for the last 60 years. The table below shows the US business cycle as defined by its main national economic forecasting service.

US recessions and recession probabilities

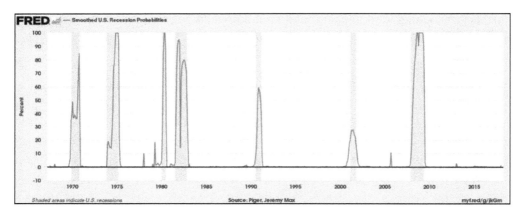

The credit cycle

Bond investors pay particular attention to a derivation of these wider business cycles called the *Corporate Credit Default cycle*. This measures what it says on the tin: the rate of defaults by corporate debtors i.e. those companies that borrow money from investors using corporate bonds.

The chart below is from Moody's; it looks at the period between 1920 and 1999, highlighting the All Corporate Default Rate and US Industrial Production Index. The latter index measures changes in US industrial output while the default rate measures the percentage of outstanding loans to companies that fall into default. There are no prizes for guessing the relationship between the two! As industrial output slows, the number of companies defaulting on their loans (bonds) increases. An increase in default rates is clearly bad news for bond investors. If default rates shoot up to say 0.10 (which means that 10% of all loans default), that means any income received from a diversified portfolio of corporate bonds (anything between 5 and 10% per annum) is likely to be swamped by defaults. Remember also that bond investors tend to anticipate these changes in the default rate and start selling off at least six months ahead of an industrial index slowdown.

Trailing 12-month All-Corporate Issuer Default Rate, 1920–1999

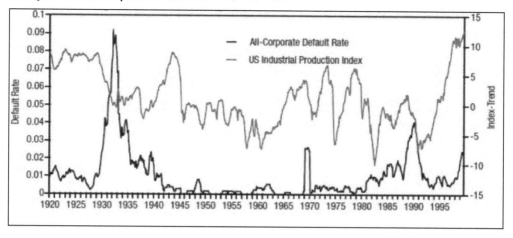

PULLING IT ALL TOGETHER IN THE ASSET ALLOCATION CYCLE!

What becomes immediately apparent is that investors are faced with a blizzard of different economic and technical cycles. They all sound very compelling but how can the investor possibly hope to make sense of them all? The key is to step back from the noise of these cycles and think about how sudden switches in key measures can have an impact on your portfolio. Investors also need to look at the quantum of change in key measures to see whether we're moving from one part of a cycle to the next.

US-based investment advisory firm Pring Turner have attempted to distil all these cycles and processes into one, simple-to-understand, asset allocation framework. There's absolutely no rocket science at work, as all of the key shifts are well known and widely discussed, but the simple diagram below does show how the business cycle over a period of between 4 and 10 years has an impact on individual investors. The *Idealized Business Cycle* and resulting *Six Business Cycle Stages* each contains its own major asset class switch – as recession deepens, you buy bonds but then as that recession bottoms out you start to buy equities. Expansion is good news for equities but as an economy reaches capacity we move into inflation-sensitive bonds and then sell conventional bonds. At the height of the business upturn we finally sell equities and then start the slow retreat into conventional government bonds as the economy slows down.

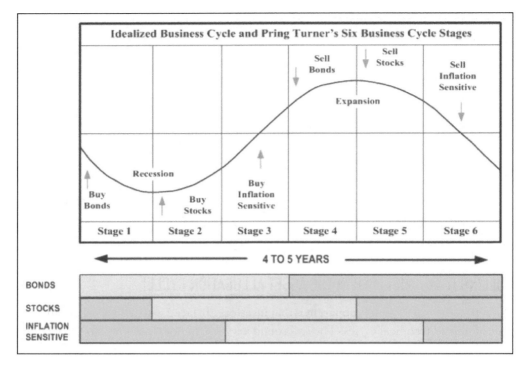

Obviously, this business cycle approach to investing is highly stylised and sometimes assets don't respond in price as we expect. Crucially spotting where we are on the business cycle is incredibly difficult unless you are very skilled at scanning through hundreds of different macro-economic measures. Nevertheless, we think this Pring Turner model is an incredibly powerful way of linking together tactical portfolio changes and the wider macro-economic environment.

THINKING LIKE A HEDGE FUND

All this discussion of macro-economic signals and cycles might strike some (cynical) investors as wearily familiar. Doesn't it sound a bit like the rarefied world of hedge funds? These once masters of the universe were supposed to be able to generate absolute gains whatever the stage of the cycle, by masterfully monitoring the key signals and then implementing them using broad, liquid investments loaded with leverage? Most hedge funds failed to live up to the promise, but we shouldn't be too quick to dismiss all the ideas about portfolio construction developed by these overpaid speculators. In particular many of the most successful hedge funds operate a strategy called macro – this involves going long and short key on national currencies, bonds and equity indices based around a big trend or idea. Crucially many of these strategies can be easily implemented using ETFs.

In this section we'll look at why macro hedge funds have become so successful, and how the ordinary investor might think about copying some of their strategies using ETFs. Later in this section we'll look in much greater detail at how macro hedge funds execute their investment strategies but in very simplistic terms macro investing involves a number of basic principles:

- Invest in simple-to-understand, liquid, popular markets – these should offer up low-cost products with tiny bid-offer spreads. Unsurprisingly ETFs are very popular with this group of hedge funds.

- Use leverage to gear up your returns.

- Be willing to long *and* short an asset.

- Think tactically and aim to get in ahead of the momentum trade and look to get early in order to minimise risk.

- Look for big trends, usually powered by insights into the economic policy and political process.

- Once you've spotted a big idea, look to see how key economic cycles interact with key financial markets such as equities, FX or bonds.

- Most macro funds base their analysis of opportunities using the three Rs as a starting point: interest rates, GDP growth rates and the inflation rate – these three macro-economic rates have an enormous influence on the way that modern financial markets operate.

HOW ECONOMIC CYCLES INTERACT WITH FINANCIAL MARKETS

We've already looked at some of the key rates and cycles – and how they interact. Research firm Parala is one firm that has tried to fuse academic thinking about economic cycles with investment strategies that look to switch between different asset classes (equities, bonds and commodities) or equity sectors. In the next three charts we can see how these myriad economic and business processes are hugely interconnected and why investors need to think about the big, macro picture.

Parala's analysis isn't unique and you'll find much of its thinking duplicates the internal research processes at the world's largest hedge funds, especially those that operate what are called macro strategies i.e. where investment strategies in equities, bonds, commodities and FX are determined by key macro-economic signals. According to Parala, its methodology is based on the large body of academic research on macro-economic predictability of financial markets and shows that it is possible to identify outperforming sectors, styles, or asset classes, "by using their prior correlations to many of the same macro-economic variables that have been shown to predict variability in the stock market's opportunity set". In simple terms, using key macro-economic signals might help you work out how different shares or financial markets will respond to changes in the economy.

What Parala's analysis[8] does do is pull together this thinking into a relatively simple framework which can be easily explained by charts.

The first chart below shows the ebb and flow of the US-based ISM Index and the Reuters CRB Commodity Index – although the two indices aren't perfectly synchronised, one can clearly see that there is a relationship between the two signals. The ISM Index monitors new orders and production among US manufacturers while the CRB Commodity Index looks at the price of a range of futures-based commodity prices including oil and foodstuffs.

Commodity price movements and US economic cctivity

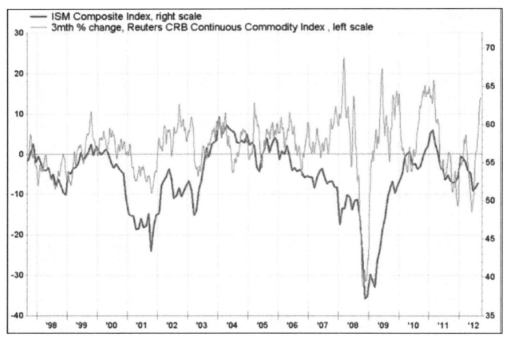

Source: Fulcrum Asset Management

The key message from this first chart is that there would appear to be a close relationship between US manufacturing output (as measured by the ISM) and commodity price indices. i.e. that as US industrial output increases, we should expect to see an increase in the price of commodities.

That relationship is indeed confirmed in the next chart from Parala which looks at another industrial confidence indicator (the PMI index – the Purchasing Managers Index for the US) and the S&P GSCI Commodity Futures Index (a rival to the CRB Index). Again, we can see that the relationship is close, though not synchronised.

---

8   www.parala.com

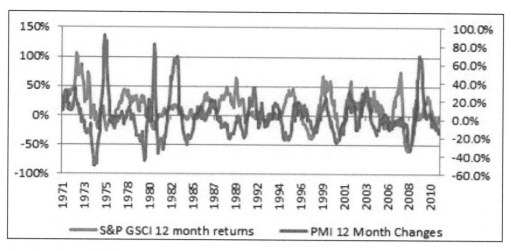

Source: Bruce Kasman, J.P. Morgan

Our last chart looks at the relationship between the ISM Index again and the benchmark equity index, the S&P 500. Again, we can see that there is clear relationship between industrial growth and *equity prices*, i.e. the price of shares is heavily influenced by wider macro-economic factors.

One small aside on the relationship between stock markets and GDP growth trends: many analysts reckon that equity markets are indeed closely correlated with changes in industrial and GDP growth. But that relationship usually involves equity investors pushing up share prices ahead of a growth upturn. In other words, they'll attempt to price in a recovery in share prices at least six months ahead of an actual upturn confirmed by data such as the ISM corporate index.

Equity price movements and economic activity – US economy

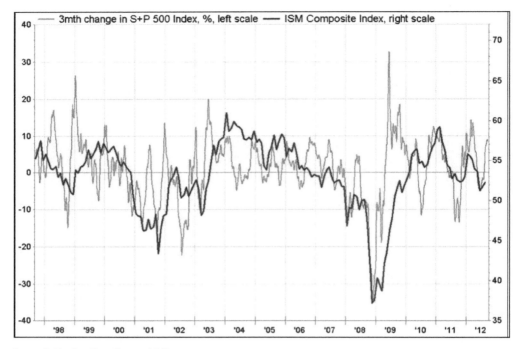

Source: An idea from Bruce Kasman, J.P. Morgan

Thinking about the impact on investments

Macro-based analysts take this thinking about the synchronicity of macro-economic signals with different asset classes and then attempt to apply it to individual equity sectors and even individual stocks. According to Parala, pro-cyclical sectors, such as technology or durable goods, outperform the broad market during macro-economic expansions, while counter-cyclicals, such as staples or precious metals, insure investors against recessions.

The key insight is that despite their best intentions, investors are slow to react to corporate news as well as developments in the macroeconomy.

Why this tardiness or slowness of response?

Some analysts think that it's because of a reluctance to take aggressive positions due to the career risk involved, i.e. very few fund managers have ever been fired for failing to predict a recession!

These behavioural forces mean that many fund managers hold on to their losers at the beginning of a downturn and then oversell their winners as the recession bottoms out.

The key for macro-based researchers is to identify a small but reliable set of macro-economic indicators that can help you build a robust portfolio of shares, bonds and commodities.

APPLYING MACRO SIGNALS TO INVESTING

"I don't play the game by a particular set of rules;
I look for changes in the rules of the game."
George Soros

Many investors obsess about risky assets such as equities, but hedge fund managers are, on the whole, a fairly dispassionate bunch. They are happy to go long or short any asset class, bonds or equities. As a rule, their core concern is to use any asset class to make money in any kind of market.

One particular breed of hedge fund managers takes this dispassionate, multi-asset class world view and then moves it on to a whole new level. Macro fund managers think across asset class and start with a top-down analysis that's inexorably linked to an understanding of how macro-economic factors affect individual markets.

In simple language that means they might start with an analysis of inflation or interest rates in different countries (they're a fairly global bunch as investors go) and then work out a strategy that involves trading in everything from bonds and FX through to equities to express that macro view.

Call it *Top-Down Thinking* but applied to different individual markets using a *Bottom-Up* analysis, i.e. they'll use those macro factors and then examine the individual dynamics of a market or security to look for an opportunity.

Macro managers can go long or short and use leverage to improve their returns. Unlike conventional managers with portfolios full of different, diversified stocks (or bonds), macro managers take concentrated positions – ideally with limited downside but with huge potential upside.

Trades usually fall into one of two major categories – directional (capturing a trend, no matter how fleeting) or relative value (one currency for instance may be undervalued compared to another).

Many macro funds are also high frequency traders, responding to news flow such as employment and GDP figures to make a large number of small bets on interest rates and stock and bond prices.

Whichever strategy is used, these macro hedge funds tend to use a fairly limited number of trading instruments:

- **FX**, usually based around the relative value or strength of one currency vs another. Currency pairs are a staple of the macro trade, and these pairs trades can be executed in markets that extremely liquid and trade 24 hours a day, 6 days a week, usually based around the interbank market. The leverage involved in these strategies can amount to as much as 100 times. Favourite ideas include the carry trade and a focus on EM currencies appreciating.

- **Interest rate** trading usually involves global sovereign (government) debt, with lashings of leverage again. Strategies include outright directional movements on government debt through to relative value trading in which a portfolio manager trades one debt instrument relative to another.

- **Equity** index trading based on a benchmark index like the S&P 500 and involving everything from simple ordinary shares through to index options.

- **Bonds and bond indices** are also massively popular with many macro hedge funds. Global bond markets are huge and very liquid and there's usually a very close link between a country's macro-economic fundamentals and its sovereign bonds.

The key insight is that macro fund managers are usually looking for long-term secular shifts in capital flows, i.e. big trends. This means that they tend to take a world view with a medium to long-term perspective. They also tend to concentrate more on fixed income products like bonds as well as currency markets rather than equity or commodity markets.

MACRO INVESTING IN PRACTICE

Macro hedge fund investors think big! They're global in scope, willing to use different asset classes whenever appropriate but also, crucially, they're likely to be internally organised in a very different way when compared to rival strategists. Most successful macro funds are run as funds of funds, where risk capital is spread out among different styles, markets and countries but all under one roof with a centralised risk control function.

Macro hedge fund managers have another peculiar focus – as traders they like to get in early to key trends or investment ideas and then exit before a market finally turns i.e. shoots up or down in value by a substantial margin.

Other key fairly unique characteristics for a macro hedge fund trader in action includes:

1. Their portfolios are usually very liquid and their funds generally offer investors redemption terms that reflect this liquidity.

2. They tend to make most of their money when volatility (in FX, bonds or equities) increases i.e. they tend to perform well during times of increased risk and uncertainty.

3. A typical macro hedge fund manager might have dozens and dozens of individual positions but in practice they all tend to relate to just a few big themes or ideas.

DIVERSIFICATION MULTIPLIED – INVEST LIKE AN ENDOWMENT FUND

The hedge funds dedicated to short-term trading and using macro signals don't seem to share a great deal with the big US university endowment investment funds. These huge multi-billion dollar outfits by contrast think long term, not worrying overly about what might happen in the next few months or even years – many use models which measure returns and income over 50 to 100 years. They also don't tend to engage in speculative investment positions. Whereas many hedge funds might make use of ETFs to express tactical views, very few endowment funds do. They're big enough to run their own passive funds which don't require a stock market listing.

But the endowment funds do think about alternative assets in the same way that many hedge funds do. Hedge funds are perfectly happy in trading everything from bonds and commodities all the way through to direct lending and alternative income. University endowment funds love alternative assets as well – and many of their best investment ideas have come from the most unusual places, along the way producing very diversified portfolios. Crucially ordinary ETF investors can mimic some of these portfolio construction ideas by using tracker funds that invest in alternatives.

But first investors need to understand the ideas behind endowment style investing. Back in the 1980s and much of the 1990s two major asset classes seemed to rule the roost in investment, namely equities and bonds. International diversification helped subtly change the mix of assets for most investors (emerging markets became a sensible choice in the late 1990s) but it's the rise of a clutch of new ideas called 'alternative assets' that's really revolutionised the debate about how to build a diversified portfolio.

These alternative upstarts include everything from mainstream hedge funds and property real estate investment trusts through to more esoteric frontier markets and even funds that invest in forests – in theory all of these alternatives could help an investor build up a diversified portfolio of uncorrelated assets. Some of the most enthusiastic early investors in these alternative assets were the large American university endowments, where investment in alternative assets has powered a huge increase in public wealth made available to higher education. Crucially these non-taxable vehicles have developed an investment philosophy that focuses on diversification, largely achieved by a relentless focus on the long term – this patience allows them to invest a very large portion of their permanent capital in illiquid assets while also being tolerant of market volatility. This means that they tend to have stable asset allocations over time, with much less reliance on market timing and lower trading costs.

PORTFOLIO IDEAS

THE YALE MODEL

The most articulate exponent of alternative assets is David Swenson, chief investment officer (CIO) for Yale University. With Swenson at the helm, Yale's university endowment has grown to over $19 billion in assets under management. Looking at returns, Yale boasts a two-decade investment record of +16.1% per year returns, a track record that easily places him as one of the best managers of institutional money in the United States. Along the way Swenson has built up something of a cult following around his 'Yale model', which involves developing diversified portfolios constructed out of alternative assets.

At the core of Swenson's Yale model is a strategy that involves buying a mix of US stocks, bonds, foreign stocks and a batch of assets that aren't highly correlated with the stock market – alternative assets. These could include everything from forestry (a major focus for Yale) through to real estate and hedge funds.

Crucially Swenson reckons that if you don't have access to his professional fund management resources you shouldn't try to pick stocks, nor should you pay anyone to do it for you – Swenson is a tireless critic of the mainstream for-profit mutual fund industry and has been an outspoken advocate of private investors using lowo-cost index funds as one way of building a diversified portfolio. In his bestselling book *Unconventional Success: A Fundamental Approach to Personal Investment,* Swenson maps out a "well-diversified, equity-oriented portfolio" for ordinary, private investors. This consists of passive, index tracking funds that invest in:

- 30% domestic stock funds

- 20% real estate investment trusts

- 15% US Treasury bonds

- 15% US Treasury inflation-protected securities

- 15% foreign developed-market stock funds (the EU, Japan, Australia, etc.)

- 5% emerging-market stock funds (Brazil, Russia, India, China, Taiwan, Korea, and the rest of the developing world)

In recent years Swenson has subtly altered his advice and currently suggests that investors have 15% of their assets in real estate investment trusts and raise their investment in emerging-market stock funds to 10%. Crucially this focus on the long term with a bias towards alternative assets has paid off handsomely for the big endowment funds – according to Frontier Investment Management the big, 'super' endowments (those with more than $10 billion under management) have generated consistently higher returns than the market. Frontier reckons that these super funds have achieved an average 10-year annualised return of 9.7%, 5.1% greater than the returns of a traditional US equity/bond portfolio (60/40).

According to the many experts who've tracked the US endowments the source of this outperformance is that long-term focus on alternative assets. Whereas most ordinary investors with a standard 60/40 split of assets (equities and bonds) will have almost no exposure to 'alternatives', the big endowments have invested a huge proportion of their funds in everything from private equity through to hedge funds. The table below – from Frontier, who've studied endowments on an annual basis since the middle of the last decade – shows the major asset classes in the very largest university endowment funds. Notice the heavy exposure to private equity, hedge funds, real estate and commodities – most ordinary investors would probably struggle to have more than a few per cent of their portfolio in each or all of these alternatives, but the endowments typically hold the majority of their assets in these alternatives.

Top 20 US endowment funds by assets

Private Equity	20%
Global Equities	21%
Hedge Funds	22%
Global Bonds	10%
Commodities	9%
Real Estate	10%
Emerging Equities	6%

Source: Frontier Investment Management and various US University Annual Reports

And what's even more startling is that these alternative assets have been growing as a proportion of their portfolios over the last decade – the next chart from Frontier shows that the endowments exposure to private equity and commodities has been increasing relentlessly over the last decade.

Super endowment asset allocation over time

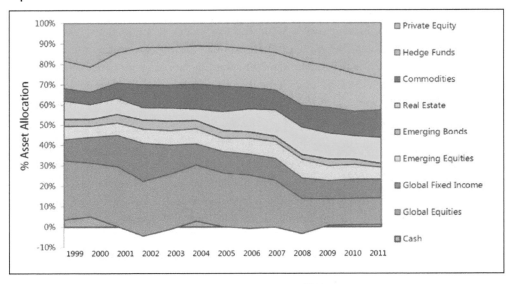

Source: Harvard University Annual Report 1999-2011, Yale University Annual Report 1999-2011

BUILDING A PORTFOLIO OF DIFFERENT ETFS – THE LIFECYCLE APPROACH

If both the hedge fund approach and the strategy adopted by the big US endowments strike the reader as perhaps a little too esoteric, another much simpler idea might appeal – and provide you with a properly diversified portfolio.

The lifecycle approach dictates a mix of asset classes that evolve and change depending on your age (or risk profile). If, for instance, you are planning to retire many decades in the future, you're more likely to take big risks in order to boost your returns – in essence you know that even if you make a mistake or two in the search for growth, you can hopefully make up for it over the next few decades. That bias towards an ability to absorb losses means that you might focus your mix of assets on riskier markets such as equities. A 60-year old, about to retire in five years' time, by contrast, is likely to be much more risk averse – that means they'll want a more conservative mix of assets including bonds and less risky assets.

This blindingly simple analysis has evolved into something called lifecycle funds, which are also known as target date funds. This involves you sitting down, working out your planned retirement age (which will nearly always be massively wide of the mark, given changing longevity patterns) and then finding a fund that has the closest equivalent to that year, called a target date. Given that it is currently the year 2018, if you are 30 now, you will probably be looking at retiring in 35 years' time, in which case your 'target date' is probably around 2053.

Some of the best work on these lifecycle funds has been done by consultants at Ibbotson Associates – they've studied many of these models and developed more than a few for their own clients. One of their recent research notes declared that "Target maturity investment solutions should help investors through the investment phases of accumulation, transition, and retirement."

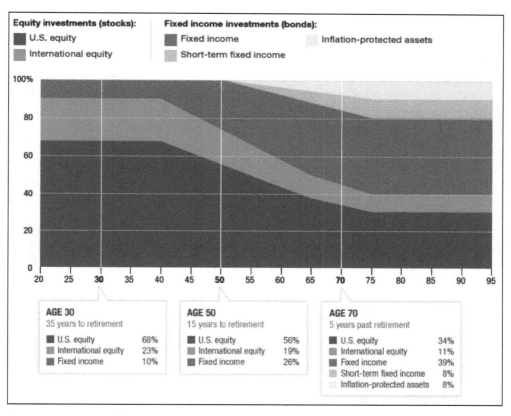

Source: National Public Radio (US)[9]

A second variation on the same model can also be found, called target risk funds, which do not specify an actual year but take a measured risk approach, suggesting a transition from ultra-high risk to ultra-low risk and all shades of risk control in between. The exact mix of assets will depend entirely on your own risk/return profile and also the views of your advisers, but most plans will feature something like the glidepath featured above – this graphical representation (from a US study of lifecycle funds) shows how at different ages, different assets may be mixed together.

---

9   http://www.npr.org/templates/story/story.php?storyId=124245298

The last piece in the investment jigsaw: what should I expect for future real returns?

Obviously, the decision about choosing a particular portfolio construction approach could be made much easier if we had some idea of likely future returns. Clearly accurate crystal balls are rare in the world of investment but there have been some methodologically detailed attempts to measure the possibility/probability of future returns.

These 'yardsticks' are nothing more than informed guesswork, but they are useful nevertheless. One key use of this forward-looking planning framework is that it allows the investor to sensibly judge how much money they need to put aside for the future. If one assumes real total returns of say 1% (that is returns above inflation of 1% per annum) then you'll almost certainly need to put aside a heck of a lot more money than if you believe future real growth rates will be closer to say 5% per annum. Clearly any exercise in crystal ball gazing needs to be taken with a huge block of salt but it's not an entirely fruitless exercise, largely because valuations over the long term do actually 'matter'. Put simply a financial asset that is already expensive using fundamental measures such as the price-to-earnings ratio is highly unlikely to produce a stellar return when compared to a financial asset that is cheap.

And if one accepts that fundamental measures of value have some relevance, perhaps the strongest long-term measure of value is something called the Cyclically Adjusted Price to Earnings ratio or CAPE. Also called the Shiller P/E ratio, this ratio was popularized by academic economist Robert Shiller, as a valuation metric that divides real prices by an average of real EPS over the prior 10 years. This approach allows the price-to-earnings relationship to be viewed in the context of multiple business cycles and is not biased by the most recent events.

Very simply as this multiple stretches beyond the average, reversion is expected to occur. Many academics and investment managers have looked long and hard at this CAPE measure and something approaching a consensus has emerged – in the short term, as a guide to what might happen with day-to-day markets it's next to useless but over the long term of many years, the CAPE measure has significant predictive power based on past returns.

Obviously, an important caveat is in order, which is that maybe in the future the relationships that power the CAPE might break down. Over the past decade for instance critics have rightly pointed out that the measure has been skewed by including depressed earnings from the financial crisis. Other critics are – in our view tellingly – worried that the CAPE measure might decline in potency in a global system where interest rates are abnormally low, perhaps allowing stocks to become much more expensive than normal and then stay that way.

Nevertheless, the CAPE measure is still useful as a guide or a pointer towards future returns. It's not foolproof and it certainly shouldn't be the only metric informing an investment strategy, but it is helpful nevertheless. And the good news is that the CAPE measure does allow us a rough approximation of a crystal ball for future returns based on current market valuations.

The idea here is to break down the various components of past returns and then use these valuation metrics to forecast through into the future based on variables such as national GDP growth rates or returns from dividends. If anyone is going to make a decent stab at this forecasting game, Rob Arnott and his colleagues at US firm Research Affiliates are likely to be among the most trusted. They've been constantly tracking returns from fundamentals-based investing for the last decade and they've recently updated their excellent Expected Returns[10] website.

The site is freely available and boasts clever tools which allow the user to compare Research Affiliates' long-term return expectations across a variety of geographies and asset classes. The chart below summarises the range of expected returns for a bunch of varying asset classes, with real expected returns compared to likely volatility.

Emerging market equities come out on top in terms of potential returns with annual returns of nearly 6% (real) likely over the next decade, but that bumper potential profit comes at a likely cost, with very high levels of volatility. Investing in emerging markets currencies looks a slightly less scary trade, with returns of over 4% but much lower levels of volatility. US small caps look a terrible idea with negative likely returns but massive volatility, while the most depressing numbers concern global equities – potential real returns of not much more than 1% per annum.

Portfolio and asset class expected returns
Time horizon: Expected 10yr

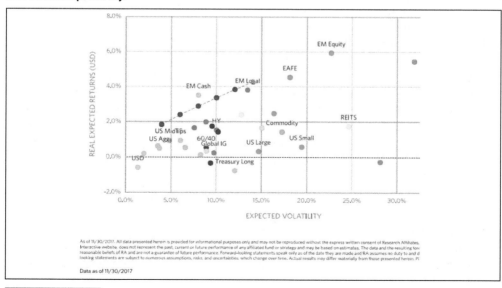

Data as of 11/30/2017

---

10   https://interactive.researchaffiliates.com

Leftfield idea for building a portfolio – use momentum

There is one last, slightly alternative, way of piecing together a diversified portfolio of ETFs – use momentum as a strategy. In simple terms this means only buying those stocks/bonds/asset classes/ETFs which exhibit noticeable 'relative strength' i.e. buy shares or ETFs which have consistently outperformed the wider market over a recent period. This period could be the last 3 months or the last 12 months. One simple implementation could be to look at the returns from companies within the FTSE 100 and then only buy the top 20 stocks that have shown the greatest relative strength (versus the FTSE 100 benchmark) over the 12 months to the end of December. In one version of this simple screen, the investor then waits one month, until February, and then buys all the strongest stocks equally weighted. This strategy could also be applied to asset classes and national markets, with the benchmark being a World All Markets index such as that developed by MSCI or S&P Dow Jones. Academics who've studied these momentum strategies suggest that momentum is in fact one of the most powerful forces in stock markets although investors do need to be aware that this momentum-based strategy has only worked during some years in the past and that when momentum fades, losses can be catastrophic!

Another version of the same argument is to use more technical measures to measure the likelihood of an asset class or national market making positive gains in the coming months. This also involves looking at sentiment through the lens of momentum but uses a more technical measure instead – the moving average of different asset classes. This 'system' suggests that investors simply make a decision to move back and forth between different assets based on a signal, namely that 'moving average'. The concept has been fleshed out by a US analyst called Mebane Faber and explained in an article for the *Journal of Wealth Management*. Faber is a wealth manager (and prolific contributor to the excellent seekingalpha.com website) and he has been trying to work out a simple way of protecting wealth by timing his equity investments. What he aspires to is a system that is simple to administer and clearly tells you when to buy and when to sell. His solution is the 200-day simple moving average, one of the most basic technical analysis indicators. It is worked out by adding up all the closing prices for the past 200 market days and dividing by 200.

According to Faber, the rule is to buy when the asset price or market shows a monthly price above the 200-day moving average and sell when it moves below. It is not really more complicated than that, although one implication is obvious: you will be spending a fair amount of time holding large parts of your portfolio in cash. To test his idea, Faber has run the data over the entire last century.

Faber's system does not really add much to total, accumulated returns – in fact, it slightly underperforms the index marginally in roughly 40% of the years since 1900. But it massively cuts down on risk, the maximum loss and volatility. On average, Faber finds that you get roughly the same returns as the index but with less risk. You get Faber's paper online at http://papers.ssrn.com/sol3/papers.cfm?abstract_id=962461.

CONCLUSIONS

Over the last few dozen pages we've investigated all manner of portfolio construction ideas that could involve buying (and selling) ETFs. They've ranged from fairly simple life-cycle approaches all the way through to hedge fund-like market-timing strategies using macro indicators. Whichever strategy you decide to use, we'd repeat ten basic principles which should guide sensible portfolio construction:

1. Diversify between bonds and equities.

2. Within bonds diversify between those that will protect you in an inflationary environment (inflation-linked bonds) and their more conventional siblings. Crucially also diversify your durations (invest in short and long dated) and credit risk (low-risk governments and higher risk corporate).

3. Within equities, those investors willing to stick with equities over the long term should consider investing in certain riskier types of shares – small caps – as well as value stocks and momentum-based strategies.

4. Gold is a useful diversifier and a sensible way of insuring against sudden increases in volatility.

5. Investors worried about a sudden increase in inflation should probably weight their portfolios towards gold, inflation-linked bonds and equities. Those investors worried by deflation are probably best off in government bonds.

6. Currency is a risk for investors over the short to medium-term but markets usually correct over the long term. This implies that international diversification is still useful and that investors shouldn't overly worry about currency risk.

7. The suitability of individual asset classes is hugely impacted by your time horizon. That means that if you are willing to sit tight for 20 to 40 years, taking greater risk through equities could well make sense. Investors with a shorter-term time horizon might be less suited to equities and should carefully consider their exposure to interest rates, capital losses, and inflation.

8. Equities are much more volatile than most investors imagine – but that can also be your great opportunity if you're either patient or intelligent.

9. Buy an asset when it's cheap – history teaches us that you have a greater chance of making above average returns, especially when the asset is very cheap.

10. Growing fast isn't always good news for investors – top line macro-economic growth (GDP growth) rarely translates into bottom line investor profits.

Armed with these principles, we can begin to put together our mix of assets, always informed by our own investment goals and our attitude towards risk. Lifecycle 'glidepaths' can help indicate a rough 'allocation' of assets within a portfolio but these 'allocations' should only ever be used as a 'model' i.e. an indicative guide which needs to be personalised. Most investors will look to depart from these 'suggested' allocations based on whether they are more or less risk averse. Cautious investors might be defensive and orientated towards value stocks within the world of equities (and probably bullish towards income-producing assets such as bonds) whereas adventurous types may be the exact opposite and be very willing to embrace the ebb and flows in sentiment. Each of the model portfolios below is precisely that – a model portfolio. They are ideas and templates which investors should personalise and make unique to their investment outlook. Crucially we've also deliberately avoided suggesting or tipping specific ETFs. We do talk about either broad asset classes or specific indices and in our experience, there'll be numerous choices available for each. At the very end of this book you'll also find our list of the top 100 ETFs based on a number of objective, quantitative measures such as sheer size or cost.

MODEL PORTFOLIOS

In this chapter we describe five model portfolios:

1. Adventurous Growth Portfolio

2. Balanced Portfolio

3. Opportunistic Portfolio

4. Contrarian Portfolio

5. Cautious Portfolio

Let's look at each of these in turn.

1. ADVENTUROUS GROWTH PORTFOLIO

At the top level, this is a portfolio about taking risks for an investor who can afford to be patient! Imagine that you are 30 years old. With a fair wind you have between 35 and 40 years before you retire, and you are suddenly starting to earn enough money to start a retirement fund. But you are faced with a huge question: how do you build a portfolio which will give you long-term growth without taking on too much risk? The core to building any portfolio is to balance risk and reward, even for younger investors. The riskiest assets tend to produce the biggest long-term gains, although over that long term the resulting volatility will be huge.

Investors have become used to the idea that over the very long-term equities are a great investment – the average over the last 100 years has been more than 6% per annum in most major developed world markets. But no one actually saves for 100 years. Most investors face a more limited timeframe of between 20 and 40 years. That matters because over this time period volatility can make a huge difference.

US analyst and adviser John Mauldin looked at this in a paper called 'While Rome Burns'. He examined the frequency of returns and the impact of volatility. He found that "in the 103 years from 1900 through 2002, the annual change for the Dow Jones Industrial Average reflects a simple average gain of 7.2% per year. During that time, 63% of the years reflect positive returns, and 37% were negative. Only five of the years ended with changes between +5% and +10% – that's less than 5% of the time".

Mauldin reminds his readers that most of the years were far from average. Almost 70% of the years were double-digit years, when the stock market either rose or fell by more than 10%. He then goes on to examine actual returns in 88 20-year periods. According to Mauldin: "Though most periods generated positive returns before dividends and transaction costs, half produced compounded returns of less than 4%. Less than 10% generated gains of more than 10%." He warns that "the stock market rarely gives you an average year. The wild ride makes for those emotional investment experiences which are a primary cause of investment pain".

But his overall message is that equities will, nevertheless, deliver substantial compounded returns, especially if you focus on a number of variables, including dividends. A number of realities emerge from this long-term financial analysis. The first is that if you are consistent and have a long enough timeframe, then equities stand a very high chance of yielding greater long-term returns.

The next is that income and dividends matter. Accumulating returns from dividends comprise a large part of total returns, but there is also some evidence that over the long term the market misprices more value-orientated companies that tend to produce a decent yield. As we've already discussed, work from economists such as Ken French and Eugene Fama at the University of Chicago suggests that smaller companies produce higher returns – called the scale premium – and you may be able to boost long-term returns by anything between 1% and 3% per annum. All these concepts sit behind this model portfolio. It is targeted at younger investors, but it could work for anyone willing to take on more risk.

Which asset classes to use

The first possibly surprising thing about this portfolio is that it does boast some income-producing bonds! Ordinarily many higher risk, adventurous-style portfolios have almost no fixed income exposure, yet our model portfolio boasts two bond-based asset classes – emerging market bonds and high-yield corporate bonds – representing 15% of the total value of the portfolio.

In practice both of these asset classes are at the riskiest end of the bond spectrum and are likely to move in line with equities and risk appetites. Our sense is that EM bonds are arguably a better way to access the emerging markets growth phenomena than equities, plus you receive a steady yield component to your returns. We have included a small amount of EM equity exposure, but this is directly targeted at investing in what we believe is the most interesting EM story – in valuation terms at least – namely mainland Chinese shares, in our case by tracking A Class shares in the CSI 300 Index.

Within the main developed world equities part of the model portfolio we have a heavy bias towards quality and dividend businesses. We've also featured two other core global equity ideas – tracking the biggest 50 global mega caps via the Dow Jones Titans Index and a Global Equity IT sector tracker, which, as the title suggests, is looking to invest in the world's very biggest technology companies.

Investing in mainstream European and Japanese equities comprises 22.5% of total assets – with Japan our sense is that we're mid-way through a strong momentum trade in favour of local equities while Europe is also mid-way through its own sustained recovery. We're probably most nervous about the US small caps exposure (through an index called the Russell 2000 Small Cap Index) largely because although we think this is a great long-term bet, our worry is that it is overpriced at the moment. Still as this is a portfolio for an investor with a 20-year time span we are also willing to build some exposure to these US small caps, although arguably UK small caps are a better bet at the moment! Last but by no means least, we have included 7.5% exposure to commodities which could be either via a broad commodity sector tracker or – our preference for this riskier style of portfolio – through a broad commodities index that uses momentum as a way of selecting different individual commodity markets.

Our hope is that over the long term this portfolio should be capable of generating a return of around 2 to 3% per annum in income (from dividends and bond coupons) with an overall total return of about 5–7% per annum.

Profile – adventurous portfolio

Asset Class	Weighting (%)	Index	Income producing
Emerging Markets Local Currency Bonds	10	Local emerging market bonds	Yes
High Yield Bonds	5	iBoxx Euro Liquid High Yield	Yes
Global Quality Income	25	SG Quality and Income Index	Yes, though use total return version
Japan	10	TOPIX Index	Yes, but low. Use total return version
Europe	12.5	MSCI Europe	Yes, but low. Use total return version
Global Large Cap Equities	7.5	Dow Jones Global Titans 50 Index	Yes, but low. Use total return version
US Small Caps	7.5	Russell 2000	Yes, but low. Use total return version
Equity Sector : World Information Technology	7.5	MSCI World IT Sector	Yes, but low. Use total return version
Chinese Equities	7.5	CSI 300	Yes, but low. Use total return version
Commodities	7.5	Thomson Reuters/Jefferies CRB Index	No

Portfolio summary – broad asset class mix

Bonds	15	Developed World Equities and Debt
Equities	77.5	Emerging Markets Equities and Debt
Commodities	7.5	Commodities

2. BALANCED PORTFOLIO

This portfolio is a mixture of assets for the more cautious long-term investor who still wants some capital growth. Let's start by looking at the bond segment of the balanced portfolio – comprising around 40% of the total holdings. We've weighted the underlying asset classes towards the riskier end of the bonds spectrum with almost no direct UK government bond exposure, bar a token 5% weighting towards inflation-linked securities.

The key idea here is that bonds higher up the yield and risk curve are likely to prove less vulnerable to any big (upwards) move in interest rates or bond yields – which seem inevitable to us at the current juncture. If long-term government bond yields did suddenly spike up past 4% for instance these riskier assets will certainly fall in value, but that generous yield likely to be between 3 and 5% in the case of corporate and local currency emerging market bonds will help mitigate some of the effects of a bond market slump. We are cautious on the prospects for all fixed-income securities in the next few years, but we nevertheless accept that many investors still want some bond exposure in their portfolio, thus our focus on riskier, higher yielding assets.

Turning to the larger equity portion of the portfolio (60% of assets) we've focused pretty much exclusively on developed world mega large-cap equities via indices such as the MSCI World Index (risk weighted) and the FTSE All-Share Index. This latter index includes nearly all UK equities but is still very much focused on UK FTSE 100 large caps. Crucially we also view UK equities as being undervalued with the real potential for decent gains in the coming years.

Both of our model portfolios featured so far include the SG Quality Income Index, largely because we think it has in effect a strong 'value' and 'income' bias. It also tries to focus on companies with a quality robust balance sheet and decent income prospects which we believe is the smart move for the long-term patient investor. These stocks might under-perform in the next 12 months or so, but our sense is that if you're willing to sit tight over the next decade, quality dividend-focused stocks should continue to outperform.

Last but by no means least, we have included two global sector indices – the consumer staples and utilities sector based on the MSCI World Index. Both should appeal to the more defensive investor looking to access businesses that should be able to maintain profits even if global growth starts to slow down (which we think is unlikely though not impossible). These sectors – rather like the SGQI Index – will probably underperform if equity markets become even more bullish over the next few months, but their generous, well-backed stream of dividends should help mitigate any market volatility.

One final word on how to manage this portfolio. This is a buy-and-hold model portfolio for the next ten to twenty years – as is the adventurous portfolio – and we wouldn't recommend any trading on a month-by-month basis. An investor could operate an annual rebalancing exercise, with an upper and lower boundary of 25% (which would mean selling an asset class that rose by more than 25% in value to bring it back to its suggested portfolio allocation, and vice versa for a stock that falls 25%) but we remain to be convinced of the usefulness of such an exercise.

Crucially we wouldn't operate any stop loss on this portfolio as we believe it quite likely that some asset classes could be quite volatile in the coming years (both bonds and equities) and it's highly likely that an artificial barrier at say 25% might force you to sell a position. So, just sit tight and remember this portfolio is only for the patient long-term investor.

Profile – balanced portfolio

Asset Class	Index	Weighting (%)
BONDS		
High Yield Euro Bonds	IBOXX EUR Liquid High Yield 30 Ex-Financial	5
Sterling Corporate Bonds	IBOXX £ Liquid Corporates Long Dated	20
EM Local Currency Bonds	Emerging Markets Broad Local Currency Bond Index	5
Inflation-Linked Bonds	£ Gilt Inflation-Linked	10
EQUITIES		
World Equities	MSCI World	20
UK Equities	FTSE All -hare	20
World Equities	SG Quality and Income Index	10
World Equities Sector	MSCI World Consumer Staples	5
World Equities Sector	MSCI World Utilities	5

Portfolio summary

Equities		60%
Bonds		40%
CORE ASSUMPTIONS		
Weighted towards income-producing assets including bonds		
Bond exposure is to higher risk asset classes with higher yield		
Equity exposure weighted towards dividend-orientated businesses		
Within equities also a heavy exposure to larger cap stocks		
Assumes both equities and bonds represent 'fair value' at best with likely low capital gains		

Target income yield across portfolio over long term	4%
Target capital gain across portfolio	1 to 2% pa over long term
Target return over long term (10 years or more)	5 to 6% pa

3. OPPORTUNISTIC PORTFOLIO

As the name implies, this is a more short-term (12 month) collection of assets designed to capture key trends and market sentiment on a month-by-month basis, based on a more speculative approach. As we've already discovered, many professional investors prefer an approach which suggests that sentiment towards key assets changes as economics-based indicators ebb and flow. These indicators are sometimes very well known – PMI sentiment indicators or jobless numbers for instance – others less so, focusing instead on risk-based factors such as the spread between different bond yields or volatility levels.

Each and every asset allocation specialist has their own personal mix or 'brew' of factors, individual to their core concerns but what we'll try to do with this portfolio is build on the knowledge of these 'experts' by merging them together to build a portfolio that should reflect month-by-month changes in sentiment towards the global economy.

The opportunistic portfolio is constructed using one very big assumption: that global growth will continue apace and that as more investors pump money into risky equities, we'll see a progressive broadening out of confidence amongst investors across different sectors and countries.

Economies such as the UK that had been viewed with some suspicion in recent years will – we hope – find themselves in demand (helped along by reasonable valuations) while sentiment will remain positive for industrial commodities as emerging markets start to benefit from increased demand. Two other trades will we think suggest themselves – continued positive momentum in Japan and continued recovery in the Eurozone. We were initially tempted to give a little more focus to both strategies, by favouring small caps in both Japan and Europe but for now we're happier sticking with large cap exposure.

The obvious omission is that of emerging markets. If confidence does recover, these growth assets should see a strong rebound *but* we're still a little nervous about capital and liquidity squeezes in places as varied as Turkey and South Africa and general jitters around the sheer scale of Chinese debt. As the contrarian portfolio shows, we think the adventurous investor will make money on these assets, but our only concern is that we might need to wait a few more months so that sentiment can turn decidedly bullish.

Profile – opportunistic portfolio

Asset Class	Index	Weighting (%)
Global Mega Caps	DJ Global Titans	30
UK Equities	FTSE All-Share Index	15
European Equities	MSCI Europe	15
Japanese Equities	TOPIX Index	15
Industrial Metals Equities	MSCI World Materials	25

Portfolio summary

Equities	100%
CORE ASSUMPTIONS	
Currently weighted towards 'risk on' assets i.e. assets that may grow in value as investors become more confident about future global growth, especially in the advanced countries. That implies no bond exposure	
Strong exposure towards cyclical commodity assets especially industrial metals and industrial metals equities	
Global exposure is vital	
Within equities also a heavy exposure to larger cap stocks	
Target income yield across portfolio over long term:	2%
Target capital gain across portfolio:	5 to 7% per annum
Target return over long term (10 years or more):	7 to 9% per annum

4. CONTRARIAN PORTFOLIO

This portfolio is designed to identify a collection of deeply out-of-favour assets that *might* benefit from a catalyst in the next 12 months which will result in a fundamental rerating of prices. Crucially we're not keen to focus on what we perceive to be 'value traps' i.e. financial assets that are likely to remain out of favour for the foreseeable future because of 'structural issues'.

The best way of explaining this qualified contrarianism is to look at Russian equities, which by virtually any definition are deeply out of favour and unloved. The challenge though for the investor is to make money from fundamental revaluations (usually prompted by a catalyst of some sort), not doggedly pursue an asset class just for the hell of it! Currently we're not convinced that anything will change investor sentiment towards President Putin's regime, except perhaps a vast upwards increase in the price of oil.

Our contrarian portfolio comprises a slightly peculiar mix of assets. First off, we have a big bet on emerging markets, especially those in Asia. We've also incorporated a large exposure to European equities, which we again think is undervalued by the markets. But perhaps our bravest bet is on bonds, which comprise 30% of the portfolio, based on equal exposure to both high-yield corporates and inflation-linked bonds issued by the UK government.

This last choice is probably the most outlandish as the consensus among many institutions is that inflation of 3 to 4% is under control. Our contrarian bet is that this is nonsense. Inflation will rear its ugly head in the next few years and inflation-linked assets will do well. We fully accept that if we assume UK breakeven inflation rates (an estimate made by the market for medium-term rates) stay at between 3 and 4% then inflation-linked securities might be viewed as expensive. But we're willing to wager that we'll see inflation rates well above trend as growth picks up speed, making these inflation-based assets seem much better value.

Profile – contrarian portfolio

Asset Class	Index	Weighting (%)
Emerging Market Equities	MSCI EM Index	30
Asian Equities	MSCI AC Asia-Pacific ex Japan USD	10
European Small Caps and Value stocks	MSCI Europe	30
High Yield Bonds	IBOXX EUR Liquid High Yield 30 Ex-Financial	15
Inflation-Linked Government Securities	IBOXX £ Gilt Inflation-Linked	15

Portfolio summary

Equities	70%
Bonds	30%
CORE ASSUMPTIONS	
A medium-term mini portfolio that hopes to buy 'cheap' assets	
Strong exposure towards cyclical commodity assets especially industrial metals and industrial metals equities	
Global exposure	
Within equities also a heavy exposure to larger cap stocks.	
In bonds we have exposure to riskier fixed income securities such as high yield as well as assets that should increase in value as global inflation increases	
Target income yield across portfolio over long term:	3 to 4%
Target capital gain across portfolio:	7 to 9% pa
Target return over long term (10 years or more):	7 to 9% pa

5. CAUTIOUS PORTFOLIO

Our last model portfolio is for the most cautious, conservative investors whose main priority is capital preservation rather than taking extra risk to boost capital growth. We think that over the long term this portfolio should be capable of generating a return of around 2 to 3% per annum in income (from dividends and bond coupons) with an overall total return of about 4 to 5% per annum – our guess is that most of the capital gains will come from riskier equities.

Profile – cautious portfolio

Asset Class	Index	Weighting (%)
UK Gilts	All UK £ Gilts	20
UK Corporate Bonds	Liquid £ corporates, long dated	10
US Treasuries 10 years +	Treasury 10 years + index	10
Emerging Markets Local Currency Bond	Local emerging market bonds	5
UK Government Inflation-Linked	All UK £ index-linked	15
Global Quality Income	SG Quality and Income Index	15
World Equities – Risk Weighted	MSCI World (equity) risk weighted	10
Emerging Markets	MSCI Emerging Markets	5
Commodities	A broad commodities index such as the Bloomberg Commodities Index	5
Equity Sectors – Consumer Staples	MSCI World Consumer Staples Index	5

MINI PORTFOLIOS

We finish with a final leftfield flourish, featuring three mini portfolios which attempt to capture a particular big idea or theme.

1. SciFi mini portfolio

Our first is what we call the *SciFi mini portfolio* – an avowedly risky portfolio of equity assets with a dominant technology theme. What we're interested in with this portfolio are cutting edge technology fields, which means that valuations will be sky high, with dividend income at rock bottom levels and long-term volatility probably at the volcanic level!

The two big bets are on robotics/automation stocks and biotech. The drivers for both are blindingly obvious – ETFs tracking this space represent 60% in total of the portfolio. Cyber security is a much more niche area, but we think that governments and consumers (as well as corporates) will be spending exponentially more money securing their networks and internet access over the next decade.

Our last theme is the emerging new electricity grid, built around renewable power and the next generation of batteries – which may in turn be powering an armada of electric cars.

There aren't many ETFs currently tracking this space, so we've put our exposure down at 20%, focusing if you can on lithium and other materials used by battery developers.

Theme: SciFi	Weighting (%)
Robotics and automation	30
Cyber security	20
Biotech	30
New electricity grid, especially lithium-based batteries	20

2. Greater China mini portfolio

The Greater China mini portfolio is also an increasingly obvious idea for momentum driven, growth-orientated investors. The emergence of a new Asiatic global economic, political and military super power presents both opportunity and risk. Most investors look to access the equity story through stocks in the developed world which have deep trading links with China – this is perfectly sensible if a little unadventurous. For this risky portfolio, we'd rather invest directly in stocks, either in China directly or more broadly within the Emerging Markets (EM) space. Crucially we're also keen to diversify by investing at either a regional or global level, expecting China to be a prime mover in both. That's certainly the case with the EM Consumer growth story which is arguably the most profound transformation currently underway globally – billions of people are being turned into materialistic consumers, for good or bad! China currently represents the single biggest, deepest, most affluent market though places such as India, Indonesia and Vietnam are catching up fast.

It's a similar story with the infrastructure revolution in emerging markets. Again, China tends to hog the headlines with its new cities and shiny high-speed trains but plenty of countries are following in its footsteps and spending tens of billions every year on new public infrastructure.

Our focus on China is most direct with the exposure to China A shares but we've also included Taiwanese stocks in our mini-portfolio. Our sense is that as Chinese consumers spend ever larger amounts of money on electronics and consumer stocks, Taiwanese businesses will be the most direct beneficiaries. Also, Taiwanese-listed businesses tend to boast the best corporate governance and the highest dividend payouts in the region.

Theme: Greater China	Weighting (%)
EM Consumer growth	25
China A shares	25
Taiwan equities	25
EM Infrastructure	25

3. Smart Beta Composite mini portfolio

Our last mini portfolio is a way of playing the smart beta theme using a simple set of four ideas. The Smart Beta Composite mini portfolio is *not* an attempt to build a complicated two, three or four multi-factor fund as described in an earlier chapter – there's a growing legion of products that effectively tap this market. By contrast we've focused on what we think most investors need. That means, first, a focus on value, and especially dividend orientated stocks.

As we've already discussed in earlier chapters we believe that dividends and value stocks are a great long-term bet – this strategy is probably a bit boring but probably fairly well rewarded in terms of returns for the patient investor. We also think that quality stocks, though currently expensive, stand a good chance of outperforming over the long term.

Our last two ideas stand in direct contrast to each other. Low or minimum volatility ETFs are a sensible bet for the investor with a low tolerance for risk, but we have our doubts about the efficacy of this strategy over the very long term. By contrast a bias towards small or mid-cap stocks is likely to prove much more volatile (and thus risky) but we also hope that the reward will be greater over the long run.

Theme: Smart Beta	Weighting (%)
Value, dividend-focused equities	30
Quality stocks	30
Low or minimum volatility stocks	20
Equal weight or mid/small cap	20

AN INTERVIEW WITH OLIVER SMITH, PORTFOLIO MANAGER AT IG

When you buy an ETF, what do you look at beyond the management fee?

Like many aspects of investing, it depends what your objective is. If I'm buying for the long-term ideally I want to see a low management fee, a tight NAV tracking error and stable or growing assets under management, which will give me comfort that the ETF will be there in the long term.

If it's for a short-term trade, assets under management and management fee are much less significant. The key for a short-term trade is the bid-ask spread of the ETF; the tighter the bid-ask spread, the lower my frictional trading costs will be. For example the iShares core FTSE 100 (ISF) has a bid-ask spread of just 0.03%, making trading nearly costless, but I would think twice about buying in and selling out of iShares Global HY Corporate Bond GBP Hedged ETF (GHYS) which has a bid-ask spread of 0.27%.

In general the more liquid the asset class, the tighter the bid-ask spread will be as creation costs are lower. Market makers have a very important role to play in ETF pricing, being paid by providers to make a market in ETFs which would otherwise have no liquidity. As the ETF becomes more popular, trade volumes increase, this attracts new market makers and the investor ultimately ends up benefiting.

How do you think investors should consider using ETFs in their personal portfolios?

For my own investments, ETFs make up a large percentage of my portfolio. I simply don't have time to actively monitor large numbers of managers across different asset classes and geographies, nor do I believe that I can consistently pick the winners in all of them.

Low ETF fees really do make a difference to long-term total returns, but in the medium term I'm concerned that capital gains tax will rise (from 20% at present), which will make switching investments very costly. Can I really take the risk of buying into a star manager and see them underperform, switch firm, or retire, only to face a large tax bill when I want to sell out? It's surely more sensible to hold a number of ETFs as a low-cost core portfolio and not trade them for many years, potentially decades, and instead be more active with a 'satellite portfolio' of best ideas. My satellite includes various shares and investment trusts.

Fixed income ETFs are a must have. A lot of private client portfolios still take large credit risk with exposure to individual corporate bonds, but these portfolios have a habit of suffering from negative skew. More often than not a downgrade will force the Portfolio Manager to sell the bond at a loss, the consequences of a default being too injurious to the client. However a bond ETF – simply buying the market – allows an investor to allocate to these stressed bonds, which have little impact on overall wealth but could recover their losses and make decent gains.

Any investments you avoid?

In general I'm not a fan of commodity ETFs, but exclude precious metals from this observation. ETFs can make some complex asset classes look very simple, but it can be difficult for even seasoned professionals to understand the dynamics behind soft and bulk commodities ETFs. If you wanted to get exposure to oil via an ETF, the ETF does not own physical oil, but an oil future; your returns therefore are susceptible to the shape of the oil futures curve. If the curve is upwards sloping ('contango'), each time the future is rolled there is a cost, but it is very difficult to find out what the shape of that curve is unless you have a market data subscription!

Looking at the GBP returns for the Bloomberg Commodity Index over three years (to 30 June 2018), the Spot Price Index – the headline numbers we see every day – is up 27.9% compared to +3.7% for the investible Total Return Index. These ETFs can be a very expensive lesson for the uninformed.

Leveraged ETFs are another where investors risk getting their sums wrong. They have their place, offering clarity on pricing as well as security, but by having daily re-setting leverage the impact on your portfolio can work rather like buying high and selling low. If the trend is in your favour you'll do better than expected, and if it's against you you'll do worse than expected. Short holding periods are fine, but long holding periods are not so wise.

Do you worry about the liquidity of your ETFs?

Not particularly as an ETF can only be as liquid as the underlying market. ETFs can give the illusion of liquidity, but as long as the ETF tracks its benchmark a buy and hold investor should not have any nasty surprises.

The advantage of trading on exchange is that there will always be a market for your stock, but it just may not be at the price you wish to sell it. In a market dislocation (say in High Yield credit) the ETF could trade at a discount to NAV, but not excessively as market participants would arbitrage away the anomaly. If you really needed to sell, you could; as long as the exchange is open someone will make you an offer. Contrast that with funds which can get gated in the event of having too many redemptions and you have a product which shouldn't give you any sleepless nights.

A lot has been written about ETFs, their supposed distortive qualities and what would happen if everyone wanted to sell at the same time. Yet there is scant evidence of this being a problem. Most of the gain in ETF assets under management has been at the expense of actively managed funds; the overall pool of assets is the same, the clients are the same, only the delivery mechanism, the fund wrapper, has changed.

What kind of nuances should investors be aware of?

As an investor I have a few rules, which I try and stick to. The first is to always buy the GBP share class of an ETF, which will help cut down my foreign exchange fees. Secondly, I will try and trade the ETF when the underlying market is open as the bid-ask spreads are slightly tighter, and thirdly I try to look at the ETF's premium or discount.

This last point is often overlooked, it being out of the control of ETF companies. Essentially because ETFs are listed, their share price is subject to fluctuations in demand. In theory all ETFs should trade at a slight premium to reflect creation costs, especially UK equity ETFs, because there is no stamp duty payable. However these premiums are not constant and at any one time ETF premiums can differ markedly amongst providers. If you were to buy a FTSE 100 ETF on a premium of 0.5% and sell it on a small discount of -0.2%, then that is the equivalent of paying a decade's worth of fees. Conversely should you buy it at NAV and sell on a premium, you've generated an extra return.

Similarly if you buy a China ETF after the local market is closed, the price you pay is not based on today's closing NAV, but on the market's expectation of what will happen tomorrow based on price action in our markets. Trade timing is important and to limit the risk of adverse pricing, you should always try and place buys and sells at the same time.

Tell us about some of the more sophisticated portfolio tilts where you use ETFs

Currency hedged products have really opened up a layer of sophistication to ETF investing, which is particularly relevant with Sterling having sold off against its peers. Using risk management software we can now identify and breakdown the sources of portfolio risk; equity, fixed income, currency, commodity and stock specifics. By isolating currency exposure, much of which is just noise, we can lower the volatility of portfolios and smooth their returns.

Previously currency hedging would have been performed using FX forwards, which was quite a complicated business rolling them on a monthly or quarterly basis. ETF providers now offer this at a very competitive cost and you can be assured that the pricing they get is superior to what all but the very largest institutions will receive.

Fixed income ETFs have also seen a lot of product development. In the main currencies you can now target a particular part of the yield curve, meaning if you think rates will rise you go short duration and can flex that exposure over time. Taking this a step further, if you don't like UK yields it's possible to buy USD bonds hedged back into Sterling.

Are there any areas of the market where you think ETFs don't work all that well?

Whilst I'm a huge advocate for ETFs – the transfer of wealth from fund manager to consumer has been immense – they are not suitable for everything. Due to their intra-day liquidity requirements, ETFs are, to some extent, restricted in what they can buy.

If you want exposure to anything smaller than midway down the FTSE 250, investment trusts and funds are a better option. This means that Smart Beta ETFs that profess to have a small-cap factor tilt are really only moving away from the mega caps. There are no FTSE Small Cap or AIM ETFs, the UK market is just not liquid enough and this applies across Europe and Emerging Markets. Similarly specialist credit vehicles and listed private equity can offer some portfolio diversification and access to those really hard to reach parts of the market.

How do you see the industry evolving?

Fee competition has been intense in the mainstream ETFs, so the onus now is on providers to do something a little bit different to make a return. This will see them try and advance further into the more traditional retail funds space, with thematic ETFs that really capture the consumer's imagination likely to see a lot of promotion.

But it need not necessarily be a story of inevitable decline for the fund providers, far from it. Technology improvements, deep resources and marketing budgets could allow them to close the gap – at the moment funds are priced once a day, but it is conceivable that some firms might launch their own ETFs or even develop a dealing mechanism to price their funds on an intraday basis.

ETFs were once just a blunt tool to get market cap exposure, but the proliferation of different strategies, index providers and asset class tilts continues to provide opportunity for investors.

TOP 101 ETFS

TOP 75

IN THIS SECTION we select what we consider the top ETFs in the London market that investors should consider. We cover a lot of ground, taking 75 ETFs in total. We have chosen ETFs from every major asset class, with products picked from every major issuer. The ETFs chosen are meant to reflect the wide range of products on offer. There is no particular method to the selection, with one exception: tracking difference. For each asset class we have picked the ETF that tracks its benchmark most closely. We have included this information because it is a helpful indicator of reliability and the data can be harder to come by.

The columns in the table are:

- Ticker: Bloomberg Ticker

- ETF: ETF name

- TER: Total Expense Ratio

- AuM: Assets under Management

- TD: Tracking Difference (provided by TrackInsight, the French data company)

Ticker	ETF	TER	AuM (£m)	TD
UK Equities				
LCUK:LN	Lyxor Core Morningstar UK NT DR UCITS ETF	0.04%	10	
CUKX:LN	iShares FTSE 100 UCITS ETF (Acc) – GBP	0.07%	450	-0.07%
VMID:LN	Vanguard FTSE 250 UCITS ETF	0.1%	685	
US Equities				
VUSA:LN	Vanguard S&P 500 UCITS ETF	0.07%	16,842	
LCUS:LN	Lyxor Core Morningstar US Equity (DR) UCITS ETF	0.04%	36	
XSPX:LN	Xtrackers S&P 500 Swap UCITS ETF	0.09%	2,537	0.63%
Japanese Equities				
XDJP:LN	Xtrackers Nikkei 225 UCITS ETF 1D	0.09%	518	
JPHG:LN	Amundi ETF JPX-Nikkei 400 UCITS ETF Daily Hedged GBP	0.18%	3	
CNKY:LN	iShares Nikkei 225 UCITS ETF – JPY	0.48%	252	-0.93%
Broad Commodities				
COMM:LN	iShares Diversified Commodity Swap UCITS ETF – USD	0.19%	989	-0.14%
CMFP:LN	L&G Longer Dated All Commodities UCITS ETF	0.30%	684	
CRBL:LN	Lyxor Commodities Thomson Reuters/CoreCommodity CRB TR UCITS ETF C-EUR	0.35%	810	
World Equities				
XWLD:LN	Xtrackers MSCI World Index UCITS ETF 1C – USD	0.19%	2,216	0.03%
LCWL:LN	Lyxor Core MSCI World (DR) UCITS ETF	0.12%	28	
VWRL:LN	Vanguard FTSE All-World UCITS ETF	0.25%	1,460	
European Equities				
UB01:LN	UBS ETF – EURO STOXX 50 UCITS ETF A-dis – EUR	0.15%	465	0.53%
XD5E:LN	Xtrackers MSCI EMU Index UCITS ETF 1D	0.15%	2,137	
VERX:LN	Vanguard FTSE Developed Europe ex UK UCITS ETF	0.12%	936	
German Equities				
DAXX:LN	Lyxor DAX (DR) UCITS ETF – EUR	0.15%	978	
XDDX:LN	Xtrackers DAX UCITS ETF Income 1D	0.09%	543	
DXGP:LN	WisdomTree Germany Equity UCITS ETF GBP Hedged	0.35%	17	
Indian Equities				
CI2U:LN	Amundi ETF MSCI India UCITS ETF - USD	80.00%	11	-2.14%
INR:FP	Lyxor MSCI India UCITS ETF C-EUR	0.85%	952	
XNIF:LN	Xtrackers Nifty 50 UCITS ETF 1C	0.85%	142	
Latin American Equities				
ALAU:LN	Amundi ETF MSCI EM Latin America UCITS ETF – USD	0.20%	167	-0.49%
LTAM:LN	iShares MSCI EM Latin America UCITS ETF (Dist)	0.74%	483	

Property				
XDER:LN	Xtrackers FTSE EPRA/NAREIT Developed Europe Real Estate UCITS ETF (DR) 1C – EUR	0.33%	353	0.13%
IUKP:LN	iShares UK Property UCITS ETF	0.40%	757	
IASP:LN	iShares Asia Property Yield UCITS ETF	0.59%	262	
French Equities				
CACX:LN	Lyxor UCITS ETF CAC 40 (DR) – D – EUR	0.25%	3,902	-0.30%
CF1:FP	Amundi ETF MSCI France UCITS ETF	0.25%	953	
Chinese Equities				
CSIL:LN	Lyxor CSI 300 A-Share UCITS ETF C-USD	0.40%	4	
XX25:LN	Xtrackers FTSE China 50 UCITS ETF (DR) 1C	0.60%	118	
IASH:LN	iShares MSCI China UCITS ETF	0.65%	44	2.20%
Precious Metals				
GBS:LN	Gold Bullion Securities	0.40%	3,042	
PHPM:LN	ETFS Physical PM Basket	0.44%	93	
XAD1:LN	db Physical Gold Euro Hedged ETC	0.59%	687	
Energy				
CRUD:LN	ETFS WTI Crude Oil	0.49%	609	
BRND:LN	Boost Brent Oil ETC	0.25%	8	
AIGE:LN	ETFS Energy	0.49%	58	
Cash				
CSHD:LN	Lyxor Euro Cash UCITS ETF EUR	0.10%	596	
XSTR:LN	Xtrackers II GBP Cash Swap UCITS ETF	0.15%	76	
SMTC:LN	Lyxor Smart Cash	0.12%	144	
FEDG:LN	Lyxor Fed Funds US Dollar Cash UCITS ETF C-USD	0.10%	32	
Agriculture				
AIGA:LN	ETFS Agriculture	0.49%	315	
WEAT:LN	ETFS Wheat	0.49%	69	
COFF:LN	ETFS Coffee	0.49%	57	
COCO:LN	ETFS Cocoa	0.49%	39	
Emerging Markets Equities				
EMIM:LN	iShares Core MSCI EM IMI UCITS ETF	0.25%	6,527	0.15%
AEEM:FP	Amundi ETF MSCI Emerging Markets UCITS ETF	0.20%	4,070	
VFEM:LN	Vanguard FTSE Emerging Markets UCITS ETF	0.25%	1,179	
MXFP:LN	Invesco MSCI Emerging Markets UCITS ETF	0.29%	562	
Developed Markets Bonds				
GIL5:LN	Lyxor FTSE Actuaries UK Gilts (DR) UCITS ETF – GBP	0.07%	126	-0.10%

MTH:FP	Lyxor Ultra Long Duration Euro Government FTSE MTS 25+Y UCITS ETF (DR) C-EUR	0.10%	43	
IBTS:LN	iShares USD Treasury Bond 1-3yr UCITS ETF (Dist)	0.20%	2,395	
XGLE:LN	Xtrackers Eurozone Government Bond UCITS ETF 1C	0.15%	1,881	
Corporate Bonds				
IEBC:LN	iShares Core Euro Corporate Bond UCITS ETF (Dist)	0.20%	6,733	0.01%
CUIH:LN	UBS ETF Bloomberg Barclays US Liquid Corporates Interest Rate Hedged UCITS ETF (USD) A-dis	0.23%	16	
SHYG:LN	iShares Euro High Yield Corporate Bond UCITS ETF EUR (Dist)	0.50%	3,784	
CREG:LN	L&G LOIM Global Corporate Bond Fundamental UCITS ETF	0.35%	27	
Emerging Markets Bonds				
JPEA:LN	iShares J.P. Morgan $ EM Bond UCITS ETF (Acc) – USD	0.45%	182	
LOCG:LN	L&G LOIM Emerging Market Local Government Bond Fundamental UCITS ETF	0.55%	203	
HYEM:LN	VanEck Vectors Emerging Markets High Yield UCITS ETF	0.40%	2	
SBEG:LN	UBS ETF (LU) Barclays USD Emerging Markets Sovereign UCITS ETF (hedged to GBP) A-dis	0.47%	72	
High Yield Bonds				
SHYG:LN	iShares € High Yield Corp Bond UCITS ETF – EUR	0.50%	3,784	-0.05%
IEBB:LN	iShares Euro Corporate Bond BBB-BB UCITS ETF	0.25%	295	
XTXC:GR	Xtrackers iTraxx Crossover UCITS ETF 1C	0.24%	161	
FAHY:LN	Invesco US High Yield Fallen Angels UCITS ETF	0.45%	50	
Infrastructure				
XSGI:LN	Xtrackers S&P Global Infrastructure UCITS ETF 1C	0.60%	254	-0.30%
MLPI:LN	L&G US Energy Infrastructure MLP UCITS ETF	0.25%	22	
GIN:LN	SPDR Morningstar Multi-Asset Global Infrastructure UCITS ETF	0.40%	63	
IEMI:LN	iShares Emerging Market Infrastructure UCITS ETF	0.74%	72	
High Yield Bonds				
TIPG:LN	Lyxor US TIPS (DR) UCITS ETF – USD	0.09%	265	-0.08%
XEIN:GR	Xtrackers Eurozone Inflation-Linked Bond UCITS ETF 1C	0.20%	533	
INXG:LN	iShares GBP Index-Linked Gilts UCITS ETF	0.25%	845	
INFL:LN	Lyxor EUR 2-10Y Inflation Expectations UCITS ETF C-EUR	0.25%	955	

THE WILD CARD 26

I N T H I S S E C T I O N we take a look on the wild side. We go through some of the more innovative products, many of which have been launched in the past few years. The 26 'wild card' ETFs go beyond the plain vanilla and give exposure to less standard asset classes, themes and factors. As well as giving an indication of where the industry is going, this section aims to arm investors with some new investing ideas.

THE TOP 26 WILD CARDS

Investors shouldn't only focus on the cheapest or largest ETFs with greatest liquidities. As we've discovered, more and more ETFs are tracking unusual indices and strategies, many influenced by smart or thematic beta. Here we identify a shortlist of 26 ETFs which have caught our eye recently.

UK Equities

1. **Smart Beta idea: UBS MSCI UK IMI Socially Responsible UCITS ETF (LSE: UKSR)** This ETF tracks larger UK companies but excludes any businesses involved in nuclear power, tobacco, alcohol, gambling, military weapons and genetically modified organisms. The ETF tracks the MSCI UK IMI Extended SRI 5% Issuer Index which caps any individual company at no more than 5% of the index. This should mean that the ETF is a bit less concentrated than would otherwise be the case. The ongoing charge for the fund is 0.28%.

2. **Worth highlighting: db x-trackers FTSE 100 Equal Weighted UCITS ETF (LSE: XFEW)** This ETF follows the equal-weighting strategy highlighted by Peter Sleep. It invests in all members of the FTSE 100 but gives them an equal weighting. So, HSBC comprises 1% of the fund as does Next and AstraZeneca. This ETF uses full physical replication. The fund has an ongoing charge of 0.25% a year.

US Equities

3. **ETF with currency risk hedged: iShares S&P 500 Hedged GBP (LSE:IGUS)** This fund has about £183 million under management and gives you exposure to the S&P 500 while also hedging your currency exposure. Imagine that the S&P 500 rises 20% over a year but the dollar falls 20% against sterling over the same period. If you put your money into plain vanilla iShares Core S&P 500 fund, your investment would

end up pretty much flat at the end of the year. But if you bought the hedged version, a large chunk of your profit would be protected. Following a big price cut in April 2017, the annual fee for this fund is 0.2% which is impressive. The fund tracks the S&P using physical replication.

4. **Smart Beta idea: SPDR S&P US Dividend Aristocrats UCITS USD (LSE:UDVD)** Dividends comprise a big chunk of the returns for long-term investors, but dividend investing can be risky, especially if many of the highest-paying stocks are in a particular sector. (This happened in the run-up to the financial crisis when many high-yield stocks were banks.) This ETF only invests in companies that have increased their dividend for at least 20 years – hence the description, 'dividend aristocrat'. Companies that consistently increase dividends tend to have sustainable competitive advantages. However constructing an ETF on this basis tilts the portfolio towards mid-cap and value stocks, which may not suit all investors. The ongoing charge for this fund is 0.35% a year.

5. **Worth highlighting: Wisdom Tree US Small Cap Dividend UCITS GBP (LSE: DESE)** This relatively small ETF also focuses on dividend-paying stocks but just small caps. Over the very long-term, small caps have historically performed better than their larger peers and if you think that trend will continue, this could be a good way to play it. The fund tracks the Wisdom Tree US Small Cap Dividend Index which comprises the smallest 25% of the companies in the Wisdom Tree US Dividend Index. This larger Wisdom Tree Index is made up of most US dividend-paying stocks that also meet some criteria for liquidity and capitalisation. The ETF is small with a fund size of £15 million and the ongoing charge is 0.38%.

World Equities

6. **Largest Smart Beta ETF: iShares Edge MSCI World Minimum Volatility (LSE:MVOL)** This ETF aims to reduce risk by investing mainly in low-volatility stocks in the MSCI World Index. Not all the stocks, however, are low-volatility. Some more volatile stocks are included to bring some risk diversification. The TER of 0.3% is low for a smart beta ETF.

7. **Featured ETF: iShares Edge MSCI World Value Factor UCITS ETF USD (LSE:IWVL)** This ETF tracks the MSCI World Value Index. This index comprises 876 value stocks across 23 developed markets. The stocks are selected using three criteria: price to book value, forward price earnings ratio and the dividend yield. The value index has a much higher exposure to Japanese stocks than the main MSCI World Index – 26% of the value index is invested in Japanese stocks, with only 38% of the fund invested in US stocks. The ETF has a relatively low TER of 0.3% and a fund size of over a billion dollars. If you want to tilt your portfolio towards value, this ETF is a useful tool to do so. There are plenty of value adherents out there who argue that value stocks tend to outperform over the long term, even if that's not been the case in recent years.

European Equities

8. **Big European Smart Beta ETF: iShares Edge MSCI Europe Minimum Volatility (LSE: MVEU)** In theory, this ETF should outperform in bear markets but be a little left behind when markets are strong. The fund mainly comprises stocks in the MSCI Europe Index with low volatility, however it does include some relatively volatile stocks to ensure adequate diversification. The ETF has an ongoing charge of 0.25% a year and there are almost 1.1 billion euros under management.

9. **ETF with currency hedging: iShares MSCI Europe ex-UK Hedged UCITS GBP (LSE:EUXS)** This ETF protects you if the euro falls even though European stock markets have risen. Currency hedging costs money so the ongoing charge for this ETF is 0.4% a year. If you take the view that Brexit will damage the UK economy compared to the Eurozone, then you might think there's a good chance that the pound will fall against the euro over the next decade. And if that's what happens, hedging won't have been necessary. But if you think that the UK will prosper outside an over-regulated Eurozone, investing in this hedged ETF makes more sense. Hedging might also be an attractive option if you have no idea what the eventual outcome of Brexit will be.

Global Emerging Markets

10. **Big Smart Beta Emerging Markets ETF: iShares Edge Emerging Markets Minimum Volatility ETF UCITS (LSE:EMMV)** This ETF tracks stocks in the MSCI Emerging Markets Index under a set of constraints. These include limiting turnover, exposure to particular names, and ensuring better diversification than in the plain vanilla MSCI Index. The ETF doesn't purely focus on low-volatility stocks, it includes some stocks with higher volatility to ensure adequate diversification. The fund has an ongoing charge of 0.4% a year and has around $550 million under management.

Japan

11. **ETF with currency hedge: iShares MSCI Japan Hedged ETF GBP (LSE: IJPH)** This ETF is priced in pounds and has a currency hedge so that you are protected from any adverse movements in the yen/sterling exchange rate. However, this protection comes at a cost with an ongoing charge (OCF) of 0.64%. It tracks the MSCI Japan Index and uses physical replication although there is some optimisation – in other words, it doesn't necessarily buy all the constituents of the index. There's also a version that hedges your investment to dollars, it's ticker is LSE:IJPA.

12. **Worth noting: Source STOXX Japan exporters UCITS ETF USD (LSE:JPEX)** This is a smart beta ETF that tracks the STOXX Japan International Exposure Net Total Return Index. The index focuses on companies in the STOXX Japan 600 Index which earn at least 50% of their revenues outside of Japan. It delivered a 24.6% return in 2016. The annual charge is 0.35%.

Infrastructure

13. **Worth noting: ETFS MLP Energy Infrastructure (MLPX)** The ETFS US Energy Infrastructure MLP GO UCITS ETF (MLPX) tracks the performance of the Solactive US Energy Infrastructure MLP Index which is in turn a benchmark for Master Limited Partnerships or MLPs which are listed and domiciled in the United States. These tax-efficient structures own energy transport infrastructure assets such as pipelines, storage facilities and other assets used in transporting, storing, gathering, and processing natural gas, natural gas liquids, crude oil and/or refined products. The fund is USD-denominated and has a TER of 0.25%.

14. **Worth noting: State Street Infrastructure Equity and Debt. SPDR Morningstar Multi-Asset Global Infrastructure ETF (LSE:GIN)** A rare multi-asset beast which tracks both equities and bonds within the global infrastructure space. It tracks the Morningstar Global Multi-Asset Infrastructure Index which consists of a broadly diversified portfolio of publicly traded global equity and global fixed income securities in 18 infrastructure-related industries. The index is equally weighted between equities and fixed income while the ETF has a low TER of 0.40%.

Bonds

15. **Leftfield idea: Lyxor EUR 2–10Y Inflation Expectations ETF (INFL)** This is a euro-denominated fund which tracks an index called the Markit iBoxx EUR Breakeven Euro Inflation Fr & Ge. This index is designed to provide exposure to breakeven inflation through a long position in inflation-linked bonds issued by France and Germany and a short position in French and German sovereign bonds with adjacent durations. This all sounds slightly complicated but in fact this is a cost-effective way of playing any increase in inflation expectations for bonds issued by Eurozone governments. The TER of the euro-denominated fund is just 0.25%.

16. **Worth noting: iShares J.P. Morgan EM Local Government Bond ETF (LSE:SEML)** Big ETF which invests in local currency, emerging market government bonds globally. This makes the underlying assets more volatile, but yields are also much higher. Clearly, FX risk is much higher as well. TER for the fund is 0.50%.

17. **Big Smart Beta bond ETF: the Lombard Odier bond series and especially the ETFS Lombard Odier IM Global Corporate Bond Fundamental GO UCITS ETF (LSE: CRGH)** This tracks the LOIM Fundamental Global Corporate Index which uses fundamental weighting to track corporate bonds. This fundamental weighting means that the fund tries to invest in the best value bonds rather most other bond indices which use market cap weighting. This latter methodology means you invest the most in the most heavily indebted businesses. The TER on this fund is just 0.30%.

18. **Worth noting: iShares Fallen Angels High Yield Corp Bond UCITS ETF** The bonds tracked in this ETF were originally issued by corporates which had an investment grade rating but have since been downgraded to high yield bond status. Fallen angels tend to be larger and well-established companies such as JC Penney, Dell, Sprint and Nokia. Relative to the broad high yield bond market, these fallen angels have traditionally averaged not only higher credit quality but also higher absolute and risk-adjusted returns. This iShares ETF, with a TER of just 0.50%, is a cost-effective way of playing the US high yield space with reasonable quality names.

Alternatives

19. **Alternative take on broad commodities: Source LGIM Commodity Composite UCITS ETF (LSE: LGCU)** This ETF aims to provide the performance of the LGIM Commodity Composite Index after fees. L&G developed this index to make sure it's representative of the broad commodity market, only features the most liquid assets and is accessible at low cost. The selected sub-indices are then equally weighted with quarterly rebalancing. The TER on this ETF is 0.77%.

20. **Worth noting: ETFS All Commodities GO UCITS ETF (LSE: BCOG)** One of the safer bets for getting access to a highly diversified basket of commodities. At the time of writing, BCOG is well balanced, with about one third of its weighting going to agriculture and livestock, energy, and industrial metal and precious metals. It has none of the energy sector bias that usually plagues broad commodity indices. The TER is 0.30%.

21. **The best: Gold Bullion Securities (LSE: GBS)** GBS is gold standard for gold ETPs. Every security is backed by allocated bullion and because it only holds LBMA Good Delivery bars, investors, if they so wish, can request the delivery of the gold that backs their ETFs. It's very rare to say with a financial instrument that nothing can go wrong. But, here, it's hard to see what can. The TER is 0.40%.

22. **Leftfield idea: ETFS Industrial Metals (LSE: AIGI)** Industrial metals are a trickier one for investors. Governments in Europe tend to ban physically holding them, because they worry about hoarding. So, this ETF uses collateralised swaps to track the Bloomberg Industrial Metals Total Return subindex, which is made up of aluminium, copper, nickel and zinc. If investors want to diversify into industrial metals, this is one idea. The TER is 0.49%.

Smart Beta

23. **New idea: Invesco PowerShares Global Buyback Achievers UCITS ETF (LSE: BUYB)** A new variation on the idea of prioritising those businesses which provide a generous dividend. In the US many businesses choose to use buybacks

rather than dividends and there is some evidence that those businesses with the biggest buyback programmes outperform the wider market. This Invesco ETF tracks the NASDAQ Global Buyback Achievers Net Total Return index which comprises corporations that have affected a net reduction in shares outstanding of 5% or more in the trailing 12 months. TER on the ETF is 0.39%.

24. **Big Smart Beta ETF: iShares Edge MSCI USA Value Factor ETF (LSE: IUVL)** One of the biggest and cheapest smart beta ETFs in Europe. This tracks US equities with a strong value tilt and the fund is very cheap when compared to most active fund managers operating a US strategy – the TER is just 0.20%.

Sector Ideas

25. **Worth noting: Invesco NASDAQ Biotech UCITS ETF (LSE: SBIO)** Tracks the NASDAQ Biotechnology Index. Biotech stocks have been surging over the last few years and this is a cost-effective way of buying into this specialist space through an ETF. The index behind the fund comprises biotechnology and pharmaceuticals companies but with some crucial controls set in place to make sure the holdings aren't too concentrated – the five largest constituents are capped at 8% with the remaining constituents capped at 4%. The TER is 0.40%.

26. **Worth noting: The ETFS ISE Cyber Security GO UCITS ETF (LSE:ISPY)** Tracks the stocks of companies engaged primarily in cyber security business activities via the ISE Cyber Security Index. The TER is 0.75%.

ABBREVIATIONS

When you first start to investigate the world of ETFs, there are many acronyms to contend with: ETN, MSCI, SPDR, AP, NAV and of course ETF. Here are some of the more common ones you are likely to come across.

AAA

This is a credit rating for prime bonds. If a bond is AAA, it means that credit rating agencies think a default is extremely unlikely. The different credit rating agencies use different categories for less secure debt. But the general principle is that the more 'Bs' or 'Cs' in the rating, the less secure are the bonds.

AMC: Annual Management Charge

A measure of the cost of investing in a fund. It's normally applied as a percentage of the fund. So if you invested £1000 in an ETF with a 0.5% AMC, you'd expect to pay £5 a year to the ETF provider – assuming the value of your investment didn't change at all. However, there will be some hidden costs on top of that £5 figure, and fund management firms find it relatively easy to massage the AMC. So it's probably better to focus on the OCF or TER which include more costs.

AP: Authorised Participant

Authorised participants are a crucial part of the ETF creation and redemption process. APs are normally market makers or investment banks. An AP signs up to support a particular ETF and it can then approach the ETF with assets that reflect the ETF's composition. The AP can then demand shares in the ETF in exchange for those assets. It can also hand in shares in the ETF in exchange for underlying assets. If the share price of an ETF moves out of line with the value of the underlying assets, the AP can make money via arbitrage. That arbitrage process means an ETF's share price is normally very close to the Net Asset Value (NAV).

CAC 40

The main stock market index in France.

CU: Creation Unit

A unit is the minimum amount of shares that an Authorised Participant can use in the creation or redemption process. Creation units can vary in size depending on the ETF, but most are between 25,000 and 600,000 ETF shares each.

DAX
Germany's main stock market index.

DJIA or 'Dow': The Dow Jones Industrial Average
Traditionally this was the flagship US stock market index. It only comprises 30 large US companies and the weightings don't reflect market caps, just share prices.

ETC: Exchange-Traded Commodity
Exchange-traded commodities are debt securities that pay no interest. They are designed to give exposure to an individual commodity or a basket of commodities. These products aren't UCITS regulated unlike ETFs. Some ETCs are physical and own the underlying commodities, some are synthetic and use futures contracts. For some commodities, such as grain, synthetic is the only practical approach.

ETCs are debt securities whereas ETFs are funds. That said, ETCs are fully collateralised which means there is no counterparty risk. If the bank that issued the ETC goes bust, you'll still get your money as there is collateral.

ETC can also stand for exchange-traded currency. These are also debt securities but give you exposure to foreign currencies rather than commodities. They're also not eligible for UCITS regulation.

ETF: Exchange-Traded Fund
These are investment funds that invest in assets such as equities or bonds. These funds are traded on stock exchanges as single entities and their share prices normally change repeatedly during the day. ETFs are open-ended which means that fresh ETF shares can be created to meet demand.

ETN: Exchange-Traded Note
These are also debt notes. They can be linked to a range of different assets or indices and are listed on the stock exchange. They're issued by a single bank. The underwriting bank agrees to pay the return of the index minus fees. Some ETNs are collateralised, some aren't. ETNs aren't UCITS regulated.

ETP: Exchange-Traded Products
This is the umbrella term that covers ETC, ETF and ETN.

FTSE 100
The hundred largest shares trading on the London Stock Exchange. There are several large ETFs that track its performance. It's the UK's flagship stock market index and is weighted towards pharmaceuticals, banks, resources and telecoms.

FTSE Russell
A large index provider. Its best-known indices include the FTSE 100 in the UK and the Russell 2000 which is the main small cap index in the US.

IOPV: Indicative Optimised Portfolio Value

This is a real-time estimate of the value of an ETF's underlying assets during the trading day.

LMM: Lead Market Maker

LMMs must offer competitive bid-ask-spreads for their assigned ETFs.

LSE

The London Stock Exchang.e

MSCI

One of the largest index providers.

NASDAQ

The second largest stock exchange in the world. Like the NYSE, it's also based in New York. It has a reputation for listing technology companies.

NAV: Net Asset Value

The value of the underlying assets in an ETF or fund, divided by the number of shares in the fund.

Nikkei 225

The best-known Japanese stock market index but perhaps not the most useful as it's calculated on the basis of share prices rather than market caps.

NYSE

New York Stock Exchange.

OCF: Ongoing Charges Figure

A measure of the cost of investing in a fund or ETF. It's more comprehensive than the AMC and slightly more comprehensive than the TER.

QQQ

The PowerShares QQQ ETF tracks the NASDAQ 100 and is one of the best-known ETFs worldwide. It's listed in the US and was formerly known as the QQQ or the NASDAQ-100 Index Tracking Stock.

S&P 500

This index comprises 500 of the largest companies listed on the US stock market. These include Amazon, Apple, Facebook and Exxon Mobil. The weightings of companies in the index are based on market caps. Also known as the 'S&P'.

S&P GSCI

A broad index of commodity futures. It used to be known as the Goldman Sachs Commodity Index, but S&P bought the index from Goldman Sachs in 2007.

S&P

A major index provider, operating indices around the world, on top of the S&P 500.

SPDR

See SSGA.

SPY or SPDR S&P 500 ETF

The world's largest ETF. It's listed in the US and tracks the S&P. It has more than $250 billion under management.

SSGA: State Street Global Advisers

One of the biggest ETF providers in the world, along with Vanguard and iShares. State Street's ETFs are known as SPDR ETFs or 'Spiders/Spyders'.

TER: Total Expense Ratio

A measure of the cost of investing in a particular fund, which might be an ETF. The TER is a more comprehensive measure than the AMC, but the OCF covers a couple of extra costs beyond the TER.

TOPIX: Tokyo Price Index

This index comprises around 1700 of the largest listed companies in Japan. It's calculated on the basis of market cap.

UCITS: Undertaking for Collective Investments in Transferable Securities

A regulatory framework for funds, including ETFs, that applies across Europe

ETF STREAM

PASSIVE IS MASSIVE

ETF Stream is the "go to" website for everything ETF related in Europe and Asia/Australasia.

Our international team of journalists cover all the new issues, highlight the people moves, and track the industry's rapid growth. We're also dedicated to educating the investor and advisor – our guides, features, analysis and data help explain the passive investment industry to a wider audience. If you've got a strong opinion on the industry, we want to hear from you ! We're also keen to hear about key people moves, new issues and new issuers, and we want to learn from the best practice of investors and advisors using ETFs.

www.etfstream.com

CPSIA information can be obtained
at www.ICGtesting.com
Printed in the USA
BVHW011810060319
541856BV00002B/2/P